What readers s

"I got into bed a few night. dozing off. The text got my adrenaline running, and I finally closed the covers two-and-a-half hours later."
— Ted Hechtman, "Smart Money," columnist
Welcomat, Philadelphia

"A fascinating book — the kind of book that, agree or disagree, you're gonna pick it up and throw it against the wall at least twice."
— Buzz Schwartz, Investor's Club of the Air
KMNY Radio, Los Angeles

"Robert Czeschin may be on his way to becoming the Robert Ludlum of financial advisors.
The Last Wave is ostensibly about how to invest your money. But it's got all the fixings of potboiling fiction — nuclear terrorists, international intrigue, presidents going eyeball to eyeball with the Soviets over the oil fields of the Mideast, and natural catastrophes bringing the world to its knees."
— John Strausbaugh, *City Paper*, Baltimore

The first oil shock of the 1970s plunged the world into the worst recession since the Great Depression of the 1930s. The second oil shock swept the Ayatollah Khomeini to power and helped push U.S. interest rates to nearly 20%. Plunging share prices after the Iraqi invasion of oil-rich Kuwait created billions of dollars in losses for investors worldwide.

Today North Korea is peddling ballistic missiles and weapons of mass destruction in the Mideast. Using only conventional explosives, Saddam Hussein was able to put Kuwait's oil fields out of commission for about three months. With a nuclear weapon, he could have taken Kuwaiti oil off the market for a thousand years.

What will happen to your future—and the futures of those you love—when the next oil shock hits?
— Robert W. Czeschin, *The Last Wave*

The 1989 edition of *The Last Wave* forecast both the oil shock of 1990 and the great stock market plunge in Japan. The 1991 edition (published before Operation Desert Storm) predicted that, given a chance to surrender to allied troops, Iraqi troops would throw down their arms by the thousands.

If you followed the investment advice in previous editions of *The Last Wave*, chances are you are already vastly richer today. Now author and investment analyst Robert Czeschin is back with a fresh set of forecasts for the final days of the 20th century.

It will not be a tame or tranquil time. But where tempest and turmoil threaten, opportunities also abound.

Find out what crises lie ahead. Better yet, follow Czeschin's prescriptions for turning these insights to your financial advantage. But don't delay. The window of investment opportunity that Czeschin sees today may no longer be open tomorrow ...

.

The Last Wave

Oil, War, and Money Shocks in the Final Days of the 20th Century

By Robert W. Czeschin

SHOT TOWER BOOKS
Boca Raton, Florida

Printed in the United States of America

Senior Editor: William Bonner
Managing Editor: Kathleen Yeakle
Production Editor: Kimberlee Lansdale
Copy Editor: Judith Strauss
Cover Designer: Pam Makie

Published by:
       Shot Tower Books, Inc.
       150 East Palmetto Park Road
       Suite 320
       Boca Raton, Florida 33432

ISBN 0-9639629-6-5 softcover

Distributed in the book trade by Atrium Publishers Group

Table of Contents

Foreword

There is a tide in the affairs of men,
Which taken at the flood, leads on to fortune;
Omitted, all the voyage of their life
Is bound in shallows and in miseries.
— Shakespeare, "Julius Caesar" —

Kim Jong Il, the erratic 50-something son of North Korean dictator Kim Il Sung, wears elevator shoes and sports a bouffant hairdo in order to look taller than he is.

He stammers when he talks and worries that he may not be able to claim the legacy bequeathed to him by his late father in the world's only Stalinist dynasty. He also has his finger on a nuclear trigger—and few qualms about pushing the button.

Meanwhile, as the year 2000 approaches, hundreds of religious cults proclaim the final days, the end of time, or other versions of the apocalypse. All three of the world's major religions—Christianity, Judaism, and Islam—envision a dramatic series of events leading up to the end of the world. What could be a more compelling vision of the apocalpyse than a nuclear holocaust unleashed by a madman?

Korea's hereditary enemy, Japan, is now well within range of North Korean missiles. Even if you do not live in Asia, you could scarcely escape the financial fallout of a nuclear attack on Tokyo.

In 1923, it took five days for news that an earthquake had leveled Tokyo to reach New York. Today, the effect would be instantaneous. Stock markets around the world would plunge into the abyss—followed by the world's major economies.

North Korea is also peddling its nuclear weapons-making technology and its missiles to Libya, Syria, and Iran. In due course, there will be no shortage of madmen with fingers on the button.

Using only conventional explosives, Saddam Hussein was able to take Kuwaiti oil off the market for several months. Had he a nuclear warhead, he could have taken Kuwaiti oil off the market for a thousand years.

Will the year 2000 mark the end of time, as a growing number of cultists shrilly and increasingly proclaim? The end of history was proclaimed after the collapse of the former Soviet Union. Yet despite the end of the Cold War, the world has scarcely become a tamer place. Particularly if you live in Bosnia. Or Somalia. Or Yemen. Or Rwanda. Or in a hundred other places outside North America, Western Europe, Australia, and Japan.

On balance, it is not a more peaceful world. And history has hardly halted. On the contrary, it seems to have speeded up.

Nowhere is this clearer than in the Middle East. Saddam Hussein was merely the first dictator to seize the opportunities created by the collapse of the Soviet Union and the growing American preoccupation with domestic rather than global concerns. Despite Iraq's defeat, he will not be the last.

The first oil shock of the 1970s plunged the world into the worst recession since the Great Depression of the 1930s. The second oil shock accompanied the rise to power of the Ayatollah Khomeini. It also helped push U.S. inflation and interest rates to nearly 20%.

Today, North Korea is sending missiles and nuclear weapons technology to the Mideast in exchange for oil. Isolated and bankrupted by lunatic economic policies, the Kim Dynasty sees no alternative but to barter terror with madmen.

Meanwhile, an expanding appetite for energy has just turned Asia's emerging superpower, China, into a net oil importer. Like the United States, China has exchanged one-time status as one of the world's leading producers for dependence on foreign supplies. Furthermore, the Chinese are securing their energy future in the same way as the North Koreans—by transferring advanced weapons technology to the Mideast.

Plunging stock prices in the aftermath of Saddam Hussein's invasion of Kuwait created billions of dollars of losses for investors worldwide. What will happen to your future—and your family's—when the next oil shock hits?

Our dependence on a particularly unstable region of the world for our energy is not, however, all that threatens a financial apocalpyse in the 1990s. Imported supplies of oil may fuel the engines of the world economy. But without imported supplies of capital, increasingly fewer engines would ever be built.

The withdrawal of Japanese capital from world markets in the midst of the Kuwaiti crisis was one of the triggers that pushed stock prices down worldwide. According to former U.S. Treasury Secretary Nicholas Brady, the withdrawal of Japanese capital also touched off the worst stock market debacle of modern times in October 1987.

In my view, the world stock market peak in the first quarter of 1994 marks the end of the last wave of economic prosperity before the dawning of a new era in which the developed nations of the Western world will increasingly find themselves under attack.

We stand on the threshold of a period in which practically everything—your investments, your livelihood, the future of those you love—will be at risk. It will be a poor time to be ill-advised.

But where upheavals threaten, opportunities abound. During the Great Depression of the 1930s, for example, the foundations were laid for some of the great fortunes of the 20th century. So it will be again during the upheavals of the 1990s. This is a book about being prepared for the future.

To a fertile imagination, the notion of a final wave immediately conjures up a formidable array of images. One is a vision of a tropical typhoon spreading destruction in its wake, or a crashing assault from the sea, itself a symbol of the domain of chaos.

Another image calls to mind the regular ebb and flow of seasons and tides, which come and go with the reassuring certainty of a known and immutable time schedule. Both are profound, and both describe important aspects of the tough times and dangerous days ahead.

As inheritors of a great tradition of political stability and orderly financial markets, members of the postwar generation of North Americans, Europeans, and Australians are unprepared by either history or temperament for the tide of accelerating chaos that looms ahead.

Americans in particular are likely to be both frightened and appalled by their increasing vulnerability to events far beyond the shores of North America.

In the decade ahead, the developed countries of the West will find themselves the victims of events on a scale not seen in more than a century. Much of this will occur because of increasing dependence on unstable foreign sources of energy and capital.

Fuel sufficiency

When wood fueled the world's economies, the great coniferous forests of North America and Europe assured self-sufficiency in energy. When coal became the principal source of fuel for home and industry, large coal reserves in Europe and North America were more than enough to assure self-sufficiency.

We have not seen the last wave of the coal-fired economy. But what displaced coal from its ascendancy as the world's premier fuel was oil—which weighed 30% less and took up only half as much space in storage.

It did not take long for the military advantages of oil-fired technology to be widely recognized. Soon, a wave of competition for reserves began that persists to the present day. As French senator Henry Berenger observed in 1925: [1]

> *He who owns the oil will own the world, for he will rule the sea by means of the heavy oils, the air by means of the ultra-refined oils, and the land by means of petrol ... he will rule his fellow men ... by reason of the fantastic wealth he will derive from oil—the wonderful substance which is more sought after and precious today than gold itself.*

As with wood and coal, the United States was blessed with abundant supplies of oil. For most of the '30s, '40s, and '50s, American wells accounted for nearly two out of every three barrels of world production.

OPEC was not the first to realize the political advantages of being a major oil exporter. U.S. Presidents Franklin Roosevelt and Dwight Eisenhower pioneered the use of oil as a political weapon.

At the end of World War II, the United States accounted for over 70% of world production. Forty years later, that fraction fell to only 16%. In 1970, America crossed the fateful threshold of energy dependence. Today, the United States is the victim of the very weapon it once wielded with impunity.

It is difficult to overestimate the financial and political implications of these developments. The worldwide bear market of 1973-74 and the debt crisis that today threatens a new depression on a scale not seen since the 1930s are both products of the OPEC-induced oil shocks of the 1970s.

Other implications go far beyond the merely economic. Oil-related conflicts lie at the heart of the wave of terrorism sweeping the globe today. And at least twice, the United States has been on the verge of launching a nuclear attack to preserve access to oil for itself and its allies.

Capital dependency

Along with a growing dependence on uncertain sources of imported supplies of oil has come a similar dependence on uncertain sources of imported supplies of capital.

For example, the United States has become utterly dependent on a continuous supply of imported capital to fund the federal budget deficit. If the Japanese—or the Saudis—stopped buying U.S. Treasury bills and notes, the government's appetite for borrowing would rapidly overwhelm domestic capital markets.

The ensuing explosion in U.S. interest rates would do more than send U.S. stocks into a tailspin. It could easily push the economy into a depression from which it might take years to emerge.

As was the case with oil, the United States is on its way to becoming a victim of the economic weapon it once wielded with impunity. As former U.S. president Richard Nixon observed shortly before his death, [2]

> *Today, China's economic power makes U.S. lectures about human rights imprudent. Within a decade, it will make them irrelevant. Within two decades, it will make them laughable. By then, the Chinese may threaten to withhold Most Favored Nation (M.F.N.) trading status from the U.S. unless we ... improve living conditions in Detroit, Harlem, and south-central Los Angeles.*

Oil and war

The Japanese are also dependent on imported oil for virtually 100% of their petroleum needs. It was the need to secure its oil supplies that led Japan into World War II. The same concern fuels the debate over Japanese rearmament in the 1990s.

Today the Japanese are world leaders in anti-submarine technology, computer-based artificial intelligence, and the flat screen display technology on which the newest generation of weapons systems depends. If they embark again on a course of conquest, few countries in East Asia would be able to stand in their way. As was the case in World War II, Japanese will first target historical Asian enemies—such as Korea and China.

ix

For Americans and those who have profited from U.S. economic prosperity, the relative decline of American influence in the world may be a truly frightening development. Accordingly, a number of authors have written popular books that both exacerbate and take advantage of these fears.

Paul Kennedy's *Rise and Fall of the Great Powers* predicts economic exhaustion as a result of "imperial overreach." James Davidson and Sir William Rees-Mogg's book *The Great Reckoning* predicts a 1930s-style depression.

But there is a sense in which this view of affairs is inappropriate. To be sure, cataclysms do occur. Rome fell. Noah's flood, if you accept the biblical accounts, was an epochal deluge that changed the face of human destiny forever.

But rarely has there been a catastrophe on such a scale that none survived—or even that none managed somehow to make a buck.

In this sense, the last wave is something of a misnomer. It is true that fearful events threaten. But the next deluge will not be the end of waves or markets, just as the conclusion of the century will not be the end of time. And neither will it be the end of those with sufficiently long-range vision to prepare for what takes everyone else by surprise.

Remember, virtually anything that happens anywhere in the world is bound to be bad news for somebody. But chances are it is also good news for someone else. Successful investing is knowing how to find the good news—even when you must look beneath the surface of seemingly forbidding waters.

Unlike most people, who live without interest in or awareness of history's great turning points, you need not be taken by surprise. In fact, I hope to show you ways to turn these apparently ominous currents of events to your advantage.

To this end, this book is divided into three sections. The first section focuses on the struggle for control of the world's supplies of oil as one of the major threats to peace and prosperity.

The second section covers the growing economic might of Asia—and how it could trigger the next worldwide economic collapse. The third section is devoted to explaining how you can turn these two broad currents of history to your investment advantage.

The age of upheavals
This book is based on the premise that the past cannot only

illuminate the present but also adumbrate the future. Accordingly, **Chapter 1** begins the story of oil and war with the history of oil's emergence as a strategic objective in World War I.

It tells how the oil-powered internal combustion engine changed the face of war forever. The story of the birth of armored warfare. How the first motorized column in military history was formed almost by accident—when Paris taxi drivers were suddenly pressed into service in a heroic defense of the City of Lights.

In **Chapter 2**, you'll learn how Hitler's nearly invincible war machine ground to a halt because of lack of gasoline. How the attack on Pearl Harbor would probably never have occurred had President Roosevelt not cut off U.S. oil exports to the Japanese. How the war might have turned out very differently indeed if the combatants on all sides had more aggressively targeted each others' fuel supplies.

Chapter 3 tells the dramatic story of the first use of Mideast oil as a political weapon—the Suez crisis of 1956. You'll find out how President Eisenhower wielded the oil weapon to project American power and ensure his own re-election. You'll also read about how the first battle for control of the canal—and its vital oil cargos—unfolded nearly a decade earlier in the arid sands of the Egyptian desert.

In **Chapter 4**, you will get the inside story of how the United States twice went to the brink of nuclear war to deter a Soviet assault on the oil lifeline of the Western world. You'll learn how the Russians, flush with the initial success of their invasion of Afghanistan, began to amass troops just on the other side of Iran's northern frontier—and how American military weakness left President Carter no choice but to contemplate the first use of nuclear weapons.

Chapter 5 examines oil and the war against civilians, or the terrorist threat.

When Kurdish rebel leader Mustafa Barzani was once asked why Yasir Arafat and the P.L.O. managed to become famous while no one ever heard of the Kurdish Liberation Movement, he replied, "because we fought *only on our own land*, and we killed *only our own enemies*."

Few terrorists since have made Barzani's mistake. As the Ayatollah Khomeini and Saddam Hussein have made clear, nothing commands world attention like the slaughter of innocents.

In this chapter, you will explore the roots of terrorism in the

1990s—that go back to the seventh century A.D. You'll also learn what you can do as an individual—to avoid becoming a hostage, or to survive if you are unlucky enough to become one.

In **Chapter 6**, you'll get a chilling account of new technological developments that are already moving the Mideast tinderbox toward a hair-trigger alert—precisely the sort of situation in which wars get started by accident. You'll also learn how to build undetectable, precision-guided cruise missiles out of cheap, off-the-shelf parts.

Finally, you'll read how Iran's radical mullahs intend to achieve what Saddam Hussein failed to accomplish: consolidation of the vast Mideast oil reserves under a single power.

Pearl Harbor II

It is one of the great ironies of history that, once set in motion, events tend to assume a life of their own. Sometimes, these currents flow back to their origins and unexpectedly inundate the ones responsible for starting them in motion. This is very much like what happened when American occupation authorities unleashed forces in postwar Japan only to see that action come back to haunt them a couple of generations later.

Chapter 7 begins with the story of the Japanese postwar economic miracle—how the country went from ruins to riches in a few short years—and how policy decisions made by the American occupation authorities in the 1940s unwittingly sowed the seeds of Japanese-American conflict in the 1990s and beyond.

Chapter 8 covers the Japanese shopping spree in the United States and throughout Southeast Asia. You'll find out how the growing need for Asian capital and markets makes us vulnerable to unforeseen events far beyond our own shores.

Chapter 9 is about the rearmament of Japan. Nuclear sabre-rattling on the Korean peninsula. The Chinese plan to develop military muscle commensurate with their growing economic clout. How any one of a dozen possible flashpoints could ignite an explosion large enough to devastate markets from London to New York to Sydney.

Chapter 10 covers Asian stock markets. In it, you'll read about the forces behind the most extraordinary bull markets of modern times. You'll get an up-to-date assessment of the likelihood of another collapse—including a discussion of an unfamiliar threat that is almost never discussed in the financial press.

Finally, you'll read about the devastating effects such a debacle could have on the stock market in the United States and the rest of the world.

Preparing for financial upheaval

The possibility that events in Japan could shake markets as far away as the United States leads quite nicely into the theme of the final section, which addresses the topic of investment survival in the decade ahead.

Chapter 11 boldly predicts the shape of the next war over Mideast oil. You'll learn how the military lessons of Desert Storm will lead to new tactics designed to resist attack by high-tech stealth bombers and cruise missiles. Why the next war will be many times more destructive than any previous conflict.

You'll also discover why governments in places like Bosnia and Rwanda defy analysis by Western political science. Why strength of character in the world's zones of turmoil is almost always associated with the ability to sustain and inflict pain.

Finally, you'll get a prescription for surviving a potentially devastating attack of millennium fever—the unavoidable crescendo of craziness as the year 2000 approaches.

Chapter 12 warns you about one of the most serious threats facing the average U.S. investor today—the approaching debacle in mutual funds. You'll find out why bear markets hurt mutual fund investors worse than any other class of investor.

In the 1930s, a run on America's banks plunged the nation into a depression. In the 1990s, a run on open-end mutual funds could result in similar investment devastation on a worldwide basis. You'll also find out what you can do to head off this and other threats to your mutual fund portfolio.

Chapter 13 outlines a demographic time bomb hanging over most of the developed nations of the world. You'll read why people born between 1946 and 1964 may well be members of a doomed generation.

Chapter 14 attempts to pull all these various themes and threads together. It is a manual for riding the last wave to prosperity and profit, for finding the good news that lies beneath the surface of what seem to be rather grim and forbidding waters.

Inevitably, perhaps, a book about money and history is a book about tempest and turmoil. I hope you will find it full of high adventure—and equally appealing as both a reader and an investor.

The fact that great upheavals lie ahead, however, does not

mean that the last wave of investment prosperity must end in despair. As an individual, you may not be able to alter the course of events set in motion in Pyongyang, Tokyo, or Washington, D.C.

But what you *can* do is take financial advantage of human folly. As long as free investment markets exist, you are never powerless.

For those armed with a discerning analysis of what lies ahead, the future is never dark. Ensuring that this is the case is what *The Last Wave* is all about.

---

1. Quoted by Anton Mohr, *The Oil War*, pp. 35-36.

2. Richard M. Nixon, *Beyond Peace*, pp. 127-128.

Section I

Oil and War

Chapter 1

Oil-Fired Engines of War

The History of Oil in World War I

You may have men, munitions and money. But if you do not have oil, which is today the greatest motive power that you use, all your other advantages would be of comparatively little value.
— Walter Long, House of Commons speech, October 1917 —

World War I marked the beginning of large-scale military use of oil-related technologies. During World War I, oil became a military objective for the first time. It was also the first time an oil strategy—securing one's own supplies while denying them to an adversary—had a measurable impact on victory.

For centuries the world had known about naturally occurring deposits of oil. It was something that seeped into and ruined drinking wells and rendered land unfit for farming. But in 1859, when Edwin Drake struck a gusher in Pennsylvania, oil, for the first time, became available in commercial quantities.

As a fuel, it enjoyed considerable advantages over coal and wood. It was more efficient, giving a greater volume of heat per unit of weight. Because it was a liquid, it could be transported through pipelines.

This made it a lot easier to handle than solid fuel—and a lot safer to handle than combustible gases, such as hydrogen (at the time used to power lighter-than-air balloons). But it also made possible a further development that was to prove even more revolutionary—the internal combustion engine.

In 1862, Alphonse Beau de Rochas constructed the first oil-powered piston engine. Building on de Rochas' work, the German firm of Nikolaus Otto and E. Langen in 1876 built a version that incorporated an electric spark ignition.

By 1883, another German, Gottlieb Daimler, had constructed

an engine-powered bicycle. His engine was the first ever to use a refined by-product of oil—gasoline. In 1892 Rudolf Diesel invented the compression-ignition engine that bears his name today.

The most important thing about the oil-burning internal combustion engine was that it delivered hitherto unachieved amounts of power for an engine of its weight. This new higher power-to-weight ratio, made possible by the new technology, was soon to produce a corresponding revolution in the art of war—in the air, on land, and at sea.

Military aviation

At the turn of the century, military aviation was confined to the use of lighter-than-air balloons. As early as the American Civil War, these balloons were used as fixed observation posts for artillery. But oil-fired technology offered a new and previously unheard of dimension of mobility. No longer would balloon operators have to choose between the tether and the random currents of the wind.

Brigadier Count Ferdinand von Zeppelin was one of the first to conceive a new kind of airship. Using a newly discovered metal—lightweight aluminum—he constructed the world's first metal-framed rigid airship. In 1900, he launched the LZ1, a 420-foot-long, cigar-shaped airship powered by two Daimler engines. It was capable of speeds of up to 17 miles per hour.

Of course the real oil-powered revolution in military aviation concerned not improvements to balloons, but the invention of the airplane. In 1903, the Wright brothers made their successful flight at Kitty Hawk, and four years later, the U.S. Army issued the world's first specifications for a military airplane.

In 1910, the U.S. Army conducted a series of tests that included dropping a dummy bomb on a target shaped like a battleship and launching a plane from the deck of a ship. The same year, the Italian army dropped the first airborne torpedo.

The British were the first to pioneer tactical air support. After experimenting with aerial bombardment in support of ground troops against the Turks, they used tactical air power in a counterattack against the German army when it broke through British lines in March 1918.

Meanwhile, the Germans were the first to attempt strategic bombing. They dropped explosives from both Zeppelins and bi-plane bombers on the British home islands. But only rarely did

4

these bombs hit their targets. However, even hopelessly inaccurate aerial bombardment proved surprisingly effective as a weapon of terror that could be used to demoralize and unnerve civilian populations.

Admittedly, these events are more noteworthy for the way they foreshadowed the future than for the way they influenced the outcome of World War I. By and large, World War I aviation was confined to reconnaissance and range finding for artillery. Even so, the war provided a powerful stimulus to innovation. By its end, the speed of the most advanced aircraft topped 120 miles per hour.

It also created a new aviation industry practically overnight. During the course of the conflict, Britain built 55,000 planes, France 68,000, Germany 48,000, and Italy 20,000. During its 18-month participation in World War I, the United States alone manufactured more than 15,000 aircraft.

Oil and war on land

Before the oil-powered internal combustion engine, war on land was critically dependent on the coal- and steam-powered railroad. Railways could carry troops and supplies vast distances and disgorge them at the nearest appropriately located railhead. But from there, the effective range of military maneuver was limited by the physical endurance of men and horses.

(Interestingly enough, military planners on the eve of World War I estimated one horse for every three men would be required. And because a horse requires 10 times as much food as an average infantryman, this created an enormous burden of supply.)

One generally unrecognized aspect of World War I is the extent to which it was a victory of the gas-powered truck over the steam powered locomotive. For example, the Germans clearly started the war with the better railway system.

Indeed, the planners on the German general staff pinned their hopes of a quick victory on the belief that a sufficiently rapid advance on the part of its invasion forces would disrupt any organized defense before it could properly begin.

They were very nearly right. By September 1914, one German line extended more than 125 miles—from Verdun to a point northeast of Paris. From there, it was joined by another line stretching clear to the Alps. In a little over a month, the German railroads had deployed an invasion force encompassing more than two million fighting men. But just as the right flank of the

German advance approached the French capital, something re-markable happened. A fleet of gas-powered taxicabs came to the rescue.

The taxi defense

Displaying the same physical courage as politicians every-where, the French government immediately abandoned the city on news of the German approach. Shortly thereafter, 100,000 civilians also fled.

The most remarkable aspect of the leadership of the French army before and during World War I was its extraordinary pigheadedness. For example, the general staff was implacably opposed to modernizing the French army, claiming that the machine gun could never be any real threat to horse-mounted cavalry.

When word leaked out that the French army also was ready to abandon the city, its commanding general was practically assaulted by the military governor of Paris, Joseph Gallieni. Gallieni was convinced by aerial reconnaissance that the Ger-mans were vulnerable to counterattack. He argued that a carefully planned counterattack could halt their advance and save the city.

Gallieni had already tried and failed to convince the British to listen to his plan. But at the last possible moment—in a dramatic late-night telephone call—he succeeded in convincing the French leadership to order a counterattack on September 6.

Taken by surprise, the Germans at first fell back. But then they brought up reinforcements. Facing fresh troops and increas-ingly outnumbered, the French forces desperately needed to bring up their own reinforcements who were awaiting orders at a staging area just outside Paris.

The problem was that there was no hope of their arriving in time. The French did not have the German genius for railroads. And what railways the French did have were hopelessly dis-rupted. If reinforcements simply marched to the front, they would arrive too late.

A master of military improvisation, Gallieni was among the first to realize what could be achieved by linking the gasoline-powered internal combustion engine to the requirements of modern warfare. At 8 p.m. on the evening of September 6, 1914, he issued an order to commandeer all the taxicabs in Paris.

All over the city, soldiers flagged down taxis and ordered the existing passengers out. The soldiers themselves then got in and ordered the driver to take them to the front. And paid by the meter.

The following day, things were a little more organized. Hundreds more taxis assembled at designated staging areas around the city, crammed with soldiers. And under the cover of darkness, they set out in convoys of 25 to 50.

It was the first motorized column in the history of warfare. It was also accompanied by a furious honking of horns and shaking of fists, as individual vehicles sped about, passing and repassing each other in a uniquely French style of driving that persists among Paris taxis even today.

In this way, thousands of reinforcements were delivered to critical points along the front lines. So strengthened, the French forces renewed their attack. And by September 9, the Germans were in retreat. Paris was saved.

Oil and the birth of armored warfare

As early as 1899, F. R. Simms, a British engineer, imagined the advantages a mechanized armored cavalry would have over the traditional horse-borne variety. First, he mounted one of Daimler's engines on a four-wheeled motor bike. Then he armed it with a Maxim machine gun mounted behind a shield on the handle bars.

Encouraged by his early successes, Simms next built a prototype of what he called the War Car, armed with a 1 1/2-pound cannon and a pair of machine guns. He successfully demonstrated it in a series of tests before British army brass, where he achieved speeds in excess of 9 mph. As is so often the case, however, the generals were preparing to fight the last war instead of the next one. He didn't get a single order.

In the face of army opposition, it was the farsighted Winston Churchill who ultimately saved the idea from military oblivion. As First Lord of the Admiralty, he formed a Land Ships Committee to consider development of the craft. Because the early models had to travel by flat-bed rail car from the factory to the proving ground, there was always a chance they might be spotted by enemy agents. So, to ensure secrecy, they were routinely covered with tarpaulins stamped with the legend "WATER TANK." In due course, tank became the code word for the new armored fighting vehicle, and later, the vernacular.

Not until much later did the real virtues of armored vehicles finally dawn upon the rest of the British military. But before I tell the story, let me first set the stage.

Before the stalemate

Popular histories of World War I often dwell on the military stalemate that resulted from the network of trenches and barbed wire that stretched across Europe. But in the early days of the campaign, it was a war of feint and thrust, of tactical maneuvers on a grander scale than the world had ever seen.

In the opening weeks of the campaign, German armies, following the battle plan of General von Schlieffen, swept westward through Belgium to open a front from which to descend upon France from the north. As the Allied powers struggled to marshal a counterattack, it seemed that the best chance for disrupting the German advance lay in a flanking maneuver to the west. If only Allied armies could get around the forward elements of the German army, they could fall upon the enemy's rear.

Of course, the Germans soon discovered the Allied intentions and kept trying to extend their line of advance—before the Allies could get around it. These mutual attempts at an outflanking

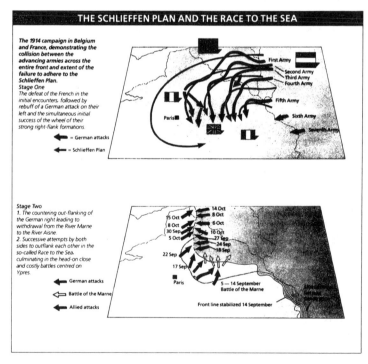

Map of von Schlieffen's invasion routes from *Technology and War: The Impact of Science on Weapon Development and Modern Battle,* by Kenneth Macksey, p. 68.

8

maneuver sent both armies in a headlong rush westward to the sea.

In 1914, some of Winston Churchill's sailors, sent over to assist the hard-pressed Belgians, witnessed a startling innovation. The Belgians, forever outnumbered and outgunned by the Germans, were forced to improvise to stave off catastrophe on the Plain of Flanders. In a desperate attempt to increase the mobility of their troops, they put 6-millimeter and later 8-millimeter armor on all the motorized vehicles they could manage to commandeer.

Much to the Germans' consternation, they found that nothing in their arsenal could penetrate 8-millimeter steel plates—except their huge fort-busting artillery. But these big guns were slow-moving and difficult to aim. And such was the state of gunnery at the time that one hit out of 30 at 100 yards was considered very good shooting. So against fast-moving vehicles, the big guns were useless.

At length, the Germans found the only way they could stop the four-wheeled armored trucks was to dig ditches too deep for them to cross. But before a network of trenches extended across the entire Western front and both sides settled down to a war of attrition, the armored car was estimated by both sides to be the military equivalent of an entire company of infantry.

This early success of the vehicles stimulated a wealth of mechanized armor building. But it was only much later, as the British grew desperate for a way to break the stalemate, that the precursor of the modern battle tank really came into its own.

In 1916, a Royal Army engineer and popular fiction writer, Colonel Ernest Swinton, designed an armored version of a vehicle based on the agricultural tractor that had been recently

British Mark I tank from *Tank: A History of the Armored Fighting Vehicle,* by Kenneth Macksey and John H. Batchelor, p. 144.

9

developed in America. It was a steel-armored tracked vehicle, powered by an internal combustion engine and armed with cannon and machine guns. Just the thing to break through the heavily fortified Hindenberg line at Cambrai.

The tanks that faced the Germans that fateful day were slow-moving and cumbersome affairs, hastily improvised out of available components. Guns and armor were taken from the navy—which, true to the oldest traditions of inter-service rivalry, tried its best to kill the project.

The world's first tank battle — Cambrai

The plan of attack called for 476 tanks, which had to be brought to the front by railroad. In those days, a tank's tracks and sprockets wore out after only 20 miles! Transport by rail also served another purpose. It ensured that the Germans were not tipped off in advance by the distinctive rumbling and clanking sounds of armor on the move.

Each tank carried huge bundles of wood (called "fascines") to dump in ditches that blocked its path. As the trenches were crossed and the barbed wire crushed down, infantry would follow. Once the defensive perimeter was pierced, cavalry would march into the open ground beyond, fall upon the German rear, and, so it was hoped, force Germany's withdrawal from northern France.

At 6:10 a.m. on November 19, 1917, the startled German defenders awoke to the ominous rumble of approaching armor. Ten minutes later, suppressive fire from 1,003 Allied artillery engulfed the enemy's forward battery positions. Smoke, fired at enemy observation posts, mixed with the morning fog and prevented early discovery of the Allied battle plan.

Breached defenses

The Germans promptly dove into their underground bunkers, content to wait until the big guns exhausted their supplies of ammunition. The enemy high command, believing in the invulnerability of the earthworks of the Hindenberg line, reached a similar conclusion.

In the underground comfort of their command bunkers, they never dreamed an invasion was possible, let alone imminent. And so they planned no counterattacks. As a result, the Allied action achieved complete and utter tactical surprise.

On the right flank, the tanks broke through almost without resistance. Grenade and rifle fire from advancing Allied infantry completely routed the terrified defenders. With speedy capture of the front-line positions thus assured, the tanks lunged ahead—at the unheard of speed of 4 mph!—down the long slope toward the vital bridges that spanned the Escaut Canal at Masnieres and Marcoing.

But when the first bridge collapsed under the weight of a single tank, the Allies knew they had a problem. Tanks were not waterproof, and portable pontoon bridges had not yet been invented.

On the left flank, the few surviving German gunners made a fortuitous discovery. In the heat of battle, their stocks of explosive artillery shells were rapidly depleted. In desperation, they resorted to solid shot, ample supplies of which were available. Although it came too late to save the German positions on the left, solid shot soon proved to be an excellent armor-piercing weapon.

Nonetheless, Allied tanks swept forward and soon outdistanced the infantry and cavalry, which were supposed to follow in close support. Just as the advance on the right was stopped by an unbridgeable canal, on the left it dissipated as effective coordination was lost between forward elements of the battle.

In those days, communication depended on the laying of vulnerable telephone cables and messengers on horseback. And it often took hours to respond to rapidly changing battlefield conditions.

Still, for the Allies, it was a tactical success, if not a strategic triumph. In exchange for 4,000 dead and 65 tanks destroyed, they captured 10,000 of the enemy, 123 artillery pieces, 179 mortars, and 281 machine guns.

Encouraged by this result, the world's first tank corps went on to even greater success. On August 8, 1918, at the Battle of Amiens, a swarm of 456 tanks tore through German lines. In this way, mechanized armor, driven by the oil-fired engines of war, changed the face of battle forever.

Oil technology afloat

The application of the oil-burning engine to ships also changed the nature of surface warfare and opened new avenues of military advantage. Oil was much easier than solid fuel to load and store. A liquid, it could be held in the numerous cavities within a ship's hull, which previously had been inaccessible and useless. The ability to use such spaces for oil storage increased a ship's fuel carrying capacity as much as 30%.

HMS Dreadnought, 1906, the first oil-fired big-gun battleship, from the National Maritime Museum collection, Greenwich, London, England.

The ability to load more fuel on a ship meant a corresponding increase in operational radius. Oil-fired boats were able to steam as much as 40% farther between refuelings than their coal-fired counterparts.

The ability to resupply at sea further increased the operational range of the fleet. Moreover, such resupply could also be accomplished without occupying a third of the crew in the effort—as was the case with coal. This was because a liquid fuel could be moved by means of mechanical pumps. Coal required shoveling.

In fact, as a ship used up her coal, an increasingly large fraction of the crew had to be diverted—from the guns, if necessary—to carry coal from bins in increasingly distant parts of the ship to the furnaces. As a result, the fighting ability of the crew was apt to decline just when it was needed most.

Because of their superior thermal efficiency, oil-burning boilers delivered more power than their coal-fired predecessors. As a result, the oil-fired ships were faster than anything else afloat.

Among the first to appreciate the advantages of an oil-fired navy was legendary British Royal Navy figure John Arbuthnot Fisher. Born to a poor farming family in Ceylon, Fisher went to sea at the age of 13 and rose to become First Sea Lord in 1904. Known for his energy, tenacity, and the sheer force of his personality, he was once admonished by none other than King

Edward VII to, "Please stop shaking your fist in my face."

But even Fisher's formidable powers of persuasion were not enough to convince the Royal Navy to convert to oil. The reason was simple. The supply of Welsh coal was abundant. But there were no supplies of oil to be had in the British Isles.

After Fisher retired, it fell to his protégé, a young politician named Winston Churchill, to take up the cause. Ultimately, the issue that tipped the balance in favor of oil was the increased speed promised by an oceangoing fleet.

The coal-fired battleships of the Royal Navy could muster a top speed of about 21 knots. The British War College calculated that it would require a top speed of 25 knots to ensure a decisive advantage over the new fleet under construction by the Germans in the years immediately prior to World War I.

Those extra four knots were not possible without converting to oil power. As commander of the navy, Churchill ordered the conversion of the entire British fleet beginning in 1912.

The war beneath the surface

Another oil-related development at sea, however, took place not above the surface, but below. The idea of the submarine, like that of the piston engine, had been around for centuries. Sketches of a submersible craft, for example, survive among the 15th-century drawings of Leonardo da Vinci.

During the American Revolution, David Bushnell built a man-powered submersible, which he launched against the flagship of the British fleet blockading New York. Driven by the muscle power of its single crewman, it made its way down the Hudson River and successfully attached a bomb to the underside of the British dreadnought.

The attack failed when the timed fuse failed to explode. But the news of the attempt was so convulsive that the target vessel was compelled to shift its berth, and in so doing, the blockade was eventually relaxed.

Development of a proper oceangoing craft, however, had to wait upon advances in materials and engine technology. But by 1900, all the pieces were in place.

In that year, John Holland put a gasoline engine in a submersible hull. On the surface, the engine not only powered the boat, but it also turned a dynamo that in turn charged a set of storage batteries. Below the surface, battery-driven electric motors supplied power. On the surface, the craft was capable of 10 knots.

Submerged, the top speed was 8 knots.

Both range and reliability improved in 1904 when Maxim Laubeuf replaced Holland's gasoline engine with a diesel. Not only did heavy oil provide greater fuel economy than refined gasoline, but its lubricating qualities reduced engine wear as well.

In addition, diesels did not require complicated spark ignition systems. As a result, they were prone to fewer breakdowns—an important consideration when you're underwater and many miles from the nearest shipyard.

Oil as a strategic objective

Besides fueling the new engines of war, oil rapidly became indispensable as a lubricant. It was also an essential ingredient in the chemistry of explosives.

As a result, oil supplies, for the first time, became a military objective. Because neither Britain nor Germany had appreciable domestic supplies of oil, both faced the logistical challenges of oil dependency. The skill that they used to anticipate and answer this challenge, as we shall see, had a major bearing on the outcome of the war.

That the Middle East was rich in oil had been known since ancient times. Indeed the biblical tale of Shadrach, Meshach, and Abednego, the victims of King Nebuchadnezzar's fiery furnace (*Daniel 3:25*), has been read by 20th-century geologists as a reference to the seepage of oil and natural gas in what are now the Iraqi mountains.

At the outbreak of World War I, oil had already been discovered in the United States and Romania. But Mideast oil was generally of superior quality. Besides that, once drilled, it generally flowed freely under its own pressure. Thus there was no need for complicated pumping equipment, and the costs of production were among the lowest in the world.

Competition for supply

By 1910, the vast bulk of British oil was coming from the Persian Gulf, a tense and nearly ungovernable region even then. So to ensure their source of supply, the British took several important steps. First, they bought their own oil company. In 1912, the British government spent £2 million to acquire control of the Anglo-Persian Oil Co., which was heavily involved in the exploitation of Persian oil fields.

Next, Britain increased its naval presence in the region. This was done to ward off any attempts by the Turkish and German navies to disrupt supply. With sources thus assured, and the Royal Navy protecting the lines of supply, the Allies were able to deploy their remaining forces in a naval blockade of Axis shipping.

Centuries of experience as a maritime power had taught British planners never to underestimate the importance of ship-building. Under Churchill's impatient supervision, the conversion of the fleet to oil proceeded rapidly, and substantial numbers of new ships were constructed. At the outbreak of hostilities, the balance of naval material stood at:

	British and Russian fleet	German and Turkish fleet[1]
Dreadnoughts	32	17
Battle Cruisers	11	6
Pre-Dreadnoughts	54	45
Destroyers and Torpedo Boats	420	178

This advantage in material, in addition to generally superior British seamanship, eventually proved insurmountable. Slowly but inexorably, the flow of oil so vital to Germany's war effort was reduced to a trickle.

The internal combustion engine also provided the Germans with their only clear advantage at sea: the diesel driven submarine. The German U-boat campaign severely restricted the flow of all Allied supplies—including oil.

By 1916, the *Times* of London reported a "dearth of petrol." In December 1917, French Prime Minister Clemenceau warned U.S. President Wilson that unless more gasoline could be found, the French army would soon grind to a halt.

In 1917, the German High Command launched its unrestricted U-boat campaign against Allied shipping. Ultimately, this may have been a strategic mistake, because it was one of the major factors in America's entry into the war. But in the short run, the effects were both devastating and immediate.

Allied tonnage lost at sea in the first six months of 1917 more than doubled what it was during the same period the year before. During one four-month period, Standard Oil of New Jersey alone lost six tankers—among them the John D. Archbold, the newest, most modern tanker then built.

The developing shortages of oil soon spurred new efforts at coordination and protection of supply. An Inter-Allied Petroleum

Conference was organized in February 1918. This was a scheme to pool, coordinate, and organize oil supplies and tanker shipments.

In addition, the development of convoy naval tactics made tankers a more difficult target for the German U-boats. The combination of fewer losses at sea plus the effort to coordinate supply, effectively solved the Allies' wartime oil supply problems. The Germans, however, were not so fortunate.

German oil woes

To be sure, the Germans suffered substantially from the Allied blockade—which effectively cut off overseas supplies. But they were also victims of their own failure to anticipate the demands of a war of attrition.

Prior to the war, the American conglomerate Standard Oil supplied 90% of Germany's needs. After the outbreak of hostilities, this supply was cut off, leaving Germany dependent on Galician oil, controlled by Austro-Hungary, and its own meager domestic supplies.

With Persia firmly under British (and Russian) influence, Germany turned toward Romania. By world standards, Romania was a relatively smaller producer. But it was the second largest producer in Europe—after Russia. For the first two years of the war, the Romanians remained neutral in an effort to figure out who was most likely to win before taking sides.

But in August 1916, impressed by recent Russian military successes on the Eastern front, Romania declared war on Austro-Hungary—which brought it into a state of war with Germany as well. The following month, German and Austrian troops began to advance against their new enemy. In October, they captured a vast Allied fuel dump on the Black Sea virtually intact.

These stocks were supposed to have been destroyed to deny them to the advancing Germans. But in the confusion of battle and the Allied retreat, they somehow were not.

In November, the Germans broke through the last line of resistance in the mountain passes above the Wallachian Plain—Romania's most productive oil-producing region. Smarting from the Allies' Black Sea debacle, the British turned to Colonel John Norton-Griffiths—to ensure that the destruction was really carried out this time.

Hell-Fire Jack

Variously known as "Hell-Fire Jack" and "Empire Jack,"

Norton-Griffiths was one of the century's legendary engineer-adventurers. At various times in his career, he had undertaken formidable construction projects in practically every corner of the world: from railways in Australia and Africa, to harbors in North America and aqueducts in Eastern Europe.

He made his wartime reputation by adapting techniques he originally developed to build the Manchester sewer system as a tactic against German trench warfare. He would simply burrow under German lines to plant large explosive charges, and then set them off as part of a coordinated attack. This technique was proven successful against the German trench network at Ypres.

Careening about the front in his two-ton, custom-made Rolls-Royce—which always seemed to be well-stocked with hot women and cold champagne—he was scarcely popular with local commanders. So despite his battlefield successes, he was eventually ordered back to London.

But when the Allies wanted to deny the Romanian oil fields to the advancing Germans, there seemed no one better suited to the mission than Hell-Fire Jack. On November 18, 1916, the day after the Germans broke through Romanian defenses, he arrived in Bucharest—this time accompanied only by a single manservant.

He did a very thorough job. Wells were spiked, equipment and pipelines wrecked, and huge storage tanks set ablaze. Before long, a steady series of local explosions mingled with the sounds of advancing German artillery.

From time to time, Norton-Griffiths insisted on personally setting the charges himself. In one equipment storage facility loaded with welding gas, the explosion went off prematurely. Hell-Fire Jack was blown out of the building and carried some distance by the force of the blast, his hair aflame.

But that didn't stop him. When his supplies of explosives were exhausted, he grabbed a sledgehammer and banged away at equipment that could not be quickly wrecked by other means. He escaped just as the crackle of small arms fire announced the arrival of the advancing German troops.

Europe's second most productive oil fields had become a blazing inferno. Vast columns of flame dotted the landscape. Heavy, asphyxiating smoke rose high in the air and blotted out the sun.

It took the Germans fully five months to get any production at all going again. Despite their best efforts, oil output in 1917 was only a third of previous production levels. But by the following year, they managed to push output to 80% of 1914 levels.

Difficult to destroy

Interestingly enough, this was history's first large scale demonstration of what would eventually become one of the timeless truths of oil and war: Oil in the ground is very difficult to destroy.

Norton-Griffiths' efforts were repeated in the Dutch East Indies ahead of the advancing Japanese in World War II. And by Saddam Hussein in Kuwait ahead of the advancing Americans in 1991. Each time, a determined repair effort was able to restore output to something approaching the previous production levels. In some cases, output actually surpassed previous levels.

Once the German infantry had secured the Romanian oil fields, it was virtually impossible to deny them access to the large underground reserves that remained. Despite his best efforts, all Hell-Fire Jack could do was slow them down.

But sometimes that's enough. By 1917, fuel shortages were already evident everywhere in Germany. Trains stopped running, and planes were forced to use substitute fuels, which degraded speed and performance.

By October 1918, the German general staff estimated that the nation's entire stock of industrial lubricants would be exhausted within six months. War industries that operated on oil would grind to a halt within nine weeks.

Although there was enough fuel to sustain naval operations for perhaps another seven or eight months, the army would be out of gas in less than 60 days. The following month, on November 11, 1918, Germany surrendered.

Despite an abundance of traditional war materials—such as coal and iron—Germany lost the war because it failed to ensure adequate supplies of what would become the most important strategic material of all.

For the victorious Allies, World War I was history's first military demonstration of a successful oil strategy. It was also a lesson that was not lost on Hitler's planners prior to World War II.

---

1. Kenneth Macksey, *Technology and War: The Impact of Science on Weapon Development and Modern Battle.*

Chapter 2

Blitzkrieg and Surprise Attack

The History of Oil in World War II

If I do not get the oil of Maikop and Brozny, then I must end the war.
— Adolf Hitler, June 1, 1941 —

By 1940, the role of oil and war was understood and appreciated by military planners everywhere. However, most accounts of World War II fail to explain the extent that the competition for oil supplies determined the shape and tenor of the conflict.

While only a minor factor in the initial outbreak of hostilities in Europe, oil nonetheless influenced the shape of German battle doctrine and enticed Hitler into a strategically fatal misstep. And in the Pacific, oil was a precipitating factor in the actual outbreak of hostilities.

Oil for the Reich

For Germany, the lessons of World War I were twofold. First, the country could never again afford to go to war without ensuring adequate supplies of oil and other vital materials. In Europe, Germany was forced to make secure supplies of oil and other vital materials a major strategic objective. As the war wore on, it was the need for more oil that lay at least in part behind the ill-fated German invasion of the Soviet Union.

The second lesson of World War I was that Germany could never again afford to let itself get bogged down in a war of attrition. In World War II, like World War I, Germany found itself hopelessly outgunned and outmanned by numerically superior adversaries. The need for a doctrine of battle that ensured swift and decisive victory was thus never more imperative.

One German officer who learned well the lessons of Cambrai

and World War I was General Heinz Guderian. A veteran of the signal corps, he saw immediately what radio could bring to the problem of coordinating an armored battle. He envisioned one man sitting before a crystal radio and directing an entire squadron of tanks from inside a mobile command post.

Such a formation, he reasoned, could outmaneuver and surprise much larger conventional formations. Out of his vision came a special new kind of armored brigade, ideally suited for a war of concentrated fire and tactical maneuver—the famed Panzer divisions.

Guderian also developed a new tactical theory for armored warfare. Instead of using tanks to attack fortified positions (as had been done at Cambrai), he proposed to make his Panzers spearheads of infiltration. Using the concentrated violence of massed firepower, he envisioned a force that could break through a defensive perimeter and then maneuver with great speed to attain vital objectives at the enemy's rear. Once the objectives were taken, however, the tanks would withdraw, leaving infantry to secure the new position with anti-tank weapons (which, incidentally, had been vastly improved in the years since World War I).

Genesis of the blitzkrieg

This line of thought meshed perfectly with the war-fighting philosophy of the German High Command. As a battle tactic, the swift shock of massive armored attack offered two important military advantages. First, it gave an adversary very little time to react. In addition, it offered the promise of quick capture of foreign stocks of oil and other raw materials, which could then be used to fuel a more sustained effort.

The Panzers' first expedition, however, was something less than an awe-inspiring success. In March 1938, Hitler incorporated Austria into the Third Reich. Although the German High Command expected no opposition to the Austrian annexation, Hitler wanted a show of force anyway. A better politician than general, Hitler had a keen appreciation of the propaganda value of pictures of cheering crowds greeting German tanks as they rolled into the Austrian capital.

Guderian himself was dispatched to Vienna at the head of the 2nd Panzer Division. The episode that followed eerily foreshadowed events that would eventually bring down the Nazi war effort: At the border, both units ran out of gas.[1]

Fortunately, it was only a case of a bureaucratic screw-up. An army fuel depot was nearby, but no one there had been informed of Guderian's advance. Moreover, the stocks had already been earmarked for other purposes (the defense of the so-called Siegfried Line).

It was late at night when Guderian arrived, and the officer in charge of the depot refused to contravene his orders—which said nothing about releasing fuel to an impatient Panzer leader at the head of a column of tanks. Because of the lateness of the hour, the depot commander could not be found, so an exasperated Guderian finally roused the mayor of nearby Passau—who was prevailed upon to provide civilian trucks to ferry fuel from other sources. He also telephoned across the border to ask the Austrian service stations on the road to Vienna to stay open—so that the German columns could buy gas along the way!

(Actually, this was not the only foul-up of the Austrian expedition. While Guderian was foraging for fuel at the border, another division arrived without any maps of the country it was supposed to invade. Guderian finally had to give the general in charge a copy of a Baedeker guidebook so that he could find his way to Vienna.)

Oil squad specialists

Annexation of Austria and later development of the Prinzdorf field contributed another 18,000 barrels per day to German oil production. But it was not nearly enough to fuel the campaign of conquest envisioned by the Nazis. Because captured supplies and conquered oil fields would be necessary to fuel the German war machine in any sustained conflict, the German high command assembled a special squad of oil-field experts to ensure that captured oil would be exploited as expeditiously as possible.

These hand-picked specialists, drawn from the ranks of domestic oil companies and various government bureaus, would be sent in to put out oil-field fires and to get production going again almost before the smoke of battle had cleared. They saw their first wartime action in Poland.

It was at dawn on September 1, 1939 that the world first saw blitzkrieg in action. Germany committed some 2,700 tanks to the attack. In devastating attacks of concentrated fire, closely coordinated with infantry and aircraft, everything that Guderian foresaw was borne out. The Panzers broke through Polish lines in short order and spread panic and confusion deep into enemy territory. In one instance, armored columns penetrated 125 miles

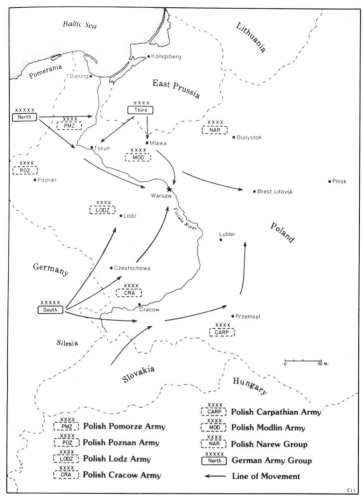

The German Attack on Poland in 1939, from *The Patterns of War Since the 18th Century*, by Larry H. Addington, p. 183.

in only five days. In three weeks, Poland was completely overrun.

Even in the midst of victory, problems surfaced that were destined to plague the German army again and again. Pre-invasion estimates of fuel consumption turned out to be vastly underestimated. Guderian's Panzer divisions consumed 1,000 gallons of gas per mile on their long drive to Vienna. But when they had to fight their way across open country, fuel consumption almost doubled. On the second day of battle, a unit of the XIX Corps was forced to halt because it ran out of gas.

Oil-field objectives

One of the major strategic objectives of the invasion was the Polish oil fields of Galacia. When forward elements of the German XXII Corps entered Jaslo, members of the oil squad found most of the structures and facilities intact. As German forces pushed farther into Galacia, however, they abruptly found Russian tanks blocking their path.

On September 17, as the German juggernaut was rolling from one victory to the next, the Russians suddenly invaded Poland from the east. Stalin, the Soviet dictator remembered chiefly for his brutal purges of political opponents, was mindful of the strategic importance of oil to Hitler. He ordered Soviet units to capture as much of Poland's oil-production facilities as possible before the Germans arrived.

The Russians won the race. When the smoke of battle cleared, 70% of Poland's productive capacity was in Russian hands—not German. As a result, Hitler was forced to dispatch Foreign Minister Joachim von Ribbentrop to Moscow to negotiate the purchase of the greater part of Polish oil output.

French offensive

Of course, the most conspicuous success of the blitzkrieg came later—on May 10, 1940, when the 94 German divisions that had been amassed along the Western front drove through the Ardennes into France and Belgium. Allied defenses—including France's much-celebrated Maginot Line—folded like matchsticks before the relentless onslaught. For a time, it seemed that no army in the world could stand before an opponent whose tactical coordination bordered on the miraculous and whose stamina was hardly taxed by a 150-mile advance in seven days.

When there was no shortage of fuel, the Panzers performed brilliantly. On June 21, the oil squads arrived at the oil fields at Pechelbronn and found that demolition by the retreating French had been sporadic and ineffective.

Altogether, more than 7 million barrels of French, Belgian, and Dutch oil fell into German hands—much of it helpfully stockpiled along the Germans' invasion routes. Captured French oil was earmarked for use by the Luftwaffe (the German air force) in what was to become the Battle of Britain.

At Cambrai, the tanks were stopped eventually by the unforeseen exigencies of a new kind of warfare. But in 1940, no such obstacles lay in the path of the German advance. In one of the

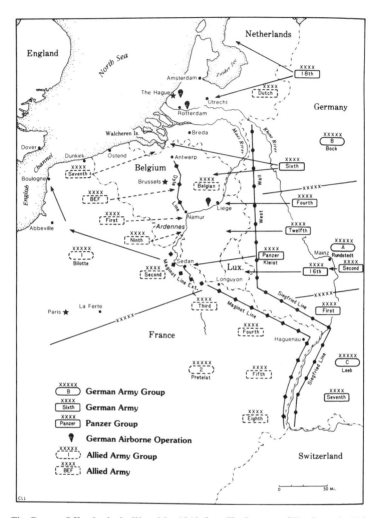

The German Offensive in the West, May 1940, from *The Patterns of War Since the 18th Century*, by Larry H. Addington, p. 188.

great ironies of history, General von Rudstedt, fearful of losses to his extraordinary tank corps, suddenly became overprotective and ordered the Panzers to halt their advance just outside Dunkirk.

Guderian and others thought it was madness not to pursue the attack—and therefore permit the hard-pressed English and French armies to evacuate by sea—but they were overruled. Had they not been, the Germans would almost certainly have destroyed the Allies at Dunkirk. The war would have been over.

Strategic shortages

In an effort to avoid the same kind of raw material shortages that hobbled Germany in World War I, Hitler and his generals had put great emphasis on accumulating stockpiles of strategic materials prior to the outbreak of hostilities. Strenuous efforts also were made to develop a domestic synthetic fuels industry.

In 1913, a German chemist, Friedrich Bergius, invented a process for extracting a high-grade liquid fuel from coal. It was called hydrogenation. In 1926, the German chemical giant, I. G. Farben acquired the patent rights to the Bergius process, and built a pilot plant which began operating in 1927.

By 1939, Germany had 14 hydrogenation plants in full operation. Six more were on the drawing board. By 1940, synthetic fuel output accounted for 46% of the country's total oil supply. Hydrogenation also produced 95% of Germany's aviation fuel. Without it, the famed Luftwaffe could never have taken to the air.

Despite the remarkable success of German efforts to develop synthetic fuels as an alternative source of supply, there was never enough oil. Once the fighting began, the British home fleet took up its war station in the North Sea—as it had in World War I—in an attempt to cut the flow of raw materials into Germany.

For a time, the spoils of war more than compensated for the effects of the British blockade. But by the end of 1940, the Germans were beginning to feel the pinch.

Oddly enough, one reason for this was the sheer size of the new German empire. Conquered territories stretched from Poland in the east to the French Atlantic coast in the west, from frigid Norway in the north to the warm waters of the Mediterranean in the south.

Even in less chaotic times, this vast area of Europe had never been self-sufficient in oil. In 1938—the last year of peace—the area then under Nazi domination had consumed 575,000 barrels a day. In 1940, the total production under German control amounted to only 234,550 barrels a day—a shortfall of 59%.[2]

Oil-driven tactics

More and more, the need for secure oil supplies began to dictate military policy. For example, Hitler was reluctant to occupy nominally neutral Romania even after it repeatedly attempted to renege on its commitment to export oil to Germany. He remembered the destruction of Romanian oil fields by Hell-

Fire Jack in World War I. (See Chapter 1.) And he was afraid of inviting a fresh Allied assault if he sent German troops to seize the fields.

(Another irony of the period is that as late as 1940, a good part of the Romanian oil industry was still run by the British. In effect, Englishmen were producing oil that the Germans then used to attack English countrymen and allies.)

By July, the shortages had grown sufficiently acute that Hitler began measuring the Soviet Union for an invasion. There was oil to be had in the Caucasus.

The invasion of Russia

Despite ample warnings from the British—who had broken German codes early in the war—the Russians did nothing to prepare for war. Stalin was preoccupied with bloody political purges at home—which eventually decimated the command ranks of the Red Army.

Hours before the attack, a dedicated German Communist from a unit assigned to the invasion force defected to the Soviet Union with word of Hitler's plans. Stalin suspected a trick and ordered him shot. So when the Germans finally did move, the Russians were quite literally caught napping.

It has been called by some military historians the greatest land war ever fought. Into the battle, the Germans threw 142 divisions, 3,350 tanks, and 2,250 aircraft. Opposing them in western Russia were 178 divisions, 10,000 tanks, and 7,000 aircraft.[3]

Despite its numbers, the Red Army was no match for its peerless adversary. When the battle began at 3:30 a.m. on Sunday, June 2, 1941, most of the Russian army was still sleeping off its Saturday night excesses. The first day, 1,489 Russian planes were destroyed on the ground and 322 in the air, with almost no losses to the Germans.

Panzer-led spearheads carried the blitzkrieg deep into Russian territory in three thrusts. Army Group North attacked the Baltic states, while Army Group Central moved against the Ukraine. General Karl-Heinrich von Stulpnagel, at the head of Army Group South, led the charge toward the Polish oil fields the Russians had seized in 1939. In only 25 days, the Panzers advanced 413 miles against their poorly trained and incompetently led opposition.

In the early weeks, it looked as if Hitler's boast about a quick

Operation Barbarossa: the German Plan of the Invasion of Russia, June 1941, from *The Patterns of War Since the 18th Century*, by Larry H. Addington, p. 198.

Russian victory would be correct: "We'll kick the door in," he said, "and the house will fall down."[4]

Scorched earth

When the oil squads finally reached western Galacia, however, they found that the retreating Russian demolition teams had been rather more efficient than the French had been a year earlier. Elsewhere, however, the Russians' headlong retreat left behind substantial stores of oil. But to their chagrin, the Nazis found that the oil could not be used without further refinement. Soviet T-34 and Voroshilov tanks ran on diesel fuel, but Guderian's Panzers needed gasoline.

From the very beginning, the Russian campaign was a race against time. And as the offensive began to bog down, time began to run out. To its credit, the Red Army was able to regroup after the frightening losses during the early weeks of the campaign.

In addition, the Japanese attack on Pearl Harbor convinced Stalin that he no longer had to worry about a Japanese invasion of the Russian Far East. That allowed him to withdraw a number of crack Siberian divisions and send them to the German front.

Logistical nightmare

More important, however, was the Germans' failure to anticipate the logistical demands of maintaining an army so far from home. Prior to the Russian invasion, the Panzers had never been in the field for more than six weeks at a time. As early as July, certain Luftwaffe squadrons were forced to begin curtailing ground support missions because they lacked aviation fuel.

On the bad Russian roads and difficult terrain, Panzer units required as much as twice the amount of fuel as had been originally anticipated. On October 9, 1941 the German quartermaster general estimated that army vehicles were 24,000 barrels short of minimum fuel requirements.

In the summer, dust choked the engines of the mechanized divisions. Fall rains turned primitive, unpaved roads into a quagmire, which did as much to slow the German advance as anything the Russian army could muster. To be sure, the Russian winter firmed up the muddy roads, but lack of antifreeze immobilized hundreds of tanks, trucks, and airplanes.

In the killing cold, even lubricating oils froze solid. All along the front, German soldiers discovered that even their rifles and machine guns no longer worked reliably.

In just six months, the campaign that had begun so optimistically became a logistical and military nightmare. By then the Germans had suffered 750,000 casualties. They had also lost some 75,000 vehicles—most to mechanical breakdowns. By December, Army Group South—the German unit nearest the Caucasus—was out of both fuel and ammunition.

It was spring 1942 before the Germans finally managed to mount an assault on the Caucasus. And it was not until August that the scorched remains of oil fields at Maikop (the westernmost of the Caucasian oil fields) were in German hands. By this time, German supply lines were so long that even the trucks carrying fuel to the front ran out of gas before they could get there.

This completely undermined the operational rationale of the Panzer units, which were designed for speed and mobility. By the time the campaign in the Caucasus unfolded, the Germans were forced to ferry oil supplies to the front on the backs of camels.

Nowhere was the crippling effect of supply shortages felt more acutely than in the Battle of Stalingrad, northwest of the Caucasus. The turning point in this campaign came during the bitter winter of 1942-43, after which the oil-starved German Sixth Army found itself on the defensive.

Ground down, frozen, hungry, its essential element of mobility gone, it was finally encircled by the Soviets. Even then, an escape route lay only 30 miles away. But there was only enough fuel to go 20 miles. So it surrendered.

But by then, all the worst fears of the Nazi war planners had been realized. Once again, Germany found itself bogged down in a long war of attrition.

My kingdom for a full tank

If the Allied victory over Germany in World War II was another example of a successful oil strategy, it is also worth noting that the war in Europe would have ended much sooner had the Allies made earlier and more strenuous efforts to target Germany's domestic oil industry.

Despite the Allies' strategic bombing campaign, synthetic fuel production more than doubled between 1940 and 1943. In the first quarter of 1944, synthetic fuels provided 57% of total supply and 92% of aviation gasoline.

One problem was that the Allied bombing generally wasn't very effective to begin with. Even under more or less continuous aerial bombardment, German factories also managed to achieve a more than threefold increase in the production of ammunition, aircraft, and weapons between 1942 and mid-1944. Tank production climbed sixfold.

Another problem was that Allied commanders didn't bother to specifically target oil until May 1944. (Even then, the British were opposed, claiming that the French railway system should be targeted instead.) On May 12, 1944, a combat wing comprising 935 bombers (plus fighter escorts) finally attacked the German synthetic fuels industry, including the I. G. Farben installation at Leuna.

On May 28 and 29, Allied bombers hit German oil installations again as well as the Ploesti oil installations in Romania. Despite nearly superhuman efforts to repair the bomb damage as quickly as possible, production plummeted. Before the first attack, synthetic production averaged 92,000 barrels per day. By September, output dropped to only 5,000 barrels.

Aviation gasoline output fell more than 90%. With the Luftwaffe operating at 10% of its minimum fuel requirements, it became more and more difficult to send fighters up to challenge attacking Allied bombers. This only further increased the destructive impact of the Allied raids.

Interestingly enough, Germany's newly developed jet fighters were just being introduced into operational air combat wings in late 1944. The development of the jet engine represented a quantum leap over propeller-driven aircraft, and would have given Germany a decisive advantage in the air. But there was no fuel to train pilots. Or even to get the new planes in the air.

It is also worth noting that the failures to take advantage of oil-related fortunes of war were not all on the Allied side. On December 16, 1944, Germany launched a powerful counterattack in the Ardennes Forest of eastern Belgium and Luxembourg. Later known as the Battle of the Bulge, it was Hitler's final blitzkrieg.

The Germans achieved complete tactical surprise and quickly broke through Allied lines. On December 17, a Panzer unit commanded by Colonel Jochem Peiper overran a small fuel depot and took the opportunity to refuel his vehicles. A few hours later, he came within three hundred yards of the perimeter of the Allied resupply center near Stavelot.

With more than 2.5 million gallons of gasoline and diesel fuel, Stavelot was the Allies' largest fuel dump in all of Europe. On the evening of December 17, it was defended by a small band of ragtag soldiers.

In a desperate attempt to improvise a defense against what they knew to be a vastly more powerful opposing force, they poured gasoline into a ditch and set it alight. Unaware of the prize that lay just beyond this thin wall of flame, Peiper ordered his Panzers off in pursuit of another military objective.

Stavelot contained enough fuel to supply the entire German offensive for a week and a half. With it—and with the Allies reeling in confusion—German units could probably have broken through to Antwerp and the English Channel.

After making what turned out to be one of history's most famous U-turns, Peiper arrived at a rendezvous where his Panzers were to be resupplied by air. But the promised supplies never arrived. In due course, his entire unit was surrounded and captured. It had run out of gas.

The war in the Pacific

While oil was an important influence on how the war was fought in Europe, it was only marginally related to the causes underlying the initial conflict. In the Pacific, however, it was the pursuit of oil that led directly to the outbreak of war between Japan and the United States.

In the 1930s, the island nation of Japan was as critically dependent on its navy, and as short of oil, as Britain had been in 1912. But unlike Britain, Japan lacked domestic resources for most other raw materials as well.

In an attempt to remedy the situation, Japan embarked on a policy of paternal domination in Southeast Asia. By 1941, the Japanese occupied Manchuria, China, and Thailand. These conquests were sufficient to assure a supply of most strategic materials, including rubber, tin, and bauxite. But a critical shortage of oil remained.

In 1939, Japan imported 80% to 90% of its oil from the United States. The rest came from the Dutch East Indies, where oil fields had been developed by Royal Dutch Shell. As early as 1930, output in the East Indies amounted to 170,000 barrels a day—as much as was produced by all Europe, excluding the Soviet Union.

With the United States and European powers preoccupied with war in Europe, the Dutch East Indies seemed ripe for the picking. And Japan knew that control of the East Indies would easily assure 100% of its oil requirements.

Additions to empire

Still, Japan was not eager for war with the Allies, realizing that would mean maintaining long supply lines at sea, which would be extremely vulnerable to attack. So instead Japan concentrated on adding to its empire in Southeast Asia, while the United States looked on nervously.

Mindful of Japanese ambitions, U.S. President Roosevelt

ordered the American Pacific fleet, then on maneuvers near Hawaii, not to return to its home base on the West Coast. Instead, it was to remain permanently on station at Pearl Harbor.

When the Japanese began their march into Indochina, however, Roosevelt felt he had to act. He slapped a trade embargo on all shipments of scrap iron and aviation gasoline to Japan.

Later that year, the Japanese signed the Tripartite Treaty, creating an alliance with Germany and Italy. Next they invaded Vietnam.

Roosevelt countered with more sanctions. In July 1941, he abruptly issued an executive order that froze Japanese assets in the United States and cut off all oil exports to Japan.

The embargo would be lifted, Roosevelt said, when and if the Japanese withdrew from all their occupied territories. Meanwhile, Britain followed with its own freeze of Japanese assets. The Dutch government in exile also ordered a cutoff in supplies to Japan from the Dutch East Indies.

A fateful choice

The Japanese were caught off guard. Their total oil reserves on the day the embargo was announced amounted to only an 18-month peacetime supply (including only a 90- to 120-day supply for the fleet). Virtually cut off from other sources, they were faced with a tough choice. They could acquiesce to American pressure and give up their newly acquired territories. Or they could seize the initiative while they still had fuel for their fleet.

As everyone knows, they chose the bolder of the two courses. On December 7, 1941, six Japanese aircraft carriers under the command of Admiral Nagumo crept undetected within 200 miles of Oahu in the Hawaiian Islands.

At first light, the initial squadrons of a 360-plane attack were launched from their decks. The first wave appeared in the skies over Pearl Harbor at 8 a.m. It was soon followed by a second wave. Two hours later, the U.S. Navy lay in ruins.

The Japanese sank five American battleships and badly damaged three others. They also damaged or sank three cruisers and three destroyers. On the nearby airfield, two-thirds of the American fleet of Army and Navy planes was in flames on the ground. American casualties totaled 3,000, two-thirds of which were fatalities. Nagumo's losses came to 29 planes and 50 airmen.

Despite its overwhelming success, the Japanese attack was

also a strategic oil-related blunder on a scale even larger than Peiper's famous U-turn. Nagumo's officers begged for permission to send a third wave of attack aircraft against the American repair facilities and oil storage tanks on the island of Oahu. But having had what he felt was extraordinary luck so far, Nagumo was in no mood to tempt fate a third time.

Meanwhile, 4.5 million barrels of oil—the entire fleet reserve—sat in aboveground tanks vulnerable to .50 caliber bullets. Had he destroyed those tanks, the United States would have been forced to bring in new supplies all the way from California—thousands of miles away. Nagumo would have effectively immobilized every surviving ship in America's Pacific fleet—in addition to those he actually destroyed.

While the bombs were falling in Hawaii, the Japanese began their advance on the East Indies. Hong Kong was blockaded and bombed—along with Singapore, Wake Island, and Guam. Japanese troops took over Thailand and invaded Malaya.

On January 11, 1942, the Japanese landed in the East Indies. Their supplies of oil were secure.

Or were they? Japan still had to move vast quantities of oil from the Indonesian archipelago to the home islands by tanker. And as the war dragged on, the vulnerability of these tankers to American submarines eventually proved devastating.

Oil and war in the Pacific

Of Japan's total wartime steel merchant shipping fleet, approximately 86% was sunk. A further 9% was damaged beyond repair. U.S. submarines—which accounted for only 2% of American naval personnel—were responsible for inflicting 55% of Japan's total losses. A further 5% was accounted for by the submarines of various U.S. allies. By 1944, sinkings far outnumbered new tanker construction.

In time, oil shortages began to have an impact on fleet operations. In the Marianas campaign of June 1944, for example, the Japanese battle fleet was so short of fuel that it could not maneuver effectively. In part because Japanese aircraft carriers sailed right at the Americans instead of taking evasive action, they suffered losses of 273 planes to the Americans' 29.

Much the same thing happened at the Battle of Leyte in the Philippines. Two Japanese battleships never even made it to the battle because of fuel. Others arrived too late to do any good—in part because they were steaming at half-power to conserve oil.

Finally the commander of the Japanese Second Fleet, who could have rained destruction on the lightly armed American invasion forces on Leyte Beach, was forced to turn back because of insufficient fuel.

Fuel shortages also forced curtailment of virtually all Japanese air operations. By 1945, for example, the Japanese were forced to halt navigation training altogether. Pilots were simply told to follow their squadron leaders to locate their targets.

Interestingly enough, the increasingly desperate oil situation was also a factor in the unleashing of the famous *kamikazes*. In Japanese, *kamikaze* means "divine wind." This is an allusion to the great typhoon that shattered the 13th century invasion fleet of Kublai Khan before it could land on the Japanese Islands.

Statistics gathered by the Japanese command showed that on average eight bombers and 16 fighters were shot down for every American aircraft carrier or battleship sunk. Careful analysis suggested the same result might be obtained at the cost of only two or three *kamikazes*.

A pilot who deliberately smashed his plane into the target was virtually certain to cause more damage than if he dropped a bomb that might or might not hit its target. Second, the pilot's commitment and willingness to die was bound to have an unnerving psychological effect on an enemy that could scarcely comprehend the fanaticism of such an act.

And finally, because the *kamikazes* were on a one-way trip, they only required half as much scarce fuel as a conventional attack.[5]

---

1. Heinz Guderian, *Panzer Leader*, Chapter 3.

2. R. Goralski and R.W. Freeburg, *Oil and War,* p. 63.

3. Larry H. Addington, *The Patterns of War Since the 18th Century*, p. 197.

4. D. Yergin, *The Prize*, p. 335.

5. Rikihei Inoguchi, Tadashi Nakajima and Roger Pineau, *The Divine Wind: Japan's Kamikaze Force in World War II*, pp. 70-80.

Forging the Oil Weapon

The Suez Crisis of 1956

The bravest men can do nothing without guns, the guns nothing without ammunition. And neither guns nor ammunition are of much use in mobile warfare unless there are vehicles with sufficient petrol to haul them around.
— German Field Marshal Erwin Rommel,
"The Desert Fox" —

While the role of oil in World War II would influence an entire generation of military strategists, it took the Suez crisis in 1956 to really establish oil as a political weapon. Shortly after British Prime Minister Anthony Eden—Churchill's successor— publicly declared that Mideast oil was so critical England would fight to protect it, Egyptian President Nasser gave him a chance to make good on his word.

Indeed Nasser's nationalization of the Suez Canal and the subsequent attempts by France and Britain to regain it amply demonstrated the West's willingness to go to war over oil. But the debacle that followed was hardly a convincing show of strength. Among other things, Western mishandling of the crisis in Egypt set the stage for the military competition that continues in the region to this day.

An ancient dream

Whence the original idea of a waterway between the Red Sea and the Mediterranean came lies shrouded in the mists of antiquity. As any student of ancient civilizations is aware, the builders of the pyramids were no slouches when it came to civil engineering. More than 2,000 years before Christ, they dug an irrigation system spanning the vast expanse of what is now northern Egypt.

Part of it included a canal extending east from Goshen to the Bitter Lakes. From there, another canal provided access to the Red Sea.

French dreams of empire

A waterway across Egypt was also sought by Napoleon, who in 1798 was searching for a way to break the British monopoly on the trade routes to the Orient. Only 100 miles of flat sand stood in the way of another potential route to India, a route 6,000 miles shorter than the alternative journey around the horn of Africa.

But because of a naval defeat at the battle of the Nile—a sound thrashing delivered by the British commander Lord Nelson—Napoleon's grandiose scheme came to naught. Soon thereafter, he was forced to return to Paris, his canal unbuilt. Years later, it took another remarkable Frenchman, Ferdinand de Lesseps, to bring the ancient vision to fruition.

De Lesseps was a French diplomat stationed in Egypt, and by all accounts he was a larger-than-life character. He was said to have awed Frenchmen with his grace in the ballroom, and Arabs with his agile horsemanship. But cutting a canal through the Egyptian wilderness was a project that taxed even de Lesseps' legendary persistence and powers of persuasion. Nonetheless, after 10 years of labor, and at a cost of 433 million francs, the waterway—100 miles long, 50 to 100 yards wide, and 26 feet deep—was finally finished. On November 17, 1869, the Suez Canal opened for business.

(In truth, the Suez Canal was only one of de Lesseps' accomplishments. At the age of 64, he married a girl of 20 and begot 12 children. And before he died, at the ripe old age of 89, he was deeply absorbed in a new canal project—this time across Panama!)

World War II exposure

As we saw in Chapter 1, Britain's dependency on Mideast oil began in the years just prior to World War I. By the time World War II broke out, the Middle East supplied not only Britain, but much of the rest of western Europe as well. A large fraction of this oil went through the canal, which made it an important military objective.

The strategic significance of the waterway was certainly not lost on Hitler's war planners. In addition to denying the Allies access to Mideast oil, control of the Suez Canal would put the Nazis squarely astride the major trade routes to East Africa and India.

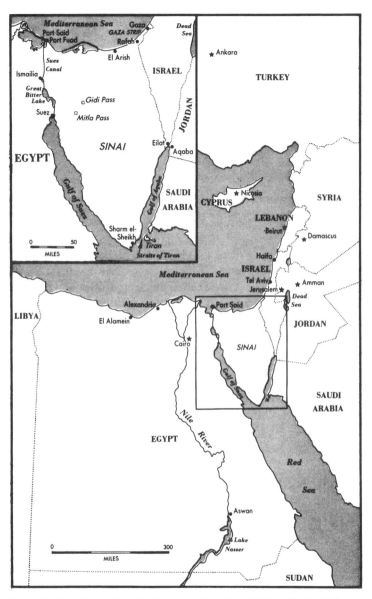

Map of the Suez Canal, from *The Lion's Last Roar: Suez 1956,* by Chester L. Cooper, p. 46.

Mussolini's muddle

In pursuit of this objective, Mussolini was dispatched to Libya, Egypt's North African neighbor to the west. In September

1940, he marched across the border at the head of an Italian army 135,000 strong. Mussolini, however, was never noted for his generalship. A few miles inside Egyptian territory, he was routed by 30,000 British troops under the command of General Richard O'Connor.

Shortly thereafter, O'Connor launched a counteroffensive that sent the Italians reeling. Mussolini, as it turned out, was no more skillful in retreat than he had been in attack. By January, he had fled back to Libya, with O'Connor in hot pursuit. And on February 9, 1941, he finally caught up with the Italians at Beda Fomm.

The carnage that day was impressive. At the cost of 500 British dead and 1,400 wounded, O'Connor destroyed 10 Italian divisions and killed or captured 150,000 Italian troops. For all practical purposes, the Italian 10th Army had ceased to exist.

Had O'Connor been allowed to push on to Tripoli, the campaign in North Africa could have been won in weeks, and the Suez lifeline would have been secure for the balance of the conflict. But British intelligence had picked up hints that the Germans were planning a new invasion of Europe. And at the time, the defense of Europe seemed much more important than the pursuit of obscure victories in North Africa.

Espionage advantage

The British, in one of the great intelligence coups of all time, broke the German command codes early in the war. As a result, they were uncommonly well-informed about the latest thinking of the German general staff. And when they learned of new German plans for a blitzkrieg in Greece, O'Connor and the vast bulk of his troops were recalled to reinforce the defense.

But superior intelligence alone is no guarantee amid the fortunes of war. As it turned out, the Allies were right about German intentions—but wrong about nearly everything else. Hitler was indeed planning an invasion of Greece. He feared that Greece—until then formally neutral in the conflict—would bow to British pressure to join the Allied cause. British air bases on Greek soil would put the R.A.F. within bombing range of Germany's major source of oil—the Romanian fields at Ploesti.

In spite of having had ample warning, Allied defenders were powerless to halt the German advance. The reinforcements that were taken from the Mideast were spent to no avail. Meanwhile, unbeknownst to the British, Field Marshal Erwin Rommel, the celebrated Desert Fox, had arrived in Libya.

Rommel's war

In Chapter 1, we saw how the oil-powered internal combustion engine freed land armies from utter dependence on the railroad, and created a whole new dimension of military mobility. There was no greater practitioner of the emerging new doctrine of mobile warfare than Rommel.

Bringing with him a fresh Panzer division from Germany, Rommel quickly rounded up the remnants of the Italian army and melded them into what was later known as the Deutsche Afrika Korps, which he built upon the twin principles of boldness and maneuver. Operating on only slender resources, he was a master at capturing supplies from the enemy. At one point, 85% of his transport was provided by captured American and British vehicles. In short order, he drove the remaining British out of Libya and sent them scurrying for cover deep in Egyptian territory.

When news of Rommel's exploits reached Europe, O'Connor came rushing back to North Africa with additional reinforcements. But it was too little, too late. To add military insult to injury, he was taken prisoner during the headlong retreat.

Rommel aimed to finish what Mussolini had begun and take the Suez Canal. But he needed time to prepare a major assault. In the interim, however, he kept the pressure on by launching raids behind Allied lines. Bombers and fighter aircraft attacked the canal and seeded the waterways with anti-shipping mines. Had the Germans been fortunate enough to sink a passing ship at a critical point, the canal might have been effectively blocked for weeks. Only strenuous measures by the British managed to keep the waterway open.

But while Rommel was preparing, the British were not idle. Field Marshal Bernard Montgomery was brought in to take command of the defense, and reinforcements poured in. Montgomery moved his troops to El Alamein—about 80 miles east of Alexandria—and prepared to make his stand for the defense of Egypt.

Defensive genius

He had chosen his ground well. For three days, direct assaults by the Germans failed to dislodge the British defenders. At length, Rommel tried a flanking maneuver that culminated in the battle of Halfa Ridge, where Montgomery's troops fought the Desert Fox to a standstill.

By now it was clear to Rommel that the Suez campaign was

in dire straits. Not only was he substantially outmanned and outgunned by the British, but the British naval blockade of Libya's Mediterranean coast made it difficult for the Germans to get reinforcements and supplies into North Africa. Germany depended on its wartime ally Italy for naval power in the eastern Mediterranean.

The Italians had a modern fleet, but they were even more short of oil than the Germans. As a result, Rommel was always being promised supplies that never arrived. Soon he was running low on both gasoline and ammunition. In contrast, the British were managing to keep a steady stream of fresh troops and supplies arriving at the front.

Furthermore, Rommel's already battle-weary troops were being weakened by long exposure to the harsh desert climate. Fearing a British counterattack on his dangerously exposed position, he cabled the German High Command in Berlin for permission to withdraw back into Libya. Hitler, however, refused his request.

When Montgomery saw that the Germans failed to make a speedy withdrawal to more defensible terrain, he attacked. For 13 days he threw everything he had at the hapless Germans. By early November, when Rommel finally struggled back to Libya, the once-formidable Afrika Korps had been smashed to pieces. Egypt, the Suez Canal, and the vital oil lifeline were all secure.

Postwar vulnerability

When peace finally came to Europe, the British and the French set themselves to rebuilding their war-torn countries. Slowly, normal trade relations were re-established, and civilian traffic through the canal resumed.

By 1955, oil accounted for two-thirds of all canal traffic. And in turn, two-thirds of Western Europe's oil was supplied by Suez shipping. Britain received 80% to 85% of its oil through the canal. France imported 90% of its oil from the Middle East, half of which came through the canal.

But while Europeans were once again pursuing the good life, the Egyptians began to chafe under British rule. A principal source of irritation stemmed from the continued presence of foreign troops on Egyptian soil. As much as a decade after World War II was over, Britain had not withdrawn its forces. Seventy-thousand British troops remained on station along the Canal Zone. Although now a member of the United Nations and a leading nation of the Arab League, Egypt still suffered the indignity of occupation by a foreign army.

Condescension and resentment

Actually there had never been any love lost between the British and the Egyptians anyway. For their part, the British found it hard not to treat the Egyptians condescendingly. The British remembered them mostly as hawkers, pimps, and thieves of unrivaled ingenuity. In two world wars, they had proved themselves nothing but liabilities. Worse, they seemed peculiarly ungrateful for the British bloodshed to save them from the Germans.

From the Egyptian point of view, the British were taskmasters to an enslaved population. Although Egypt was formally ruled by a nominal monarch, the ineffectual King Farouk, British influence was pervasive. Indeed, the popular perception that the British were behind everything—from the country's abject poverty to its catastrophic defeat at the hands of the Israelis in the 1948 War of Independence—made it easy to blame all the nation's ills on foreign manipulation.

The British recognized the signs of growing unrest. But after the painful and reluctant release of India to independence, they were in no mood to surrender yet another overseas possession. And they were certainly not inclined to turn over something as vital as the Suez Canal to the notoriously untrustworthy Egyptians.

Blood in the streets

By the summer of 1951, the tension had reached a flash point. Egyptian civilians employed by the Suez Canal Co. walked off their jobs. Food supplies to the British garrison at the canal's base were interrupted. But most disturbing of all was a mounting campaign of guerrilla attacks against British installations. Among those chiefly responsible for the attacks were the Muslim Brotherhood (a radical Islamic group) and the Society of Free Officers (S.F.O.), a dissident faction within the Egyptian army.

In exasperation, the British finally decided to strike back by attacking what seemed a local center of insurgency—the police headquarters in Ismaili. The news of the British assault spread like wildfire, and the reaction was instantaneous. Xenophobic mobs took to the streets looting and burning foreign property.

For the entire day, Cairo was in flames, and a number of unlucky foreign nationals lost their lives at the hands of the crowd. Finally the Egyptian regular army was called in to restore order. But orders to subdue fellow citizens who were only venting their frustration on the hated foreigners were not easy to obey.

A year later, members of the S.F.O. were ready to act. On July 23, 1952, the S.F.O. seized control of the army. At the head of the movement was a popular veteran of the war with Israel, Major General Neguib. Second in command was S.F.O.'s chief ideologue and major driving force, a man named Gamel Abdul Nasser.

Four days later, the army surrounded the Ras-el-Tin palace in Alexandria. And that same evening, King Farouk—the last surviving member of the 150-year-old Mohammed Ali Dynasty—was sent into exile.

Nasser immediately installed Neguib as president and himself as prime minister. But it soon turned out to be a tempestuous marriage. Neguib was popular with the Muslim Brotherhood, while Nasser was not. And when a member of the radical Islamic group took a shot at Nasser as he addressed a crowd of supporters from a balcony in Alexandria, he seized the opportunity to remove the president from office. Two years after the initial coup, Nasser stood alone at the pinnacle of Egyptian power.

Patriotic agenda

Nasser was not content with merely articulating Egyptian aspirations. As soon as he was able to consolidate his power, he set himself an agenda designed to remedy long-standing grievances among his people and to bolster national self respect.

First on his list was the problem of the hated British presence. In May 1953, he opened negotiations with London that dragged on for more than a year. Finally, in October 1954, Nasser was able to sign an agreement that committed the British to phased withdrawal over 20 months. At the end of that time, only a cadre of civilian technicians would remain to operate the canal.

Second, Nasser set about trying to repair the damage done by the Israelis to his country's armed forces in 1948. That, however, required modern arms and equipment that Egypt could not produce. So Nasser went shopping.

When U.S. President Eisenhower demurred and British Prime Minister Churchill equivocated, Nasser asked the Soviets. The Russians could scarcely believe their good fortune. Ever since 1945 they had been angling for ways to undermine Western influence in the region. Now, this upstart Egyptian seemed about to drop Europe's vital oil lifeline right into their laps.

In September 1955, Nasser triumphantly announced that Czechoslovakia would supply the Egyptian army. Although the specifics were not announced at the time, the deal included:[1]

- 300 of the latest Soviet model medium and heavy tanks
- 200 MIG-15 fighter aircraft
- 50 Ilyushin heavy bombers
- 100 pieces of armored artillery
- 2 naval destroyers
- 4 minesweepers
- Large quantities of rifles, small arms, radar, and spare parts

The third and final item on Nasser's agenda was the High Aswan Dam. Nasser staked not only his personal prestige on this development project, but as it turned out, his entire political future as well. The original Aswan Dam, built across the Nile by British engineers in 1898, had served its purpose well. But Nasser wanted a new one, four miles upstream from the original and vastly larger.

As originally conceived, the new dam would increase Egypt's arable farmland by 17%—an important matter for a desert country struggling to feed its teeming millions. It would also make Egypt self-sufficient in electric power.

The ink was hardly dry on the Czech arms deal when the Russians, trying to make the most of a good thing, offered to build the dam as well. But Nasser had few illusions about Soviet intentions. After all, his military was already dependent on Moscow. To permit Russian influence over the economy as well would be tantamount to re-accepting the yoke of foreign domination—something he had so recently and painfully thrown off. So Nasser turned instead toward the West—where he got a lukewarm reception.

Without much enthusiasm, the British and American governments agreed to open negotiations with Egypt and the World Bank concerning financing for the project. But as the negotiations unfolded, Nasser, true to form, began to bridle at restrictions on the Egyptian economy that Western bankers seemed certain to propose.

Trouble in Washington

The real crisis, however, was in the United States. The Israeli lobby was up in arms over the possibility that the American government might be party to an agreement to aid a hated enemy. In addition, U.S. Secretary of State John Foster Dulles was personally furious at Nasser for his diplomatic recognition of Communist China. Furthermore, with the Korean War recently concluded, the American Congress was in no mood to increase foreign-aid appropriations.

But worst of all, it was a presidential election year. And to President Eisenhower's political advisors, it seemed a poor time to go out on a limb for a none-too-friendly country that had just signed an arms deal with the Soviet bloc. So when Eisenhower got cold feet, Churchill's successor, Anthony Eden, backed out as well, and the deal fell through.

An act of political desperation

It was a crushing blow to Nasser's prestige. And in the West, at least, there were few to mourn his predicament. As the Western press and his Arab detractors gleefully speculated on his political demise, it became clear that Nasser had only one option. With his political survival at stake, he decided to hit back, and hit hard.

On July 26, 1956, he addressed an exultant crowd from the same balcony in Alexandria where he had escaped death at the hands of the Muslim Brotherhood two years earlier. As the crowd roared its approval, he announced that the Suez Canal would be nationalized and that its annual revenues of 35 million pounds sterling would be devoted to building the new Aswan Dam. Even as he spoke, Egyptian commandos were quietly taking over offices and installations all along the Canal Zone.

The sheer audacity of Nasser's bold move stunned the Western world. But to the men who occupied the corridors of power in both London and Paris, it was an outrage that simply could not be tolerated.

Fury at Nasser and concern for oil supplies created a degree of political consensus not seen between Europe's leading powers since the days of World War II. From the outset, it was clear that both Britain and France were spoiling for a fight.

Conflicting aims

The major difficulty was deciding which objective should come first. Was it "knocking Nasser off his perch," as British Prime Minister Anthony Eden put it, or securing the safety of the canal with its precious cargo? As the crisis unfolded, it became clear that Britain and France could not do both.

Securing the Suez Canal would mean that the British and French invaders would have to strike first at offices and installations along the Canal Zone—before startled Egyptian technicians could sabotage the waterway. But the canal itself was 100 miles long, and even airborne troops would need a certain amount of time to deploy along its entire perimeter.

That would give the Egyptian army plenty of time to organize a counterattack. Worse, a landing of foreign troops would bring forth an outpouring of patriotic fervor that would likely make Nasser stronger and more politically secure than ever.

On the other hand, if the principal policy aim was to depose the Egyptian president, then the British and French would have to destroy his power base—the Egyptian army—and occupy the capital. This would require landing an expeditionary force on Egypt's northern coast and an overland push south to Cairo.

The problem with this strategy, however, was that it too would take time to execute. Even if the tide of battle went all the Allies' way, under no conceivable circumstances could they hope to destroy the entire Egyptian army in one fell swoop. And whatever elements survived were certain to launch retaliatory strikes at the vulnerable installations along the canal.

Russian wild card

One problem with either strategy was assessing the military impact of Egypt's brand-new shipment of Eastern bloc arms. Nothing much was known about the quality of Egyptian pilots and tank crews. But there was always the chance that the equipment might be manned by some of the many East European advisors known to be in the country. That raised the unsettling possibility of a direct confrontation with the Soviet Union.

An even greater problem was the matter of public opinion. While Nasser was loved by no one in the West, it was by no means certain that another foreign adventure would be welcomed by voters whose memories of World War II were all too fresh.

Failure to come to terms with this fundamental incompatibility of aims virtually ensured from the start that neither objective would be achieved.

Ignoring clear-sighted advice to the contrary, the Allies tried to do both. They would drop troops in the Canal Zone and invade the country as well. They would tell the public that the operation was necessary to ensure the safety of international shipping in the Canal Zone.

Israeli connection

In retrospect, it seems incredible that experienced politicians actually thought such an implausible story could be sustained. But the most preposterous part was yet to come. The French conceived the half-baked notion of involving the Israelis.

To be sure, the Israelis had a score to settle. Not only had Egypt banned Israeli ships and Israeli-bound cargos from the canal, but it had been an enthusiastic sponsor of the bloody raids by the P.L.O. guerrillas that so plagued Israeli settlements. When the French approached Israeli Chief of Staff Moshe Dayan about the matter of starting a war with Egypt, he was intrigued at once.

This was the plan. On October 29, Israel would launch a reprisal attack on Egyptian positions in the Sinai with the intention of advancing as far as the canal. The next day, after formally appealing to both sides for a ceasefire, Britain and France would ask Egypt to permit Anglo-French troops to temporarily occupy the Canal Zone. This was necessary, they would claim, to ensure the safety of this waterway.

It was a request Nasser was certain to deny. But his refusal would give Britain and France an excuse to launch their planned invasion under the guise of protecting free trade and separating the belligerents.

The attack unfolded pretty much as planned. The Israelis attacked as scheduled, but they followed their own military agenda, which did not take them anywhere near the canal. As anticipated, Nasser rejected the Anglo-French request to land troops in the Canal Zone.

With the Israelis so far away, he probably thought the British and French were seizing an opportunity to bluff their way back into Egypt. Anglo-French forces landed more or less as planned along the Egyptian coast.

Soviet bluster

Interestingly enough, Egypt's new benefactors, the Russians, did nothing. They had their hands full with a crisis of their own. The captive peoples of their East European empire were growing restless. And on November 1, 1956, the third day of the Suez operation, Russian tanks rolled to Budapest to crush a Hungarian political effort toward liberalization. In truth, they were probably delighted that so much of the world's attention was focused elsewhere.

That did not, however, stop them from trying to make the

most of their newly self-appointed role as guardian of Mideast peace. Soviet Foreign Minister Bulganin sent thinly veiled warnings to Washington, London, Paris, and Tel Aviv. To Eisenhower, he proposed a joint American-Soviet military operation to "curb aggression" in the Middle East.

In messages to London and Paris, Bulganin warned that "we are fully determined to crush the aggressors and to restore peace in the Middle East through the use of force." More persuasive to the British than Bulganin's bluster was an intelligence intercept outlining orders to the Russian air force to mobilize for an attack against Britain.[2] In a message to the Israelis, he threatened the very existence of the Jewish state.

While the operation went reasonably well, at least in its early stages, the cover story convinced no one, least of all the Americans. In the years since World War II, the French had grown used to fractious run-ins with Washington. But the British had at least hoped for benevolent neutrality.

Ike's ire

Eisenhower, however, was livid. It seemed to him that the British and French were deliberately endangering world peace to execute a personal vendetta against Nasser. And with the American presidential election less than a week away, the timing could not have been worse. After months of campaigning before the electorate as one of the world's elder statesmen, here he was in danger of being undone by a new war—and one started by allies!

The international outcry was intense, and within days the British began to waver. Some members of the British government took the Russian threats seriously, and British Prime Minister Anthony Eden came under heavy fire in Parliament. Eventually he was forced to convene the Cabinet to consider a unilateral withdrawal.

Edge of financial collapse

The day the Cabinet met, the situation seemed grim indeed. Nasser had effectively closed the canal by scuttling Egyptian ships in the channel. A run on the pound was underway in foreign markets, and the country's foreign exchange reserves were being drained at the alarming rate of 15% a day. Worst of all, British industry was down to less than a month's supply of oil.

As early as 1938, U.S. oil production accounted for more than 60% of the world's total. As a result, the United States was able to use oil as a political weapon in much the same way as OPEC nations did some 20 years later.

When Eisenhower cut off oil shipments to Europe and demanded an immediate cessation of hostilities in Egypt, the British had no choice but to throw in the towel. After briefly wondering if they should not finish the job themselves, the French also acceded to demands for a cease-fire and subsequent withdrawal.

It was an inauspicious moment for the West. Not only was the canal lost, but the Israeli attack had enabled Nasser to cement his supporters with the age-old rallying cry of Zionist aggression. In the aftermath of U.N.-supervised withdrawals, he remained stronger than ever. Only the Israelis managed to achieve their military objectives.

Legacy of defeat

The effects of the Suez crisis were profound. In the oil-rich Mideast, Western influence plunged to a new all-time low. The public humiliation suffered by both Britain and France played a prominent role in the decision by both nations to develop their own nuclear weapons. In England, the Suez crisis brought down the government.

France, furious over what it saw as pusillanimous behavior on the part of the British and bullying tactics on the part of the United States, withdrew from NATO.

Nasser, in his marriage of oil to Mideast nationalism, created a powerful weapon that would be used again and again by other ambitious leaders of oil-producing nations. And the Soviet Union, eager to seize the initiative in the wake of Western humiliation, established itself as a power to be reckoned with in the region for years to come.

And within a few short years, super-power competition for Mideast oil would bring the United States to the brink of launching a nuclear attack. Precisely how this came about is the story of the next chapter.

---

1. Chester L. Cooper, *The Lion's Last Roar: Suez 1956.*

2. Peter Wright and Paul Greengrass, *Spycatcher*, p. 107.

Chapter 4

Persian Gulf 1980

The Untold Story of America
on the Nuclear Brink

No matter how well-fed, equipped, or officered, without oil and gasoline, the modern army is a hopeless monster, mired and marked for destruction.
— T. H. Vail Motter, U.S. Army historian —

At the conclusion of the Suez Crisis of 1956, the power of oil as a political weapon could no longer be seriously disputed. And if anyone required a further demonstration, the Soviets were quick to provide one. In the late 1950s, they imposed an oil embargo to bring down a Finnish government that had somehow neglected to include the local Communist party.

Even so, Western nations were slow to grasp the political disadvantages of oil dependence, and of dependence on Mideast oil in particular. As a result, they found themselves utterly unprepared for events to come—the rise of OPEC and the 1973 oil embargo, to name just two—which could have been anticipated.

By the end of the 1970s, OPEC was approaching the zenith of its power and had pushed the price of crude above $30 a barrel. The West had grown more dependent on energy imports than ever. In 1979, the United States depended on foreign imports for nearly half its oil supplies. Eighty-seven percent of annual consumption in Europe came from foreign sources. And Japan imported 100% of its annual needs.

Importer and Percentage of Oil Imports in 1979[1]

Exporter	United States	Europe	Japan
South America	8	2	—
North Africa	8	10	—
West Africa	6	5	—
Indonesia	3	—	13
Mideast	15	60	77
Spot or other	8	10	10
Total Percent of Oil Consumption Imported	**48**	**87**	**100**

To make matters worse, virtually all Mideast oil came by tanker from the Persian Gulf. A cursory glance at a map of Southwest Asia quickly reveals that the Persian Gulf is almost a landlocked lake.

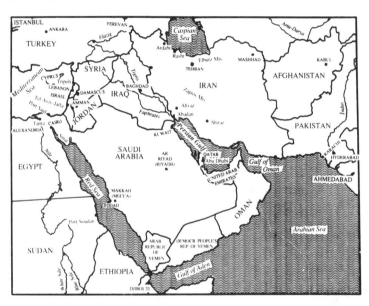

The Persian Gulf and the Middle East.

Only by passage through the narrow Straits of Hormuz at its extreme southern end can tankers reach the Indian Ocean and thereafter the open seas. The northern shore of this vital chokepoint is Iranian territory. The southern shore belongs to the tiny emirate of Oman.

Indeed, Western oil vulnerability had grown so serious that U.S. President Carter numbered the Persian Gulf among the vital interests of American foreign policy. In his last State of the Union Address, he declared:

> *Let our position be absolutely clear: An attempt by any outside force to gain control of the Persian Gulf region will be regarded as an assault on the vital interests of the United States of America, and such an assault will be repelled by any means necessary, including military force.*

Persian ally for the Persian Gulf

Unfortunately, brave words could no longer mask the empty arsenal that lay at the heart of U.S. ability to execute its declared oil strategy. For years, American policy in the Persian Gulf had rested on the stalwart good will of the pro-Western Shah of Iran. As the autocratic master of an oil-rich country situated on the northern shore of the Persian Gulf and commanding the north bank of the vital Straits of Hormuz, he made a formidable ally.

Although fiercely committed to an ambitious plan to modernize backward Iranian society in a single generation, the Shah never forgot his debt to the West. During the 1973 oil embargo, he stood almost alone continuing shipments to the West.

But he was also a tyrant noted for the brutal suppression of his domestic political adversaries. And it was this fact that made it difficult in early 1979, as his grip on power was slipping away, for the Carter administration to come to his aid.

Perhaps it is unrealistic to suppose that with vigorous American support pro-Western leadership in Iran might have been indefinitely sustained. On the other hand, those who urged American acquiescence in deposing the Shah on moral grounds can scarcely claim a moral victory in his successors. And without a doubt, the Shah's departure was an unmitigated catastrophe for Western policy in the Persian Gulf.

In the absence of a pro-Western Iran to police the Persian Gulf, U.S. power to influence events in the region suddenly became practically nonexistent. In the event of a military emergency, American troops would have to be flown in from the United States—a distance of more than 7,000 miles.

Worse, the lack of sufficient airlift capacity meant the troops would have to go without tanks or heavy arms. As then U.S. Defense Secretary Harold Brown had noted the previous year in congressional testimony, the United States had just enough airlift for a suicidal show of force in the Persian Gulf.

This loss of power in a strategically vital region of the world did not go unnoticed. On Christmas Eve 1979, the first Soviet military transports began landing in Kabul.

The Afghan invasion[2]

Three days later, columns of T-54 and T-64 tanks, supported by the heavy artillery of the Soviet 40th Army, began crossing the Oxus River into Afghan territory. At the same time, a special KGB hit team supported by airborne commandos attacked the fortified Duralaman Palace, the official residence of the Afghan president, Mohammad Hufizullah Amin.

The Soviets had clearly planned this operation with great care. Most of the strategic objectives in and around Kabul were taken in short order—many without firing a shot. The original plan for neutralizing the Afghan president had been no less meticulously thought out. During an elaborately planned banquet that evening, Amin and his bodyguards were supposed to be drugged by their Russian cooks.

Amin ate heartily. But the plan faltered when a number of the guards were inadvertently omitted from the guest list. When the Russians inside the palace tried to pay a postprandial call on the Afghan president, they were surprised to find a contingent of clear-headed palace police blocking their path.

Revolution on a schedule

Now, staging a coup or fomenting a revolution is an enterprise of considerable complexity. Timing is often critical, and the history of revolution is littered with examples of uprisings that got off schedule and, as a result, fell apart. So the Russians were understandably upset when a platoon of unexpectedly clear-eyed bodyguards threatened to make a shambles of their carefully crafted timetable.

In exasperation, an armored column was called in to assault the palace. But the Soviets were further chagrined to discover they faced an opponent who refused to surrender, even in the face of overwhelming odds. It was a sobering experience, and one destined to be repeated again and again in subsequent years as the Soviets would try without success to conquer the defiant Afghan freedom fighters.

The battle for the palace lasted four hours. By this time,

Amin, even in his half-drugged state, must have finally realized what was going on. But all attempts to call for help failed. Communications between the palace and the outside world were completely cut off. Soviet demolition teams had done their work well.

Crimes against the people

When the last defenders were finally dispatched, Soviet troops wearing Afghan army uniforms burst in and shot Amin as he stood by the palace bar, sipping a drink. According to one report, one of a number of KGB agents who had infiltrated the Amin household, threw up his hands and pleaded in Russian for his life, thereby escaping instant annihilation.

In an effort to ensure there were no witnesses, the Soviets machine-gunned everyone in the presidential family, including seven children. The next day Radio Kabul announced that Amin had been tried, found guilty, and executed by a Revolutionary Tribunal for committing "crimes against the people."

Moscow had chosen its moment well. In the United States, the administration was preoccupied with the brutal taking of American hostages in Iran. Much of the rest of the world was caught up in merrymaking to celebrate the new year.

In Afghanistan, heavy snow blanketed the ground, making it difficult for opposition to the Soviets to organize. As a military operation, it was strictly invasion by the numbers—a swift, decisive *fait accompli* about which the world could protest, but in the end, do nothing.

Fruits of conquest

To the hard men inside the pre-*perestroika* Kremlin, a puppet pro-Soviet regime in Afghanistan appeared to confer a number of strategic advantages. First, it eliminated a hotbed of opposition to the Soviet regime. For more than 100 years, Afghanistan had been a check on Czarist ambitions to the north (and, to a lesser degree, on British ambitions in India to the south).

When, for example, civil war broke out in Russia in 1917, the Afghans vigorously supported their fellow Asians in Turkestan and Uzbekistan—both of which had long been under Czarist domination.

In the 1970s and 1980s, Afghan opposition took the now-familiar form of Islamic fundamentalism. A puppet regime in Kabul offered Moscow some degree of insurance against the tide of Islamic fervor sweeping into Soviet Central Asia from the south.

Second, the puppet regime afforded a strategic position for some later effort to break through to the Indian Ocean. Possession of a warm-water port—free from ice year round—has been a principal aim of Russian expansionism since the time of the czars.

But above all, Afghanistan's strategic significance was measured in terms of the 20th century's most recent index of power—oil. Hardly had the dust of travel been shaken from the khaki uniforms of the airborne commandos when a second army of geologists and oil-drilling technicians appeared, intent on exploiting the captive country's considerable natural resources.

Although the Soviet Union was the world's largest oil producer, the rate of increase in production had already been falling steadily for a number of years.

As wells in major oil-producing regions near the Caspian Sea were depleted, deposits located in the hostile climates of Siberia and the Soviet Arctic began to account for an ever-growing fraction of total reserves. Inferior Soviet technology was incapable of exploiting these reserves.

Burdened with responsibility for supplying the oil needs of its Eastern European empire, and increasingly desperate for the hard currency only oil exports to the West could produce, it is scarcely surprising that Soviet General Secretary Brezhnev began to cast an acquisitive eye toward Afghanistan.

Moreover, once Afghanistan was safely added to the Soviet orbit, Russian troops could safely take up positions on both the northern and eastern borders of a country vastly more important in the ongoing epic of oil and war—Iran.

Centuries of intrigue

Actually, Iran has been high on the list of Russian ambitions for several centuries. In the past 200 years, Iran has been attacked from the north nearly a dozen times.

In fact, the territory that now comprises Soviet Azerbaijan was the fruit of conquest in one such campaign. During World War I, Czarist troops invaded and occupied what remained of Iranian Azerbaijan. Eventually, it too would have probably been absorbed into the Soviet empire. But in 1917 the Boleshevik Revolution threw the country into chaos, and the Russian troops were called home.

But once the Communists had firmly established themselves in power, interest in Iran revived. Soon Soviet agents were again at work in Iran's northern provinces. While the doctrinaire atheism of Communist orthodoxy was anathema to most Iranians, both the Kurds and Azerbaijanis longed for independent homelands, and thus were no friends of the central government in Tehran. In Soviet eyes, such aspirations made them ripe for subversion.

For the Soviets, World War II began on June 22, 1941. On that day, German Panzer divisions rolled across the Soviet border and instantly transformed what Soviet propaganda had been calling the Second Imperialist War into what would soon be christened the Great Patriotic War. (See Chapter 2.)

Earlier that same year, German agents had managed to incite a rebellion by the followers of Rashid Ali in British-controlled Iraq. Already reeling under the onslaught of their erstwhile allies, the Russians began to worry about yet another German attack—this time from the Mideast. In due course, the Stavka, the Soviet general staff, began to draw up contingency plans for an invasion of Iran.

By summer, the Russians were ready to move. The following account of the start of that campaign comes from Schulze-Holthus, the German intelligence chief in the northern Iranian city of Tabriz.[3]

> *I had relied on consistent reports from my agents that no troop concentrations had been observed on the North Persian frontier. But the Russians had outdone me in cunning. They had concentrated motorized units farther north, which were only thrown late at night on the frontier. On Monday Aug. 25, we were attacked brutally out of our sleep at 5 a.m. by the sound of heavy anti-aircraft fire. In the meantime came the hollow thuds of the first bombs.*

Invasion by the numbers[4]

The invasion began, just as the war planners had envisaged, with a two-pronged attack into Azerbaijan from along both sides of the Caspian Sea coast. Farther east, Soviet troops advanced in two additional waves: a thrust southward from Quchan toward Shabzevar, and another eastward from Sarakhs toward Meshed.

Iranian resistance was sporadic and uncoordinated, and Soviet forces were able to advance as far as 40 miles in the first day alone. Russian fighters were unchallenged in the sky above the

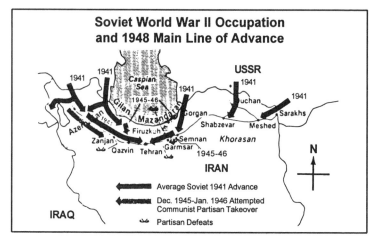

Soviet World War II Occupation and 1946 Main Line of Advance, courtesy of *Armed Forces Journal International,* February 1987, p. 30.

battle, and Soviet bombers emptied their loads on just about every town of any size in northern Iran.

Although ostensibly concerned with securing their southern flank against a German counterattack, once they were established in northern Iran, the Soviets began taking steps aimed at extending their control all the way toward the warm waters of the Persian Gulf. They provided arms and money in support of the nationalist ambitions of Azerbaijan separatist Jafar Pisherari.

Near the western border with Iraq, they encouraged the Kurds to set up an independent state. And on February 1, 1944, the Supreme Soviet accorded official recognition to both.

No exit

When World War II finally came to an end, the Russians somehow weren't in much of a hurry to leave Iran. In November 1945, they began large-scale distribution of arms to local insurgents, who they hoped to incite in open revolt against the central government in Tehran.

Before long, sporadic fighting broke out in the north. And on at least one occasion, troops dispatched by the central government in Tehran to put down unrest were stopped by Soviet uniformed forces at Qazvin, just a short distance outside the Iranian capital.

It was the Shah's intelligence services that discovered the plot against the capital itself. As soon as he learned that Soviet-backed forces were preparing to march on the city, he called for reinforcements.

Within hours, staunchly anti-Communist troops from distant provinces began to arrive in the capital. Guns and ammunition were smuggled into anti-Communist troops inside the Soviet zone of occupation. Other troops were sent out to hold the mountain passes that guarded the approaches to the city. Inside Tehran, the garrison was reinforced and placed on full battle alert.

Loyalist victories

Such vigorous measures so promptly taken apparently caught the rebels by surprise, and the plan to attack the capital never materialized. In fact, only two battles were actually fought: one at Shahi in the north, and another near Garmsar to the southeast of the capital. In both cases, the Soviet-backed insurgents were put to rout. With their local allies on the run, it soon became clear that if they wanted Iran, the Soviets would have to take it themselves.

With the conclusion of World War II, the Russians were obligated by treaty to begin withdrawing their troops from Iran by the spring of 1946. By March 1946, American and British troops

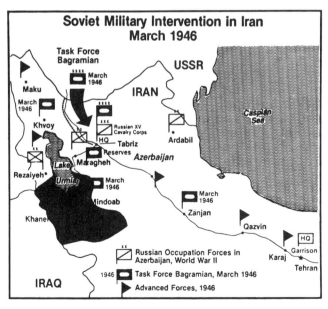

Soviet Military Intervention in Iran in March 1946, courtesy of *Armed Forces Journal International*, February 1987, p. 32.

had already departed, leaving them unopposed. On the morning of March 3, the men inside the Kremlin decided to seize their opportunity.

Within hours, Soviet armored divisions began moving *en masse* southward across the border into Azerbaijan. Several days later, the legendary Soviet tank commander, Marshal Ivan Bagramian, arrived from Moscow to take command of the Russian army of occupation. To provide as much political legitimacy as possible for the operation, Azerbaijan separatist Pisherari was instructed to issue a public statement thanking the Red Army for ousting the "tyrannical regime in Tehran."

The details of exactly what happened next are not clear. What is clear is that the Soviets were apparently on the verge of achieving a centuries-old aim of Russian foreign policy—namely, a warm-water port free from the ice that bottled up the Russian fleet every winter in its home waters. Even without benefit of hindsight, the Kremlin must have also realized that seizure of Iranian oil fields would have given the Soviets a strategic advantage of near inestimable value.

Nuclear ultimatum

On the verge of achieving all this, somehow the Soviets were persuaded to back down. Perhaps the vigorous defensive efforts of the Shah persuaded Soviet leaders that the campaign would be long and difficult.

It should be noted, however, that the prospect of a difficult campaign did not keep them from invading Afghanistan some 35 years later. More likely, the Soviet leaders were dissuaded by a blunt private message from President Truman threatening an American nuclear strike if they did not stand down.

Truman, of course, was well-known for his plainspokenness. But in public, he was careful to leave the Soviets a face-saving avenue of retreat. The U.S. State Department duly issued the following public protest to the Soviet Foreign Ministry:

> *The government of the United States has the honor to inform the government of the Soviet Union that it is receiving reports to the effect that there are considerable movements of Soviet combat forces and materials of war from the direction of the Soviet frontier toward Tabriz and outward from Tabriz in the direction of*

> *Tehran Mahabad and various points in North-western Iran.*
>
> *The government of the United States desires to learn whether the Soviet government instead of withdrawing Soviet troops from Iran as urged in the Embassy's note of March 6 is bringing additional forces into Iran. In case Soviet forces in Iran are being increased, this government would welcome information at once regarding the purposes therefore.*

As public pronouncements go, this is hardly anything that would have backed the Soviets into a corner. In private, however, the men inside the Kremlin must have concluded that it was a fool's gamble to test the resolve of an American president who had twice demonstrated the awesome power of the bomb in the skies above Japan.

Hence, there is little reason to doubt U.S. President Truman's version of events when he says in his memoirs, "We had to send an ultimatum to the head of the Soviet Union to get out of Persia." It was not, as we shall see, the last time the United States would go to the nuclear brink to stave off a Soviet invasion of Iran.

Many years later, it was discovered that the Soviet general staff had already drawn up a detailed plan for the invasion of Iran in early 1941. But when German troops stormed across the border in June, defense of the motherland suddenly took military priority over foreign adventures.

However, a copy of these plans apparently fell into German hands as the Red Army fell back in disorderly retreat before Hitler's Panzer divisions. The documents finally surfaced in the West during the early 1980s, when a historian doing independent research on captured German war files stumbled across them. (See Appendix to Chapter 4.)

Needless to say, they created quite a stir at the highest levels of the American government. Inasmuch as the invasion routes hadn't changed in 40 years, U.S strategists presumed the documents still cast considerable light on what the Russians might do in any future attempt to bring Iran into the Soviet empire. Accordingly, the U.S. Department of Defense commissioned the Stanford Research Institute to update the plan to reflect the present balance of power in the region.

This was done in 1981. Iran was very much on the minds of

U.S. defense planners just then, because a few months earlier, in a dramatic series of events known only to senior figures of the Carter administration, the United States had nearly been forced to launch a nuclear strike to forestall a Soviet thrust through Iran to the Persian Gulf.

In late 1980—barely nine months after Soviet tanks rolled into Kabul—American military analysts were forced to concede that Soviet forces could overrun Iranian oil fields and seize the northern bank of the vital Straits of Hormuz in only seven to 10 days. Worse, the United States could do absolutely nothing to stop them—short of outright nuclear attack!

Only this time, the United States no longer had a monopoly on the bomb. Sooner than anybody thought, the worst fears of Western military strategists came suddenly to the very edge of frightful realization.

America on the brink[5]

Although Western intelligence had picked up signs of unusual activity around the Moscow-based 105th Soviet Airborne Division prior to Christmas Eve 1979, news of the Afghan invasion came almost as a complete surprise to most Western capitals. The United States, in particular, had reportedly suffered a satellite failure over Southwest Asia at a critical moment.

As a result, considerable effort was devoted to bringing fresh intelligence assets to bear on the region during the early days of the Soviet occupation. By late summer, these new sources were reporting very disturbing news indeed. For all practical purposes, it looked as if the Soviets were gearing up for another invasion—this time, of Iran.

This is a story that until now has never been told. Well guarded among the official secrets of the Carter administration, it is a story that former administration officials have been notably reluctant to discuss. A fuller accounting of those tension-filled days of August 1980 will have to wait upon the eventual declassification of documents in years hence.

What is known is based on the minutes of a meeting held between then-Secretary of Defense Harold Brown and the Joint Chiefs of Staff. The minutes were obtained by *Armed Forces Journal International* and written about in the September 1986 issue.

Distant early warning

Sometime in July 1980 American intelligence began picking

up ominous indications of a major Soviet military operation in Southwest Asia. The 28 Soviet divisions in the Turkestan, Trans Caucasus, and North Caucasus military districts, normally held in a relatively low state of readiness, were suddenly upgraded to a status equivalent to that of elite Soviet forces facing NATO defenses in Europe. Both their radio frequencies and their communications codes were abruptly switched to types believed by Western intelligence to be reserved for imminent hostilities.

A number of units moved from their garrison to the field and took up what looked suspiciously like an order of battle poised for a lightning strike to the south. Some key units suddenly began observing electronic silence, thus making their movements and intentions even more difficult to fathom.

Tactical fighter-bomber wings in the region were reinforced, while stockpiles of ammunition and aviation fuel were increased to levels never before observed by Western intelligence. An airborne division in Eastern Europe was placed on high alert. Finally, units of Spetsnaz (elite forces trained for deep penetration raids behind lines) were moved to positions from which they could easily reinforce or spearhead an attack into Iranian territory.

Consternation in the halls of power

Alarmed, the Carter White House quickly convened a series of meetings to consider American options in the event the worst-case scenario came to pass and the Soviets struck south toward the Persian Gulf. But the agonizing truth of the matter was this: Short of a nuclear attack, the United States had almost no options.

The 28 Soviet divisions on alert included about 3,400 tanks, 370 combat aircraft, 350 helicopters, nearly 4,000 artillery pieces, and upward of 8,000 armored personnel carriers and infantry fighting vehicles. Opposing all this, the United States had absolutely nothing!

Concerned about the power vacuum left by the fall of the Shah, Carter had in fact already proposed the creation of a rapidly deployable Indian Ocean task force for just such an emergency as this. But in any match up of this force against the Soviet army amassing along the Iranian border, U.S. forces would be outnumbered 6 to 1 during the first week of mobilization. After two weeks, the ratio would be 10 to 1 in favor of the Soviets, and after 30 days, 14 to 1.

As the grim truth dawned, American planners were forced to look for help in the geography of likely Soviet invasion routes.

Troops moving through western Afghanistan—one of the few countries in the world without a railway system—would have to traverse difficult terrain with roads that were either primitive or nonexistent.

Tortuous invasion route

Nor would moving an army through eastern Iran be any easier. By air it was only 250 miles to the Iranian capital and only 600 miles to the shores of the Persian Gulf—35 minutes flying time for the newest Soviet jets.

But on land, the tortuous miles through the Elburz and Zagros mountains would number upward of 1,000. Furthermore, among the 15,000-foot peaks were literally hundreds of potential choke points—bridges, canyons, and narrow mountain passages that could accommodate barely a single tank at a time.

The best defensive position for American forces would be in the mountains to the north, before Soviet forces could debouch into the plains surrounding Tehran. Someone suggested dropping in U.S. special forces teams by parachute to attempt to block and hold a number of the most promising potential choke points.

The problem was that these measures were unlikely to stop a determined invader. For one thing, Soviet airborne forces could leapfrog blown-up bridges and blocked mountain passes. Second, choke points, even if blocked by artful demolition, wouldn't stay blocked forever. Unless they were defended, they could always be cleared by the Soviet engineer corps.

Unfortunately, U.S. special forces are lightly armed and therefore ill-equipped to take and hold ground against a determined adversary. And inadequate American airlift capacity meant that any air-dropped reinforcements would also have to take the field without heavy weapons. Without tanks and artillery, they would find themselves hard pressed to hold even the most promising defensive positions.

Thinking the unthinkable

That left only one alternative—tactical nuclear strikes against the Soviet army as it attempted passage through the mountains. It was a topic no one was eager to consider. But it was all that was left.

It is clear from the information obtained by *Armed Forces Journal International* that the matter was discussed at the highest levels of American military command. Together, U.S. President

Carter and U.S. Secretary of Defense Brown made up the National Command Authority, the bureaucratic unit of the American government with the power to approve a nuclear strike.

However, somehow a nuclear war was averted. For the second time in 35 years, Soviet forces, which had been brought to the fevered pitch of combat readiness, began to stand down. How they may have been persuaded to do so must await a fuller retelling of events.

But we do know that then Undersecretary of State Warren Christopher was dispatched by President Carter to Europe. At least in part, his mission was to consult with heads of state in Britain, France, and then West Germany on how best to coordinate warnings to the Soviets to stay out of Iran. To date, Christopher has declined to be interviewed on the subject.

Persian Gulf 1990

Much has changed in the decade since these fateful events took place. The Soviets have withdrawn from Afghanistan. Communist rule has collapsed in Eastern Europe. The Soviet Union itself no longer exists.

But in the aftermath of Operation Desert Storm, Western defense planners are still contemplating the likely effects of weapons of mass destruction. And wondering how many lives will be at risk as the next chapter unfolds in the epic tale of oil and war.

---

1. Benjamin F. Schemmer, "Was the U.S. Ready to Resort to Nuclear Weapons for the Persian Gulf in 1989?", *Armed Forces Journal International,* September 1986, p. 98.

2. This account of the last days of independent Afghanistan draws upon the excellent work of Edward R. Girardet in *Afghanistan: The Soviet War.*

3. Quoted by Marshall Lee Miller. "How the Soviets Invaded Iran," *Armed Forces Journal International,* February 1987, p. 30.

4. This account draws on the work of Marshall Lee Miller, which appeared in his feature on Soviet military developments in *Armed Forces Journal International,* January 1987 to February 1987.

5. Benjamin F. Schemmer, *op. cit.*

Appendix to Chapter 4

In 1941, Stalin ordered his general staff to draw up plans for an invasion of Iran. Among them were the following maps showing the planned line of advance between Zhulfa and Tabriz and on to the Iranian capital, Tehran.

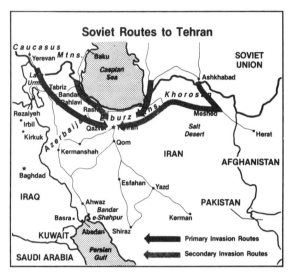

Soviet Routes to Tehran, courtesy of *Armed Forces Journal International*, January 1987, p. 28.

Soviet Main Line of Advance to Tehran, courtesy of *Armed Forces Journal International*, January 1987, p. 30.

Soviet Line of Advance Between Zhul'fa and Tabriz, courtesy of *Armed Forces Journal International*, January 1987, p. 30.

Chapter 5

Oil and War Against Civilians

The Terrorist Threat

I see heads before me that are ripe and ready for the plucking, and I am the one to pluck them. I see blood glistening between the turbans and the beards. Oh people of Iraq, people of discord and dissembling and evil character, I swear by Allah that you will keep strictly to the true path, or ... by God, I will strip you like bark ... I will beat you like stray camels ... what I promise, I fulfill; what I propose, I accomplish; what I measure, I cut off.
— Speech delivered by Iraqi governor
al Hadjadj ibn Yusuf al Thaqafi in 694 A.D.
and memorized by Iraqi schoolchildren today —

One of the most chilling contemporary examples of the age-old connection between economics and war can be seen in the increasingly brutal attacks on unarmed civilian populations. Of course, from the point of view of military history, the use of terror as a tactic is scarcely anything new.

In Greek mythology, the twin horses that pulled the chariot of the god of war were named Dread (Demios) and Terror (Phobos). In his fourth-century B.C. epic *The Peloponnesian War*, Thucydides reports the use of "unheard of atrocities" as an instrument of rebellion.

Iraqnophobia

In 1256, the grandson of Genghis Khan, Hulagu, sacked Baghdad and massacred its inhabitants. Historical accounts of the period say the Tigris ran red with blood. To ensure that no one would ever forget this grisly spectacle, Hulagu built a tower using the skulls of the thousands of dead as bricks.[1]

Visit the Killing Fields of Cambodia today, and you will find a memorial to the victims of Pol Pot. It, too, displays the skulls of his victims. Not that much has changed since the 13th century.

Deliberate displays of excessive cruelty have also often been the means by which governments headquartered in Baghdad have projected and sustained an image of invincibility. For example, on January 5, 1969, the Baathist government led by Saddam's cousin Ahmad Hassan al-Bakr hanged 14 people on gallows specially erected in Baghdad's Liberation Square.

The executions were carried out before a crowd of 200,000 that had been especially assembled for the occasion. After the executions, a festival was declared. And the corpses were left to dangle during 24 consecutive hours of celebration.

On August 8, 1969, in the village of Dakan, the Iraqi army knowingly incinerated 67 women and children who had taken refuge from artillery bombardment in a cave. (The victims were all members of the nation's rebellious Kurdish minority.) Far from treating it as an embarrassment to the government, Iraqi officials later went out of their way to allow the United Nations to document the atrocity.

Every year, hundreds of reports of torture surface—of victims with eyes gouged out, genitals cut off, fingernails missing, and the like. (For a chilling account of terrorist tactics used against Iraqi scientists, see *New Scientist*, April 2, 1981, p. 4. See also *Iraq: Evidence of Torture*, Amnesty International Publications, London, 1981.)

Ahmed Mattar, an Iraqi poet living in London, penned the following lines in memory of a friend who died at the hands of Iraqi torturers: [2]

> *They imprisoned him*
> *before they charged him*
> *They tortured him*
> *before they interrogated him*
> *They stubbed out cigarettes in his eyes*
> *and held up some pictures in front of him*
> *Say whose faces are these*
> *He said: I do not see*
> *They cut off his lips*
> *and demanded that he name*
> *those "they" had recruited*
> *He said nothing*
> *and when they failed to make him talk*

they hanged him
A month later they cleared him
They realized the young man
was not the one they really wanted
but his brother ...

While other governments that engage in similarly unsavory tactics go to great lengths to hide the bodies of those they have tortured to death, the Iraqis are in the habit of flaunting their handiwork. Bodies with parts missing or otherwise bearing the marks of torture are routinely returned to their families for burial—or dumped in the street to be seen by passersby.

Slaughter of innocents

Today, oil and war in the Mideast have spawned a whole new generation of fanatics bent on destruction. Kurdish rebel leader Mustafa Barzani was once asked how Yasir Arafat and the P.L.O. managed to become famous while no one ever heard of the Kurdish Liberation Movement. He replied: "Because we fought only *on our own land* and we killed *only our own enemies.*"

Few terrorists since have made Barzani's mistake. As the Shi'ite Muslims and the Palestinians have proved, nothing commands world attention like the slaughter of innocents.

The institutionalization of international terrorism began in 1967 when the Soviets began to establish training camps for guerrillas bent on avenging the Arab military debacle in the Six Day War against Israel. In the 1970s and 1980s, the Iranians, Syrians, and Libyans began to replace the Soviets as godfathers of the international terrorist movement. In the 1990s, leadership passed first to the Iraqis, then to the Iranians.

In the past, terrorism tended to be indigenous to a specific revolution or particular military campaign. Today, it is international in scope. In the past, the aim of the individual terrorist usually was the assassination of generals and emperors. Today, the march of technology has raised the frightening specter of a band of dedicated fanatics somehow getting their hands on a nuclear weapon.

In this chapter, we will examine the roots of terrorism in the 1990s. We will assess the fitful efforts to combat the rising tide of international hostage-taking. And finally, we will explore what you can do as an individual—to avoid becoming a hostage, or to survive if you are unlucky enough to become one.

69

Bitter harvest

One reason that terrorism is so popular is that it has been increasingly adopted as an element of foreign policy by nations on the fringe of civilization. Most experts mark the beginning of this development with the end of the Six Day War in 1967.

After their crushing defeat at the hands of the Israelis, there was little alternative, from the Arab point of view, to some sort of guerrilla campaign. In an effort to expand their influence in this oil-rich part of the world, the Soviets began to offer training and equipment to Palestinian guerrillas.

During the 1967-1969 period, several commando training camps were established in Czechoslovakia, staffed with Soviet, East German, and Czech instructors. In time, the camps began to accept not just Palestinians but members of other terrorist groups—including Baader Meinhoff and the Red Brigade. In return, these groups offered aid and comfort to the P.L.O. outside the Middle East.[3]

By 1969—within two years after their smashing military triumph—the Israelis were reporting more than 1,200 incidents of terrorism and sabotage along their borders.

The Soviets also armed Libya's Qaddafi, who has been called "the Daddy Warbucks of terrorism." Qaddafi has offered aid to almost every international terrorist group—sometimes in the form of training camps, financing, and weapons supply, other times by offering Libyan embassy facilities abroad as support bases for operations against targets in host countries.

Unlike the Soviets, who rarely directed operations abroad themselves, Qaddafi has for years conducted terrorist operations against his own people. In the opening months of 1980, he warned all Libyan expatriates to return home or face the threat of a homegrown hit squad. Since then, U.S. records note 14 attacks in seven countries by the colonel's assassination teams. Eleven Libyan exiles were killed, one wounded.[4]

Mother of mayhem

In recent years, Iraq also emerged as a major sponsor of international terrorism. For example, Iraq has been an arms supplier of the Irish Republican Army. In 1982, a British court convicted an Iraqi intelligence officer for leading the hit squad that attacked Shlomo Argov, the Israeli ambassador to London.

Nor have Iraqi attacks been confined to the Middle East. The Iraqi Istikhbarat (Department of Military Intelligence) has executed enemies of the regime in Egypt, Lebanon, and Sweden. At least one assassination was attempted in Paris. And in North America, four assassinations of Iraqi exiles in Detroit between 1977 and 1983 were very likely the work of Iraqi agents.[5]

The notorious Abu Nidal, mastermind of the bloody airport raids in Rome and Vienna in 1985, has maintained offices in Baghdad since the early 1970s. Saddam Hussein also enabled Abul Abbas and his band of cutthroats—who hijacked the cruise ship *Achille Lauro*—to escape arrest by offering them sanctuary in Iraq.

Russian revenge

As we shall soon see, even the Soviets found it occasionally useful to employ Mideast-based terrorists as surrogates—especially in connection with East European affairs. Perhaps the most striking example of this was the attempted assasination of Pope John Paul II.[6]

When Poland's independent labor movement acquired an ally with the election of the first Polish pope, the Soviets knew they had trouble ahead. Throughout 1979 and 1980, John Paul II worked behind the scenes for the peaceful creation of Solidarity, the trade union movement headed by Lech Walesa.

But on Monday, August 4, 1980, he received reliable intelligence to the effect that the Russians were on the verge of ordering Polish authorities to conduct a nationwide purge of Solidarity's leadership.

Anticipating that this might provoke rebellion in the countryside, the Russians already had put tank crews on alert. Suddenly, all the smoldering tension of the past 18 months seemed poised to erupt in a blood-chilling paroxysm of violence.

Knowing that he had to act, John Paul II sat down to write one of the most extraordinary letters ever penned by a pope. It was a single, handwritten page in Russian, on his personal stationery, bearing the papal coat of arms. It was addressed to the then General Secretary of the Soviet Communist Party, Leonid Brezhnev.

In it, he told Brezhnev that he believed a Russian invasion of Poland was imminent. And if that happened, he warned, he would relinquish the throne of St. Peter and return to man the barricades with his fellow countrymen. The letter was signed, "Yours in Christ."

Sometime during the second week in August, the letter was

hand-delivered to the Kremlin by Bishop Paul Marcinkus. A notorious curmudgeon, Marcinkus was selected because of his command of Russian and the pope's belief that he would not be intimidated by a face-to-face meeting with the most powerful man in the Russian empire. (Two years later, Marcinkus achieved notoriety of his own in connection with the Vatican's financial scandal, in which he was deeply involved.)

After the delivery, there were two months of tense and highly secret negotiations between Rome, Moscow, and Warsaw—which eventually resulted in the historic November 1980 agreement between Solidarity and the Polish government.

At this point, Brezhnev, echoing King Henry II of England, probably muttered: "Will no one rid me of this troublesome priest?" The then head of the KGB, Yuri Andropov, was listening. And a year later, the 12th-century murder of Archbishop Thomas à Becket by the minions of Henry II had its 20th-century parallel played out in St. Peter's Square. On May 13, 1981, a few minutes past 5:15 p.m., Mehmet Ali Agca shot the pope three times.

After the shooting, Italian investigators assembled a wealth of evidence that the Bulgarian secret service had mounted the operation at the Soviets' request. Agca received his small arms training at a camp in Libya.[7]

Islamic jihad

The dominant religions of the West—Christianity and Judaism—have long been known for their centuries-old traditions of non-violence (despite the Crusades and the military exploits of the modern nation of Israel). As a result, the frankly martial character of Islam often comes as something of a shock to the Western mind.

The Prophet Mohammed himself led troops into battle. In fact, his successful attack on a commercial caravan at Badr in 624 A.D. is celebrated in the Koran as an expression of divine will.[8]

The term *jihad*, usually translated as "holy war," literally means a great striving in the name of Allah. Of course, this encompasses military struggle. But the great striving also includes political and economic pressures, subversion and propaganda, the penetration and conversion of non-Muslim societies, and terror.

Ayatollah on jihad

During his years in Paris, the Ayatollah Khomeini wrote:

> *Holy war means the conquest of all non-Muslim territories. Such a war may well be declared after the formation of an Islamic government. It will then be the duty of every able-bodied adult male to volunteer for this war of conquest, the final aim of which is to put Koranic law in power from one end of the earth to the other.*[9]

By tradition and prescription, *jihad* is war without scruple, a war that makes easy targets of unarmed civilians.

Indeed Muslim tradition says that those who are martyred in a holy cause are guaranteed free entry into heaven, regardless of the sins they may have committed in earthly life. This *kamikaze*-like quality makes Islamic terrorists formidable foes. As Western hostage negotiators have learned through bitter experience, it's not easy to bargain with someone determined to die for his cause.

The use of terror tactics in general—and assassination in particular—goes very deep in Islamic tradition. The grandfather of the Muslim *kamikaze* was Hassan al Sabbah. Born in 1007 and, according to legend, a classmate of Omar Khayyam, he established himself in a mountain stronghold 50 miles from the Caspian Sea in what is now northern Iran. As his fame grew, he came to be known to his followers as the "Old Man of the Mountain."

Lacking the resources to raise and maintain a standing army, he created a secret society dedicated to pursuing a campaign of terror against his opposition—the orthodox Sunni Muslims who ruled from Baghdad—then, as now, a focus of Iranian hatreds and ambitions.

The instrument of his power was a band of fearless political killers that he himself trained. Displaying a flair for indoctrination rarely equaled in subsequent centuries, he elevated ritualized murder to a high art, and established a tradition whereby the techniques of assassination were transmitted from one generation to the next.

Hashish and paradise

His training methods combined the most powerful symbols of Islamic mythology with the most advanced behavioral and biochemical techniques the 11th century had to offer. He recruited his men from among the tough Bedouin tribes that inhabited the neighboring Alumet Mountains. In small numbers, they were drugged with hashish—a concentrated resin from the marijuana plant—and taken to a special hidden garden cleverly appointed with all the trappings of the Muslim heaven.

His aim was twofold: To establish a vision of paradise so desirable that these superstitious folk would willingly die to get there; and to establish his credentials as a great prophet.

Marco Polo was one of the few Westerners who managed to meet the direct descendants of Hassan al Sabbah face to face. In 1273, Polo wrote the following account of how the Old Man of the Mountain maintained his stable of assassins:

> *He kept at his court a number of the youths of the country, from 12 to 20 years of age, such as had a taste for soldiering, and to these he used to tell tales about Paradise ... then he would introduce them into his garden, some four or six or 10 at a time, having first made them drink a certain potion which cast them into a deep sleep, and then causing them to be lifted and carried in. So when they awoke, they found themselves in the garden ... so charming ... they deemed that it was Paradise.*
>
> *Now this prince, who we call the Old One, kept his court in grand and noble style, and made those simple hill folks about him believe firmly that he was a great prophet. And when he wanted to send one of his 'ashisisnon' on a mission, he would cause this potion to be given to one of the youths in the garden, and then had him carried into his palace. So when the young man awoke, he found himself in the castle and no longer in Paradise; whereat he was not over well pleased ...*
>
> *So when the Old Man would have any prince slain, he would say to such a youth: 'Go thou and slay so-and-so; and when thou returnest my angels shall bear thee into Paradise. And should'st thou die, nevertheless even so will I send my angels to carry thee back into Paradise.'*
>
> *So he caused them to believe; and thus there was no order of his that they would not affront any peril to execute, for the great desire they had*

to get into that paradise of his. And in this
manner the Old One got his people to murder
anyone whom he desired to get rid of.[10]

First fedayeen

Sustained by this powerful vision of heaven, and convinced beyond all doubt of al Sabbah's special place at the hand of Allah, these men formed a corps known as the *fedai*—or "men of sacrifice."

Fedai is the root of the 20th-century generic term for Islamic guerrillas—the fedayeen. Because of the special role of hashish, these men were also known as *hashishim*—according to the Oxford English Dictionary, one of the roots of the most familiar term for political killers—assassins.

So eager were the assassins to die, that al Sabbah often paid his fedayeen in advance—so they could give the money to their families before setting out on a mission from which they would never return. By the time of his death in 1091, al Sabbah's influence stretched from the Persian Gulf to the Mediterranean Sea. And military commanders, kings, and religious figures everywhere all wore chain mail as undergarments to protect against the daggers of the feared assassins.

Hasan al Sabbah was an Ismaili, an offshoot of Shi'ism that is itself an offshoot of Islam. Although Shi'ites have historically been a minority, they are arguably the most visible Muslims today. In large measure, they owe their notoriety to Ayatollah Khomeini and the Islamic fundamentalist revolution.

Origins in blood

Shi'ism was born in a bloody dispute over the true successor to the prophet Mohammed. In fact, the original term was Shi'at Ali—or follower of Ali. Ali was the fourth caliph—or Islam's official representative on earth. He also was cousin to the prophet, and son-in-law by marriage to Mohammed's daughter Fatima.

When Ali was murdered in 661 A.D., the majority Sunni Muslims chose the next caliph from outside the Ali-Fatima line. But Ali's followers named his son Hasan as their own successor, thereby insuring that they would forever be viewed as heretics by the Muslim orthodoxy. Hasan later resigned the honor bestowed upon him. But that was not enough to save him from assassination.

The first of the suicide attacks for which the Shi'ites are now renowned occurred in the year 680. Hussein, grandson of the prophet, set out with fewer than 100 troops to defend the family's line of succession to the caliphate. Of course, this was a challenge the sitting caliph was not inclined to take lightly. Accordingly, he sent an army numbering in the thousands to defend the throne. The two forces met at what is now the Iraqi town of Karbala—where Hussein and his entire band of 100 followers died gloriously.

Today, Islamic mourning houses and religious study centers are called *Husseiniyehs*. And the annual re-enactment of Hussein's martyrdom at Karbala is one of the most important events on the Shi'ite religious calendar.

Ayatollah's crusade

When the Ayatollah Khomeini came to power, he lost no time in building on the institutional infrastructure for international terrorism that the Soviets had begun years earlier. Nor has his death resulted in any real cutbacks in government support for terrorist activity.

In some sense, the current wave of Shi'ite terrorism dates from a crisp spring day in March 1982, when 380 men wearing large turbans and severe expressions presented their religious and revolutionary credentials at the former Hilton Conference Center in Tehran.

At the conclusion of the meeting, four things were decided: 1) Religion could not be separated from politics; 2) true independence only could be achieved by a return to Islamic roots; 3) there could be no reliance on outside powers; and 4) a large-scale offensive should be undertaken to cleanse the Muslim world of the satanic influences from both the East and the West.

It was the start of a crusade that would rock the world. The nerve center, communications hub, and organizational center for recruiting and deploying cadres of the faithful to spread the revolution was a plain-looking building in downtown Tehran, nicknamed Taleghani Center by the American CIA. There, personnel from Syrian and Libyan intelligence services worked hand in hand with a nearly endless supply of local fanatics.

Often, the lights burned late.

Nuclear nightmare

One of the ultimate terrorist nightmares, of course, would be a small nuclear device in the hands of Shi'ite fanatics, the proverbial "suitcase from Allah."

Tactical weapons of Soviet manufacture—such as nuclear artillery shells—have apparently already appeared in unknown quantities on the black market. In January 1990, Azerbaijani guerillas attacked an arms depot near the Soviet city of Baku that reportedly contained about a hundred tactical warheads. Although the Red Army was hastily dispatched to restore order, it is not known how many of these weapons it was able to recover.

Seven months later, events in Europe led to the wholesale emptying of Soviet arsenals in East Germany. After the dramatic breaching of the Berlin war (but before political union between East and West Germany), there was an interval in which nothing any longer prevented Soviet soldiers stationed in East Germany from simply walking to freedom in the West.

But when the July 2, 1990 monetary union brought hard currency to East Germany, Russian soldiers suddenly discovered they had the means to raise significant amounts of hard currency before deserting. They simply began selling off equipment and supplies. Grenades, rifles, bazookas, ammunition, gasoline—even surface-to-air missiles—all were auctioned off to the highest hard currency bidder. In some cases, entire arsenals were nearly stripped bare.

Of course, no one knows how many tactical nuclear weapons were officially stationed in East Germany before this fire sale began. And in light of the sorry state of Soviet record keeping, it is likely no one will ever know how many subsequently disappeared.[11] That some of the weapons now unaccounted for will eventually wind up in the hands of hotheads in Baghdad, Tehran, or Tripoli is virtually a foregone conclusion.

Do-it-yourself nuke

If a would-be terrorist cannot afford black market nukes—which, after all, are still rare enough to command premium prices—one alternative may be to make a bomb himself. Nuclear technology is increasingly within the reach of the do-it-yourself terrorist. For example, the U.S. Public Broadcasting Service series *Nova* featured a 20-year-old Massachusetts Institute of Technology student who produced an accurate technical design for a fission bomb in March 1975. A year later, a 21-year-old Princeton physics major designed a bomb with information available solely from public documents.[12]

Nuclear explosives, however, require more than technical know-how. They also require fissionable materials like uranium or plutonium. That supplies of fissionable materials are rare and monitored by a host of international agencies, however, provides only a limited degree of reassurance. In the United States alone, more than 9,000 pounds are missing from the books through 1981.[13] It only takes about 20 pounds of plutonium to make a bomb.

For terrorists unable to build bombs themselves, attacks on nuclear installations make an excellent alternative. As the Soviet nuclear debacle at Chernobyl makes clear, an explosion at a power plant can easily spread radioactive contamination over an enormous area.

In recent decades, there have been 155 incidents—among them, bombings, other attacks, and violent demonstrations—at sites of civil nuclear installations in Europe and the United States.[14] With more than 370 power plants operating in more than two dozen countries—and a similar number under construction, there is no dearth of likely targets.

That all these fears are to be taken seriously is confirmed by no less an authority on terrorism than Vladimir Kryuchkov, chief of the KGB's foreign espionage directorate from 1974 to 1988. In this capacity, he directed KGB support of terrorist training camps in Cuba, Libya, South Yemen, and Syria. Working through satellite intelligence services in Eastern Europe, he was also indirectly responsible for terrorist attacks against targets in Britain, France, Germany, and Spain.

Promoted to KGB chairman under Gorbachev and later deposed for his involvement in the August 1991 failed coup attempt, he nonetheless issued the following warning to members of the Supreme Soviet: [15]

> *The threat of nuclear terrorism is for us very dangerous. Several hundred tons of enriched uranium has vanished from various stockpiles in various places around the globe. Nor is it technically difficult to make a nuclear device. This will mean that individual groups can terrorize not only towns, but even entire countries.*

Chemical and biological warfare

A low-tech terrorist threat of almost equal fearsomeness is the possibility of attack with chemical or biological weapons. Like terrorism itself, chemical and biological weapons are not new. The Greeks used sulphur fumes at the siege of Delium in 424 B.C. in what probably was the world's first gas attack. The first recorded use of a biological weapon occurred against a fortress on the Black Sea more than 600 years ago. Plague-infected cadavers hurled over the walls by catapult are generally credited with breaking the three-year siege of Feodosiya in 1346.[16]

The formula for VX, one of the most potent nerve gases in the modern arsenal, has been declassified by both the United States and Britain. It is very cheap to produce. No laws prohibit the manufacture or possession of nerve gas by private citizens.[17] Moreover, the U.S. government has acknowledged that a small amount of its own inventory of VX is unaccounted for.[18]

T2 toxin, the agent known as "yellow rain"—used by the Soviets in Afghanistan and by the Vietnamese in Indochina—has from time to time been reported available through mail order in the United States.[19]

What is most frightening about biological weapons is their potency. Botulinal toxin (the cause of botulism) is much more lethal than plutonium, one of the most toxic elements known to man. Less than an ounce, properly administered, could kill every human being in North America.

Bacillus anthracis, which causes anthrax, once known as "wool-sorters' disease" is several thousand times more toxic than the most modern nerve gases. Sprayed in aerosol form, a small amount could cover an area of hundreds of square miles. During World War II, Britain experimented with anthrax as a military weapon on Gruinard Island off the coast of Scotland. And only in 1990 was the island finally deemed sufficiently safe for public access.

The pre-*perestroika* Soviet Union was also an avid developer of an anthrax bomb. In April 1979, an accident at the heavily guarded Military Compound 19, in the southern Chkalov district of Sverdlovsk, allowed a tiny amount of germ-laden spray to escape into the atmosphere. According to official Soviet sources, 64 people downwind of Military Compound 19 lay dead within days. The actual number is almost certainly much higher.[20]

According to the director general of Britain's Chemical and Biological Defense Establishment at Porton Down in Wilshire, approximately 10 nations either already possess biological weapons or are in the process of developing them.[21]

After the Iraqi defeat in Operation Desert Storm, United Nations inspectors visited Saddam Hussein's biological complex at Salman Pak, south of Baghdad. Although key facilities were removed before the inspectors arrival, they still found evidence that the Iraqis were hard at work on weapons using anthrax, botulism, brucellosis, and gas gangrene.

Since World War I, chemical weapons have been banned by international treaty. And the violations of the treaty that occurred in Afghanistan and Indochina generally were on a very small scale. Much larger use was made by the Iraqis in the war against Iran, where chemical weapons proved to be one of the most effective means of breaking the human wave attacks mounted by the Iranian Revolutionary Guards.

(Chemical weapons were also extraordinarily effective in cooling the revolutionary ardor of thousands of young fanatics eager to die for Islam. It is one thing to die gloriously in a hail of bullets, charging enemy positions with the name of Allah on your lips. But it is quite another to gasp out your life in some tribal hospital as your insides slowly dissolve.)

Against the Iranians, and later against his own Kurdish citizens, Saddam Hussein used both mustard gas and several nerve agents—including sarin and tabun.

Toward a counterterrorist strategy

One of the major difficulties in combating terrorism, of course, is that the terrorist is typically a very elusive foe. As a result, it should come as no surprise that governments have mostly floundered in their efforts to combat the terrorist menace.

Perhaps the most basic counterterrorist strategy is simply to make airports and other popular terrorist targets more secure. For example, tightened airport security and creation of a special corps of air marshals has sharply curtailed airline hijacking inside the United States.

There is a limit, however, to what can be achieved by barricades and checkpoints. The experience of the U.S. government in Washington is typical in this regard. Out of concern about bombings inside the Capitol, new procedures were laid down that require all visitors to pass through a metal detector. Concrete barriers were erected to limit approaches to the building. For the most part, public reaction to these measures was muted.

But when White House officials, worried about the use of car and truck bombs, sought to close Pennsylvania Avenue to the public, the outcry was intense. Clearly, officials can go only so far before members of Western society will fight to maintain some of their most fundamental values—such as freedom of movement and the right not to be inconvenienced.

Failed policy of appeasement

One approach that clearly does not work is giving in to terrorist demands. In 1977, fearing disruption of their Mideast oil supplies, the French actually released one of the most notorious terrorists ever to fall into their hands. His name was Abu Daoud, and he was a commander of the infamous Black September movement. Black September, you may recall, was the group responsible for killing the 11 Israeli Olympic team members during the 1972 Munich Games.

Although the agreement was never admitted publicly, the French Secret Service was believed to have reached a tacit accord with a number of international terrorist organizations. They reportedly agreed to allow terrorists free passage through French territory in exchange for a promise from the terrorists that they would not stage attacks on French citizens or installations.

In 1986, however, the French began to reap the bitter harvest of their policy of appeasement when six bombs exploded in Paris within less than a fortnight. Overall, the 12-day campaign of terror claimed eight lives and injured more than 172 Parisians.

Of course, the French were not the only ones trying to solve the terrorist problem by giving in to terrorist demands. The United States did the same thing in the well-known arms-for-hostages scandal. Of course, that might never have happened had attempts to fight terrorism through counterintelligence and military operations been more effective.

Origin of failure

The slowness of the United States to develop much of an anti-terrorist capability stems in part from the scandals and budget cutbacks of the post-Vietnam era. U.S. intelligence services lost 25% of their personnel in the 1970s. At one point, fewer than 50% of CIA analysts even spoke the language of the country they were supposed to cover.

With the end of the Vietnam War, the new intelligence objective became arms control verification—and this pretty much claimed the lion's share of remaining resources. More than anti-terrorist capability was neglected. Training and recruitment fell to such low levels at one time that nearly 75% of CIA foreign station chiefs were old enough to be eligible for retirement.

There were other setbacks as well. On at least two occasions, the agency was itself the victim of a devastating terrorist attack. With the seizure of the U.S. embassy in Tehran, the CIA lost its entire network of intelligence assets in Iran. Another similar debacle occurred in Lebanon a few years later.

The KGB approach

Sometimes, however, a high-minded refusal to match the ruthlessness of one's adversary merely puts you at a severe tactical disadvantage. When four pre-*perestroika* Russian diplomats were seized by Lebanese terrorists in 1985, the KGB replied in terms well understood by terrorists all over the world. After identifying the hostage-takers, Soviet intelligence operatives seized a number of their relatives and friends. They killed one and mailed parts of his body to the kidnappers along with a note demanding release of all Soviet personnel.[22]

The diplomats were released in short order, and no doubt the terrorists were suitably chagrined. They probably also decided it would be much safer to steer clear of the Russians in the future.

The fight against terrorism also suffered from the kind of bureaucratic paralysis that routinely prevails in Washington, D.C. One example of this is bureaucracy's difficulty to even define the problem. One study noted 109 different definitions of terrorism formulated by U.S. government officials between 1936 and 1980.[23]

But if bureaucratic bungling is characteristic of the U.S. government, it is a hallmark of its armed forces. And nowhere has that been more visible than in U.S. handling of terrorist attacks against U.S. Marines in Lebanon. Along with French and Italian troops, U.S. Marines were sent to Lebanon on a peace-keeping mission in 1982 as part of a United Nations multinational force.

Marine Corps debacle

At 6:20 a.m. on October 23, 1983, a yellow Mercedes Benz stakebed truck roared past Lance Corporal Eddie DiFranco's guard post at the perimeter of the Marine encampment. As he scrambled to load his weapon—on higher authority, the Marines had been ordered to stand guard with their weapons empty—the driver looked right at him ... and smiled.

Seconds later, the building housing 350 sleeping Marines went up in what the FBI later termed the largest non-nuclear explosion since World War II. For the Marines, it was the worst loss of life since the Vietnam War.

Of course, when something like this happens, the American government has to blame somebody. A Pentagon commission headed by retired Admiral Robert Long recommended that the Marine commander, Colonel Timothy Geraghty, be punished "for failure to take the security measures necessary to preclude the catastrophic loss of life."[24] Of course, no one remembered that Geraghty had been a vocal opponent of orders from above that had specifically violated the Marines' claim to neutrality and made them virtual participants in the Lebanese civil war.

A month before, when the predominantly Christian Lebanese army suddenly found itself under strong attack by several of the local armed militias, it appealed to Washington for help. The Pentagon ordered the Marines to support the Lebanese army.

Only Colonel Geraghty seemed to appreciate that military action on behalf of the Christian-dominated army would violate the Marines' claim to a neutral peace-keeping role. Once the United States was perceived as taking sides in the factional fighting, the Marines would become just another armed militia—and another target.

Officers who were present on September 19 when Geraghty received the order to fire in support of the Lebanese army report that he argued vehemently against it: "Sir, I can't do that. This will cost us our neutrality. Do you realize if you do that, we'll get slaughtered down here? We could be severely attacked. We're totally vulnerable. We're sitting ducks."[25]

Of course, he was overruled. And he was exactly right. Only 34 days later, the smiling truck driver blasted 241 sleeping Americans to kingdom come.

A few minutes after the Marine blast, another truck bomber struck the Beirut headquarters of the French peace-keeping forces. And 10 days later, a third one struck the headquarters of the Israeli defense forces in Tyre.

Uncertain retaliation

Immediately after the attack, Israeli warplanes struck back. Two days later, so did the French air force. Interestingly enough, the French attack had been originally conceived as a joint U.S.-French counterterrorism strike. On board the U.S. aircraft carrier *Kennedy*, air crews were awakened several nights in a row and ordered to man their planes.

But each time, the raid was called off at the last minute. In spite of the president's avowal on national television that "those who directed this atrocity must be dealt justice, and they will be," the U.S. government could not make up its mind.[26] Finally, the French flew alone.

At length, the only thing the U.S. chain of command could agree on was that daily reconnaissance flights be sent to try to spot any additional threats against the Marines. On December 3, while on such a mission, the crew of an F-14 Tomcat from the *Kennedy* spotted several corkscrewing exhaust trails coming in their direction—the telltale sign of heat-seeking surface-to-air missiles.

The missiles missed, and the F-14 returned safely. But this time the brass was determined to react. Within 24 hours, the Pentagon had recommended, and the president had approved, a raid against Syrian anti-aircraft sites in Lebanon. As David Martin and John Walcott remark in their book, *The Best Laid Plans*, "Having failed to shoot back when 350 Americans were blown up, the Reagan administration had no difficulty deciding to retaliate against a few shoulder-fired missiles that had missed."

Even then, Washington could not go ahead without making a hash of everything. After the Joint Chiefs determined the specific targets against which to retaliate—Syrian anti-aircraft sites in Lebanon—the task of planning the raid became the responsibility of Rear Admiral Jerry Tuttle, the commander of the U.S. fleet off the coast of Lebanon. Tuttle was a former carrier pilot, well-known for being an aggressive and hard-driving officer.

Among the ranks he was renowned for his caustic sarcasm—which, from time to time, he also turned upon himself. (He once awarded himself the nickname, SLUF—an acronym for "short, little, ugly fucker.") In short, he was the kind of commander who either inspired utter devotion or undying hatred.

A man of strong and unvarnished opinions, he was not pleased with Washington's choice of targets. Because the Syrian anti-aircraft sites were too small to reliably show up on radar, his pilots would have to go in low and slow enough to spot them visually. This meant they would be exposed to anti-aircraft fire from not just the Syrians, but any local militia man with a shoulder-fired anti-aircraft weapon.

To minimize the risk to his airmen, he planned to attack at high noon. At least that way anti-aircraft gunners would have to look straight into the sun to spot his planes. At 3:30 a.m. on December 4, having worked out the last details of the strike plan, he lay down for a few hours sleep aboard the aircraft carrier *Independence*. While he slept, however, he was countermanded by higher authority.

Somebody in Washington had the bright idea that the raid would have greater political impact if it took place within 24 hours of the original attack. And that meant the planes would have to strike just after dawn. New orders were issued accordingly.

General ignorance

Not only did the four- and five-star idiots in the Pentagon overrule the well-reasoned judgment of their commander in the field, but they rescheduled the raid at an hour when the targets would be in shadow and American pilots, not anti-aircraft gunners, would have to be looking directly into the early morning sun.

The new orders arrived on board the *Independence* at 5:33 a.m. As soon as Tuttle was awakened with the news, he called back to say there was no way to launch on such short notice. He was ordered to do it anyway. He requested a delay long enough at least to get his air crews properly organized. He was denied.

For better or worse, military men are trained to follow orders—even when issued by imbeciles. Having exhausted the available alternatives, Tuttle scrambled his airmen, told them they had only minutes to review maps and pictures of their targets, and ordered them to their planes.

On the aircraft carrier *Kennedy*, two of the fliers scheduled for the mission, lieutenants Bill Davis and Tom Corey, raced for the flight deck. But when they arrived, they were astounded to discover that their A-6 aircraft had not even been armed with any missiles or bombs.

With only minutes to flight time, they screamed at the ordnance men to attach some in a hurry. Unfortunately, the only munitions at hand were 1,000-pound iron bombs, great for attacking large fortifications, but notoriously inaccurate against small targets like the one they were assigned to assault.

Even so, inaccurate bombs were better than none at all. But there was time only to strap on a pair of the thousand-pounders before the plane was ordered to the runway. It was almost like going to battle unarmed.

Worse, it was the rule rather than the exception. Only one of the A-6s took off with a full load of munitions, flown by lieutenants Mark Lang and Robert Goodman. Only the fact that theirs was the last plane in the take-off line had allowed sufficient time to make sure it was fully armed.

And a few moments later, it was tumbling out of control, the victim of a surface-to-air missile. As the flaming wreck spun toward the ground at two-thirds the speed of sound, Goodman and Lang somehow managed to fire their ejection seats. Lang's parachute barely had time to open before he hit the ground.

As a result, he landed with such impact that his left leg was severed. He bled to death under the gaze of the gunners who had shot him down. Goodman also landed hard, breaking a rib and separating a shoulder in the process. The remaining planes from the *Kennedy* were so lightly armed that all of their munitions could have been carried by a single plane.

Another plane was shot down, but its crew was safely rescued. So, at the cost of one American dead, another captured, and two planes lost, a pair of Syrian gun positions were damaged, and an anti-aircraft radar was put out of commission for about 48 hours.

Brass hat cover-up

Back in Washington, the chain of command was busily covering up what a disaster the raid had been. Not surprisingly, no one was willing to admit responsibility for making a dangerous mission more dangerous because of an irrelevant political consideration. It's a wonder the brass didn't find a way to blame Admiral Tuttle as they did Colonel Geraghty.

Not only did the United States fail to avenge the fatal terrorist attack on the Marines, but it could not even manage to effectively defend reconnaissance aircraft whose mission it was to help protect the Marines from further attack. According to the peculiar logic of the defense bureaucracy, there was apparently nothing to be done but give up reconnaissance. A short time later, all flights over the most dangerous areas of Lebanon—and therefore the ones most in need of watching—were quietly halted.

Even where international terrorist incidents involving Americans have been brought to a successful conclusion, the U.S. government has frequently been more of an obstacle than a help. Consider, for example, the case of U.S. Brigadier General James Dozier, a NATO commander assigned to Verona, Italy.

Unscheduled guests

On December 17, 1981, just as Dozier was sitting down to

dinner with his wife, somebody started ringing the doorbell. He went to the door where he found two men in coveralls who explained (in Italian) that they were trying to find the cause of a leak in the apartment below. Once inside, they pulled silenced pistols.

In short order, the general was gagged, blindfolded, and dumped in a steamer trunk. A couple of hours later, Dozier was taken out of the trunk and chained to a steel cot inside a pup tent that was set up inside an apartment.

His captors announced that he was a prisoner of the Red Brigade. To make sure they could not be overheard, they strapped headphones on him, and treated him to rock music at amplitudes sufficient to cause permanent hearing damage.

When news of the kidnapping reached the U.S. Defense Department, a new bureaucracy swung into action. The commission that had investigated the failure of the Carter administration's effort to rescue the American hostages in Iran found that the operation had been done in by the lack of a proper organization to direct the mission. The bureaucracy's solution, predictably, was to create another bureaucracy. In this manner, the Pentagon's Joint Special Operations Command (J.S.O.C.) was born.

The J.S.O.C. immediately sent a six-man team of intelligence and communications specialists to the Mediterranean. But once they arrived in the operating area of the European Command (E.C.), E.C. commanders claimed them. As a result, America's elite and highly trained counterterrorist force spent its first few weeks on the job arguing about who was in charge.

Psychic insights

No stranger to inter-service rivalry, the Air Force figured out a way to outdo the J.S.O.C. in the race to leave no stone unturned. Displaying a flair for imagination rarely found in military organizations, operation Distant Viewing was launched. This consisted of consulting a number of local psychics who claimed they might be able to find the general by means of extrasensory perception.

One said he was being held on a farm in Austria; another said he was confined in the hold of a ship. Again, every lead was duly catalogued and turned over to the Italian police. None led anywhere. Finally, the overburdened Italian investigators had to ask the Americans to stop trying to be of so much help.

Another effort to aid the investigation was the offer of a

$500,000 reward for information leading to a rescue. No sooner had the reward been announced than it was discovered that no office, embassy, agency, or branch of service involved in the case had legislative authority to dispense reward money outside the United States. The U.S. government, which never has any trouble overspending its multi-trillion dollar budget, somehow could not manage to come up with a half-million dollars of reward money.

Bureaucratic gridlock

It was a good thing the money was never needed. But it is worth noting that the one man who finally was able to break the bureaucratic logjam was a young Marine major who had originally come to the White House as one of the nameless assistants whose duties included handling charts, slides, and other visual aids for his superiors. A few years later, he would become legendary for his ability to circumvent Washington's perpetual bureaucratic paralysis. His name was Oliver North.

That Dozier was ever rescued owed more to the thoroughness of the largest manhunt in Italian history—involving some 5,000 officers—and the shrewdness of the U.S. ambassador to Italy than all the hamstrung efforts of the U.S. government. Aware that many captured leaders of the Red Brigade were still directing operations from behind bars, Ambassador Maxwell Rabb persuaded the Italian Minister of the Interior to put all jailed members in one place and cut their lines of communications to lawyers and relatives.

Soon, the now leaderless kidnappers began to falter. The first major break in the case occurred when police picked up the brother of one of the imprisoned brigade members. He revealed the name of one of the men who had carried Dozier out of his apartment.

As part of a plea bargain, this man led police to a second-floor apartment in Padua where Dozier was being held. After watching the apartment for several days, the Italian counterterrorist brigade stormed the building, using the sounds from a nearby bulldozer to mask the noise of the assault. Dozier was rescued unharmed— except for his hearing loss. Five terrorists were captured along with a cache of weapons and ammunition. And not a shot was fired.

Preferred target

Few Western countries present a potential terrorist with a more tempting array of targets than the United States. For example, virtually the entire natural gas supply to the U.S. Northeast comes through one of two pipelines—both of which are essentially unguarded. Furthermore, both pipelines run on special high-pressure pumps of foreign manufacture. If destroyed, they could take weeks to replace.

The lion's share of rail traffic in the Northeast passes over one of two bridges—one across the Potomac near Washington, D.C., the other across the Ohio River near Cincinnati. Neither is guarded.

Fewer than a dozen switching stations control almost all telephone traffic in U.S. major metropolitan areas. In the spring of 1989, for example, a fire in a Hinsdale, Illinois switching station blacked out telephone service at O'Hare Airport and most of Chicago. Repairs took three months to complete.

Among human targets, Westerners also rank near the top of every terrorist's list. The director of the CIA recently reported that U.S. persons, property, and institutions are victims in one out of every two terrorists incidents.[27]

It is not hard to see why. First, as we have observed, governments are rarely able to react with decisiveness or dispatch. And that helps minimize the terrorist's personal risk. Second, Westerners make ideal hostages. Because of the Western preoccupation with individual human rights, hostages become an instant media event. And as a result, network communication facilities wind up at the service of the hostage-takers.

As of this writing, the odds of becoming the victim of a hostage-taking still are very low. (They're about the same as your chances of being struck by lightning.) One thing, however, is certain. As terrorists around the world continue to zero in on Westerners, those chances are going to increase. Hence, it is only prudent to investigate what you as an individual can do to avoid becoming a victim.

Hotlines and second passports

The U.S. State Department maintains a telephone hotline that you can use to stay abreast of security conditions in countries around the world: 202-647-5225. An updated listing of these briefings also is available on-line to computer owners through the Compuserve Information Service. (GO STATE.)

Usually, the first thing a hijacker will do is collect passports from his band of victims. From these, he can easily identify each person's nationality. If, for example, you are an American or an

Israeli or a citizen of any other country against which the terrorist has a grudge, you may be singled out as a special target for abuse. One way to avoid being identified in this way is to carry a second passport.

Unfortunately, the intricacies of establishing and maintaining dual nationality are far beyond the scope of this book. And along with the advantages may come certain disadvantages. For example, if the country in which you hold dual citizenship has a military draft, you could find yourself called for military service.

Nonetheless, a second passport can be a valuable anti-terrorist defense. For details on how to obtain one, see "Second Passports and Dual Nationality," Agora, Inc., 824 E. Baltimore St., Baltimore, MD 21202, Phone: 410-234-0515, Fax: 410-837-1999. Or "The Passport Report," Scope International Ltd., 62 Murray Road, Waterlooville, Hants, PO8 9JL, U.K., Phone: 44-705-592-255, Fax: 44-705-591-975.

Bulletproof windbreakers

If you are worried about a direct assault on your life, you may want to invest in bullet-resistant clothes. Dramatic advances in the development of synthetic fibers has made possible new light-weight clothing that can protect the wearer from bullets, stab wounds, even blast effects and shrapnel. Nor do you have to look like you're wearing a SWAT-team flak jacket.

For example, you can now buy dress shirts, down vests, t-shirts, windbreakers, fur coats—even London-Fog-type rain-coats capable of withstanding a blast from a fully automatic Uzi. (Children's clothes are also now available.) However, these are not inexpensive items. For example, you can easily pay $1,000 and up for a bulletproof windbreaker or raincoat.

Another worthwhile precaution recommended by Peter Savage in his excellent book, *The Safe Travel Book—A Guide for the International Traveler,* is to develop a series of simple code words for emergency communications. To order a copy, contact the publisher, Lexington Books, at 800-223-2336; or from outside the U.S., call 201-767-4990.

In the event you are abducted and your captors allow you to communicate with outsiders by phone or note, using these key words could convey valuable information about your condition or whereabouts.

For example, Savage suggests the following key words be assigned an alternate meaning:

Key word:	Real meaning:	Sample key word phrase:
Sad	I am being beaten or tortured.	"... *sad* to miss you"
Health	I am injured or sick.	"I'm in good *health.*"
Alarmed	I am in an urban area with street noises.	"Don't be *alarmed.*"
Lonely	I am in a rural area with no street noises.	"I am *lonely* for you."
OK	I am OK, treated well.	"I am *OK.*"
Many thanks	I am among many armed captors.	"*Many thanks* for your love and support."

(Note that as an aid to memory, the first letters of the key words comprise an acronym—in this case, SHALOM.)

Surviving as a hostage[28]

If you are unlucky enough to become a hostage victim, there are a number of things you should—and should not—do to maximize your chances of emerging unharmed.

The most dangerous period of a kidnapping or a hostage-taking is the initial capture. At this moment your first impulse may be to freeze or to run or to fight. The safest thing to do is to freeze. At all costs, avoid sudden movements. They can easily get you killed.

If there is shooting, put your head down. Better still, lie on the floor. That way you'll be a smaller target. If you wear glasses or other aids, protect them. Slip them into a pocket. Don't put them down.

If shooting breaks out on an airplane in flight, there is some likelihood that a bullet will penetrate the aircraft's outer skin. A handful of bullet holes, however, will not be enough to depressurize the aircraft. A greater danger is the possibility that a stray bullet might hit a fuel tank somewhere in the plane's hull.

(To minimize this risk, the ammunition used by U.S. air marshals is specially designed for use in confined spaces. While lethal within a range of 50 feet, at greater distances these bullets rapidly lose power and are unlikely to penetrate aircraft bulkheads.)

Listen carefully to what your abductors say, and follow their instructions precisely. If you have to endure a beating, try your best to roll with the punches as much as possible. Fortunately, you can probably count on your body's own coping mechanisms—adrenaline and shock—to increase your tolerance to pain. Most former victims report that they felt very little pain when abused during a capture.

In the event of a rescue attempt, you should not under any

circumstances attempt to disarm any of your captors. Nor should you try to seize a gun during the confusion. Your rescuers will be trained to shoot anyone holding a weapon—and there will not be time to explain that you are not one of the "bad guys."

The period of confinement in a hostage-taking may be as short as several hours or as long as several years. Many of the insights on how best to survive an extended period of captivity come from the experience of William Niehous, a vice president of Owns-Illinois' foreign subsidiary in Venezuela, who was kidnapped and held captive for 1,219 days.[29]

Five points of survival

Niehous outlines a five-point plan for surviving an extended confinement. Taken together, these five points comprise the acronym FACES.

F stands for *faith* that you will be able to endure the emotional roller coaster of captivity. There is a range of psychological reactions that you are likely to experience immediately after capture. The most common emotions are incapacity, fear, denial, and withdrawal.

Initially, you may be so afraid that you think you won't be able to cope. Knowing that anybody in the same boat would go through the same thing may help you control your fear. Many former hostages have expressed surprise at their own capacity to endure what appeared unendurable.

Be aware that overwhelming fear sometimes manifests itself in neurotic reactions. Claustrophobia is a typical example. In an airplane especially, you may panic at being confined by seatbelts, or even the plane itself. Escaping into irrational behavior may be an effective form of denial, but it is an unconstructive one. A better strategy would be to seek relief in the minutiae of your experience rather than in total unawareness.

Try to distract yourself by memorizing every detail of your captors and what they do. Write a diary in your head and include everything you observe—including colors, smells, and textures. Omit no details—no matter how trivial they seem. Not only will the effort help you control your emotions, but the information may be useful later.

A is for *aspirations or goals*. William Niehous reports that he sustained his spirits by setting himself objectives. "I would live until a specific date, whether it was my son's graduation, or my wife's birthday, or Christmas. As the date came and went, with my release not imminent, I did become despondent; however, I then set another goal for life sometime in the future. I kept telling myself that those holding me surely would release me by the date of my next goal."

One way to combat the sometimes overwhelming sense of powerlessness is to organize the space allotted to you. Even if all you have is a cramped economy-class airline seat, designate special places to keep different objects. Make it one of your goals to keep your area orderly. External order will help your internal order.

C is for *communication*. If you have a medical problem that requires special medication or attention, inform your captors at the first non-threatening opportunity. They may accommodate you. Generally, it is in their interest that you stay healthy. A sick hostage is a burden and a liability.

If you are given a chance to read newspapers, try to stay abreast of events in the outside world. If you are allowed to send letters to relatives or loved ones, putting your thoughts on paper can have a beneficial effect—even if they are never delivered.

If you are allowed to communicate with other hostages, take care not to spread any suspicions you might have concerning any of them. Discord can only further devastate the morale of the entire hostage group. If held together with other hostages, do not hoard food without group consent. Secrets are hard to keep in captivity. And if you are found out, it may make you a target for hostility.

E is for *exercise*. Contrive to establish some form of exercises that can be done in your confined circumstances and do them regularly. Maybe all you can do is wiggle your toes and fingers. But even that much will aid circulation—especially if you are being held in cramped conditions.

Moreover, it is important to do what you can to keep your body as agile as possible. If a chance to escape presents itself, you don't want to be so debilitated that you cannot seize it.

Stockholm Syndrome

S is for the *Stockholm Syndrome*—the well-documented emotional attachment that frequently develops between the captive and captor. (The term comes from a barricade-hostage incident that took place during a 1973 bank robbery in the Swedish capital.)

Falling in love with the hostage-taker is a common manifestation of the Stockholm Syndrome. Sometimes this attachment is strong enough to cause a hostage to become so eager to please his captors that he acts against his own best interests and that of his fellow victims. For example, hostages have been known to help terrorists escape.

The degree to which a hostage experiences the Stockholm Syndrome varies by individual. Some remain largely unaffected, while others are nearly blinded by it. According to one study of hostage incidents, more than 80% of the kidnap victims experienced some degree of fear and anger toward the police—especially if the police overtly threatened the hostage-takers.[30]

Be aware, however, that this attachment works both ways—and you can therefore use it to your advantage. For this reason, you should seize every opportunity to establish a personal relationship with your captors.

If you have a chance, for example, try to get them talking. Be as friendly as they allow you to be, but not so friendly that you lose their respect. The more that you can get them to think of you as a fellow human being—and not as a depersonalized political objective—the greater your chances of emerging unhurt.

One further note: Ever since Kozo Okamato, the surviving terrorist of the Lydda Airport massacre, admitted "a strange ecstasy" in meting out death to innocents, a number of authorities have warned that women terrorists may be more inclined to engage in acts of senseless violence than their male counterparts.[31]

Indeed, a host of studies confirm that terrorist acts by females have thus far been characterized more by gratuitous violence than those of their male counterparts—whose use of force usually appears more calculated and directed toward some well-defined political goal. Whether this will continue to be the case is, predictably, a matter of considerable dispute.

Hopes for the future

In view of the statistics that show terrorism is growing steadily worse, and the befuddlement that has plagued efforts to combat it, what hopes should we have for the future? In the great game of military competition, high technology traditionally has been one of America's strong suits. And while technology can scarcely persuade fanatics to take up more leisurely pursuits, it can be pressed into service to make the task of the unrepentant more difficult.

Black powder markers

One promising possibility lies in steps that could be taken to reduce the anonymity of explosives. Back in the early 1970s, a 3M Company research chemist developed a means of tracing explosives by seeding them with tiny chips of multilayered melamine plastic. These tiny chips, no bigger than one-thousandth of a millimeter across, could contain as many as 10 separate layers, each with a different color laminate.

Dubbed microtaggants, these chips could be mixed in with explosives early in the manufacturing process without affecting their chemistry or performance. More importantly, they would always survive among the explosive debris, providing a positive link to a particular production batch. Government regulations require considerable record keeping on the buying and selling of explosives. These microtaggants would for the first time make it possible to link a particular explosion to a particular recorded purchase of explosives.

A dramatic real-life test occurred on May 10, 1979, when a truck exploded in the parking lot of Bethlehem Steel near Baltimore, killing the driver and severely wounding his passenger. After sweeping the area, technicians from the Bureau of Alcohol, Tobacco, and Firearms (A.T.F.) discovered the telltale taggants among the debris.[32]

A call to 3M revealed that the color code matched a batch of Tovex 220, a water gelatin explosive widely used in road construction and quarrying. Records showed that this particular batch had been sold to the Jenkins Explosives Co. in Martinsburg, WV. A visit there led federal agents to James McFillin, the man who had purchased the explosives. He also was the murderer.

The di-electric scanner

Another promising technology was developed by William Gregory of the physics department at Georgetown University. Called "di-electric analysis," it works on the principle that different materials exhibit distinctive behavior in two important respects—their abilities to store electric charge, and to conduct electric current.

Gregory built a simple device that measures these two characteristics—and found that virtually any material he tested exhibited a characteristic fingerprint. By compiling a library of these fingerprints, Gregory maintains that a set of portraits could be developed covering just about any innocent items found in a suitcase—socks, shaving cream, blow dryers, etc. Security personnel could hand-inspect anything the machine didn't recognize.

As it turns out, di-electric analysis is especially sensitive to the chemistry of explosives. This gives it an important advantage over the x-ray machines and metal detectors now in service. Neither of these can pick up the presence of an explosive, especially if it is packed in some innocent-looking container—such as a tube of toothpaste. Furthermore, the di-electric scanner should be able to easily spot the metal detector's newest nemesis—the ceramic and plastic handgun.

Gregory got a chance to prove his device when the U.S. Information Agency (U.S.I.A.) was plagued by a rash of letter bombs. With considerable public fanfare, a scanner was installed in the mailroom of the U.S.I.A.'s Washington headquarters in February 1977. Apparently the mere announcement was enough to deter aspiring bombers. The year that the scanner was in operation, no additional explosive packages were received.

As helpful as adoption of these technologies might be, at best they merely complicate the terrorist mission. Any effort to truly strike back at international terrorists inevitably amounts to another military mission of the kind that have gone awry so often in the past.

The grim conclusion is that most countries probably will never be able to match the surgical precision and efficiency of the Israeli defense forces in the battle against terrorists. As we have seen, it almost looks as if the surest way to screw something up is to put the American military establishment in charge.

Some might argue that while military miscarriages inevitably make the headlines, successful counterterrorist operations may never be publicized for fear of revealing too much about U.S. intelligence assets and techniques. This may indeed be the case. But if the whole truth were known, surely more debacles than we yet know of would also come to light.

Hidden blunders

Consider, for example, the case of an Itavia DC-9 bound from Bologna to Sicily on the evening of June 27, 1980. Somewhere over the Mediterranean, the jet exploded and crashed into the sea, killing all 81 aboard.

At the time, this was thought to be just another in a wave of terrorist bombings. But now the true story finally can be pieced together.

Not much was ever found of the plane. Thirty-nine bodies were eventually fished out of the sea, along with a few seat cushions, but it was the cushions that provided the first clue.

Tests performed on the debris in England revealed traces of a chemical known as T4, a military explosive commonly used in air-to-air missiles. Furthermore, small particles of the explosive were found deep inside the fabric of the cushions, which suggested that they had been traveling at extremely high speeds—speeds much higher than would have been caused by a bomb inside the plane.

Twenty-two days after the explosion, shepherds in a remote area about 300 miles from the scene of the crash made a startling discovery. There, on the side of a mountain, lay the wreckage of a Soviet-built MIG-23 jet fighter. The body of the pilot was still in the cockpit. Both the pilot and his craft bore the markings of the Libyan air force.

When word leaked out, authorities immediately sealed off the area. And, although the date of the crash was never officially established, the state of decomposition of the pilot's body suggested that it certainly could have occurred on the same day that the DC-9 exploded.

The Italian government has denied any link between the two events. But NATO documents confirm that a major military air exercise was conducted over the Mediterranean in June 1980. They also indicate that a squadron of four Libyan MIG-23s overflew the exercise area almost every day.

A radar study by the National Traffic Safety Board in the United States found that an unidentified object flying at high speed crossed the DC-9's flight path shortly before the explosion. Events of the final seconds of the flight, however, are obscured by a mysterious eight-minute gap in military radar reports at the time of the crash.

Although the Italian Defense Ministry has denied that any NATO planes were in the air at the time of the crash, it is difficult to avoid the conclusion that an aerial dogfight must have broken out between NATO pilots and the Libyan flyers. One MIG-23 was shot down by NATO fighters. It is also clear that the unarmed DC-9 must have suffered a similar fate.

What we don't know is which side fired the missile that brought it down.

---

1. Bernard Lewis, ed., *Islam: From the Prophet to the Capture of Constantinople, Vol. 1: Politics and War*, p. 23-24.

2. Judith Miller and L. Mylroie, *Saddam Hussein and the Crisis in the Gulf*, p. 243.

3. Special National Intelligence Estimate, prepared by CIA analyst J. Azrael, 1981.

4. *ibid.*

5. Samir al Khalil, *Republic of Fear*, p.14.

6. This account draws on the excellent work done by Gordon Thomas and Max Morgan-Witts, *Pontiff*, p. 406.

7. *ibid.*

8. *The Koran, 1:119.*

9. Quoted by J. Laffin, *War Annual 1*, p. 61.

10. Quoted by B. Lewis, *The Assassins: A Radical Sect in Islam*, p. 7-8.

11. "Nuclear Weapons on Sale for Hard Currency in Eastern Europe," *Taipan*, August 1990, p. 1; see also: "Bad Blood in Germany—The Soviet Army Can't Leave Soon Enough," *Newsweek*, November 12, 1990, p. 42.

12. *Princeton Alumni Weekly*, October 25, 1976.

13. Rear Admiral Thomas Davies, "Terrorism's Nuclear Potential: What Might the Means and Targets Be?," p. 3.

14. "International Task Force on Prevention of Nuclear Terrorism," cited by Louis R. Beres in *Terrorism and Global Security: The Nuclear Threat*, p. 40.

15. "Nuclear Weapons on Sale for Hard Currency in Eastern Europe," *op. cit.*

16. Stockholm International Peace Research Institute, *Weapons of Mass Destruction*, p. 41.

17. R. C. Clark, *Technological Terrorism*, p. 110.

18. N. C. Livingston, *The War Against Terrorism*, p. 110.

19. *Washington Post*, September 23, 1981.

20. Peter Gumbel, "Anthrax: the Survivors Speak," *Asian Wall Street Journal*, October 24, 1991.

21. White, David, "Uphill Battle to Tighten Biological Weapon Controls," *Financial Times*, September 6, 1991, p. 3.

22. Gerald F. Seib, "Soviets' Big Stick Gets Better Results Than That of U.S. Gulf Actions Show," *Wall Street Journal*, August 10, 1987.

23. David C. Martin and John Walcott, *Best Laid Plans: The Inside Story of America's War Against Terrorism*, p. 53.

24. Report of the U.S. Department of Defense, Commission on Beirut International Airport Terrorist Act, October 23, 1983.

25. Robin Wright, *Sacred Rage: The Wrath of Militant Islam*, p. 78.

26. P. Taubman, *New York Times Magazine*, April 14 , 1985.

27. W. Webster, Speech before American Bar Association meeting, Toronto, August 9, 1988.

28. Francine Modderno, *Traveler's Health and Safety Handbook*.

29. "How to Survive as a Hostage," Diplomats and Terrorists: What Works, What Doesn't—A Symposium, Institute for the Study of Diplomacy, Georgetown University, 1982.

30. Francine Modderno, *op. cit.*, p. 9.

31. D.E. Georges-Abeyie, "Women as Terrorists," in L.Z. Freedman and Y. Alexander, *Perspectives on Terrorism*, p. 78. See also: E. MacDonald, *Shoot the Women First: Inside the Secret World of Female Terrorists*.

32. Stephen Kindel, "Catching Terrorists," *Science Digest*, September 1986, p. 37-82.

Chapter 6

Oil and War Today

The Battle After Desert Storm

We have drawn a line in the sand.
— Thomas R. Pickering, U.S. ambassador
to the United Nations
during the 1991 Gulf War —

Fine. Now let us pray you can control the wind.
— Sympathetic Arab diplomat
(speaking off the record) —

After the Iran-Iraq war ended in an uneasy truce, and the Soviets withdrew from Afghanistan, many in the West naively thought that an enduring peace had finally come to the Mideast. They were encouraged in this view by both the collapse of Communism in Eastern Europe and the winding down of the military competition between Russia and the United States.

In the aftermath of the 1991 Gulf War and the first peace agreements between Arabs and Israelis, it has once again become popular to imagine the curtain has finally rung down on a thousand years of violent and turbulent history. Like those who saw the end of history in the end of the Cold War, today's dreamers are merely destined for disappointment (and surprise) the next time war erupts, and oil again hangs in the balance.

While the risk of nuclear confrontation between the super-powers has indeed diminished, the likelihood of bloody regional wars has not. On balance, it is not a more peaceful world.

Nowhere is this clearer than in the Middle East. Iraqi President Saddam Hussein was merely the first dictator to seize the opportunities created by the collapse of the Soviet Union and the growing American preoccupation with domestic rather than

99

global concerns. Despite Iraq's defeat, he will not be the last.

In the fourth edition of *The Last Wave*, published shortly after the end of the first Gulf War between Iran and Iraq, I predicted that the growing sophistication of military hardware would make the next Mideast war far more destructive than any previous ones.

This forecast was borne out by the events of Operation Desert Storm. In addition to the countless thousands of Iraqi dead and wounded, the second Persian Gulf War also resulted in the destruction of oil wells on a scale unseen in any previous conflict. It also ushered in the first large-scale use of missile warfare in the Mideast.

Even more disturbing has been the extraordinary proliferation of these missiles—many of them specifically designed to carry either conventional warheads or weapons of mass destruction—that has taken place in the region since the allied victory.

Syrian Scud scare

Syria, for example, has purchased more than 150 Scud-Cs from North Korea at a cost of more than a half-billion dollars. (Ironically, some of the money to pay for them came from the more than $2 billion given by Saudi Arabia to Syrian President Hafez Assad for contributing troops to Operation Desert Storm.)

The Scud-C represents a quantum leap in Mideast missile technology. Vastly more accurate than Saddam's Scud-Bs, it has an effective range of approximately 350 miles. That means almost every important oil field in the Mideast is within range. (So is every city and military base in Israel.)

Through its Lyongaksan Import Company, North Korea has also sold entire factories for the manufacture of Scud-Cs. Sometime in the second quarter of 1993, Syria began producing Scud-Cs at two such facilities in Aleppo and Hama.[1]

One big advantage of this is that it helps the Koreans escape surveillance of their missile sales. Missiles sent by surface ships can often be observed by satellite. Missiles built in factories of the purchasing country cannot be so easily spotted.

The Scud-C can carry three times the payload (about 11,500 pounds) of the Scud-B. And the Syrian versions were specifically configured by the North Koreans to be able to carry chemical or biological weapons without any degradation in accuracy.

With the defeat of Iraq, Syria presently has one of the only two remaining advanced chemical weapons programs in the Mideast. The other belongs to Iran.

100

Missile midwifery

Interestingly enough, North Korea's missile business was born in the late 1970s when military technicians began reverse engineering Soviet Scud-Bs purchased from Egypt. Forty of its earliest copies were sold to Iran in 1988, which subsequently used them in its war against Iraq.

Among the benefactors of North Korea's growing arms industry are the Chinese. In addition to technical expertise, the Chinese have also supplied critical subassemblies—such as rocket motors and guidance systems (some of which the Chinese, in turn, obtained from Russia and the Ukraine).[2]

China's arms exports (both direct and indirect) have long been an important source of hard-currency earnings. Fear of imperiling this profitable export partnership also helps explain why the Chinese have been so reluctant to put much pressure on North Korea to halt its nuclear weapons program.

Chinese weapons, such as the Silkworm anti-ship missile, have also been sold in quantity to Iran. CSS-2 missiles have been sold to Saudi Arabia. And Chinese M9 missiles have also been offered to both Iran and Syria.

While China supplied the know-how, Libya supplied hard-currency capital. Colonel Qaddafi has bought more than $1 billion worth of Scud-Bs, Scud-Cs, and other military equipment.

Profits from the Libyan sales were quickly reinvested in upgraded production facilities such as the ingenuously named Central Repair Workshop, a Korean-built Scud-C factory near Tripoli. North Korean engineers also helped Egypt build a Scud-C production plant outside Cairo.

In addition, the development of North Korea's next generation missile, the Rodong-1 (also called Nodong-1), was at least party financed by Libya. The Rodong-1 is a multistage, liquid-fueled, intermediate-range ballistic missile (I.R.B.M.) with a range of more than 600 miles.

In the sixth edition of *The Last Wave*, I predicted North Korea's successor to the Scud-C would become operational by 1993. Sure enough, in mid-1993, Western and Japanese intelligence services observed four successful test firings of the Rodong-1 in a remote area of the Sea of Japan.

In August, North Koreans themselves finally acknowledged the development of the missile.[3] (Needless to say, this also upset the established balance of military power in Asia. See Chapter 9.)

I now expect the Rodong-1 to start showing up in the arsenals of the world's most erratic regimes—such as Libya, Syria, and Iran—as early as late 1994 or early 1995. From bases in Libya, Colonel Qaddafi could use the Rodong-1 to hit much of Europe, including parts of Italy, Greece, and Bulgaria—as well as Western Turkey.

North Korean development efforts haven't stopped with the Rodong-1. Two larger, follow-on versions, tentatively titled Taepo Dong-1 and 2, will have ranges of approximately 1,200 miles and 1,600 miles respectively. If present development trends continue, they will become operational sometime in 1995 or early 1996.

Hair-trigger alert

The widespread proliferation of ballistic missile technology is a profoundly destabilizing development in an already unstable region. That is because such missiles are extraordinarily difficult to defend against.

Anyone who watched the 1991 Gulf War on the Cable News Network (CNN) may have been impressed with what appeared to be a remarkable performance by the U.S.-built Patriot antimissile system against Scud attacks launched from Iraq.

However, postwar analysis of radar and telemetry records has revealed that as many as half of Saddam's Scud-B and Al-Hussein missiles were so poorly engineered that they fell apart entirely on their own in midflight.

In other words, the Patriot's presumed near-perfect hit record was not so at all—because its targets had a strong propensity to self-destruct anyway.

Furthermore, Saddam Hussein never managed to launch more than a couple of missiles at a time. Slow-moving rockets, launched singly or in pairs, are the easiest for any antimissile system to shoot down.

For this reason, the standard offensive tactic against almost any kind of antimissile defense is simply to attack your target with several dozen rockets—preferably from many different directions—all at once. The best antimissile system in the world is unlikely to get all of them.

And if you arm your missiles with weapons of mass destruction, only one of them really needs to get through. This is especially the case if you are attacking a soft civilian target, such as a large city.

Thanks to North Korean and Chinese technology, future

belligerents in the Mideast will be able to launch more, faster, more accurate, and more powerful rockets at targets much farther away than ever before. Where ballistic missiles are concerned, technology favors the offense.

Note that the proliferation of advanced missile technology enormously increases the military value of preemptive attack strategies. Because these rockets are almost impossible to stop once they are launched, the only really effective defense is to destroy them on the ground.

This "use-them-or-lose-them" character of an increasingly missile-oriented offense means that the Mideast will increasingly be on hair-trigger alert. And that is precisely the sort of climate in which wars tend to start by accident.

For example, imagine some poorly trained radar operator who mistakes a flock of birds for an incoming attack. With only seconds to decide whether to launch his own missiles—or risk having them destroyed—there will not be time to investigate possible errors or malfunctions.

Poor man's cruise missile

One of the most memorable aspects of the allied victory in the 1991 Gulf War was the virtuoso performance of various high-tech military systems. For example, using the American Defense Department's $10 billion network of 24 Global Positioning Satellites (G.P.S.), allied troops were able to navigate flawlessly in the trackless Iraqi desert.

G.P.S. is the most accurate navigation system ever devised. In recent years, a civilian version of G.P.S. became available to civilian airlines and other commercial applications.

Among the dazzling displays of high-tech weaponry, nothing was more impressive than the performance of American cruise missiles. Cruise missiles are small, low-flying, robot-driven aircraft capable of hitting a target hundreds of miles away with pinpoint accuracy.

In the second Gulf War, they were used against Iraqi radar-based anti-air defenses in the initial assault on Baghdad. Once those defenses had been destroyed, the Iraqi capital was completely open to attack by allied warplanes.

The small size of cruise missiles combined with their low altitude flight capability makes them almost impossible to track by radar. In fact, they were originally developed by the United States during the Cold War as a means of penetrating what were then thought to be formidable Soviet air defenses. Because they are considerably cheaper than ballistic missiles, cruise missiles can also be produced in much greater numbers.

But no longer is the ability to manufacture and launch cruise missiles a monopoly of technologically sophisticated military powers such as the United States. Using commercially available G.P.S. equipment, it is now possible to achieve cruise-missile accuracy on the cheap.

In fact, it is now possible to build a precision guidance system with only about the level of technical expertise it requires to assemble a personal computer out of off-the-shelf parts. Here's how.

Simply put, the G.P.S. network transmits signals that can be used to compute your position anywhere on the surface of the earth. The signals come in two versions.

A coded military version, which can only be used by specially built equipment, is accurate enough to locate any position on the surface of the earth to within 38 feet. The civilian version, now used in civilian aircraft and commercially available G.P.S. receivers, can be used to locate any position within about 328 feet.

What some clever engineers have now done is to combine the commercially available G.P.S. signal with a second signal from a known, land-based beacon. A personal computer then compares the two, and analyzes the difference. The result is so-called "local differential G.P.S.," which is capable of navigating within an accuracy of only 10 feet.

In other words, using inexpensive, off-the-shelf parts, it is now possible to build a cruise missile guidance system that is almost three times more accurate than the pinpoint navigation systems everyone was so impressed with during Operation Desert Storm. Among the nations currently hard at work incorporating this technology into a new generation of cruise missiles are North Korea and Iran.[4]

Like ballistic missiles, cruise missiles are virtually impossible to defend against. Like ballistic missiles, they encourage both preemptive attack strategies and hair-trigger, launch-on-warning alert postures. Unfortunately, the danger created by the proliferation of cruise missile technology is not confined to the Mideast.

Unlike ballistic missiles, cruise missiles can be launched from almost any platform: planes, ships, trucks, even submarines. From a ship safely in international waters, such a missile could deliver a weapon of mass destruction against virtually any city on the face of the earth.

According to the U.S. Office of Technology Assessment, it would require only 90 kilograms of anthrax spores or about enough enriched uranium to fill up a fruit bowl—to wipe out Washington D.C. And as yet, there is no feasible defense.[5]

Oil strategy—Persian version

Syria is not North Korea's only Mideast customer. Scud-Cs have also been sold in quantity to Iran. Iran has also requested shipments of the Rodong-1. In addition, North Korean experts were involved in helping Iran integrate into its air force the more than 130 advanced Iraqi warplanes that fled destruction at the hands of the allied forces during Operation Desert Storm.

One reason the first Gulf War between Iran and Iraq dragged on for so many years is that a lot of people calculated that it wasn't altogether a bad thing for the two nastiest regimes in the Persian Gulf to exhaust themselves fighting each other. As former U.S. Secretary of State Henry Kissinger once observed, the unhappiest thing about the Iran-Iraq war was that its combatants couldn't both lose.

Ever since the fall of the Shah, Iran's fundamentalist Shi'ite government has been widely feared throughout the Islamic world. In part, this is because the Iranians have been among the most vigorous supporters of terrorism—and not just against America, Israel, and its allies. (See Chapter 5.) They have also promoted subversion by a variety of fanatical fundamentalist groups, from those who took over Sudan to those who attempted to take over Algeria. Egypt has also been a target.

But a special target has always been oil-rich Saudi Arabia. Within Islam, the Shi'ites and the Sunnis have had a murderous quarrel going for more than a thousand years. And the two holiest cities of Islam, Mecca, and Medina lie within the Sunni-dominated kingdom of Saudi Arabia.

In part, the Saudis are also high on the Iranian hit list because they helped bankroll Saddam Hussein during the Iran-Iraq war. And in part because of a long-running dispute within OPEC about oil prices.

With enormous oil reserves and a small population, the Saudis can afford to take a long-term view. For them, that means keeping oil prices low enough to discourage the development of alternative energy sources elsewhere.

With a large population and relatively small reserves (at least by Mideast standards), Iran has always been an advocate of the highest possible oil prices. (During the first oil shock in 1973, for example, the Shah was also the first to raise prices.)

A dedicated nationalist to the core, the deposed Shah envisioned Iran as the policeman of the oil-rich Persian Gulf. The ruling mullahs in Tehran today have no less grandiose regional ambitions.

Note that this helps explain Tehran's interest in Sudan. A Sudan firmly in the Iranian camp is a geopolitical step toward encirclement of Saudi Arabia. And Sudan's long Red Sea coastline borders a potential second choke point for international oil shipments—after the straits of Hormuz at the mouth of the Persian Gulf.

Iran's regional ambitions also lie behind its enormous expenditures on arms. Now that rival Iraq has been defeated, nothing stands in its way.

In addition to ballistic missiles, the Iranians also have a sizeable chemical weapons program. This is not surprising. After all, they were victims of dozens of gas attacks at the hands of Saddam Hussein. However, Iran also has perhaps the most aggressive and advanced nuclear weapons program in the Mideast (after Israel, of course).

Since the second Gulf War, the Iranians have aggressively courted the Muslim populations of the Central Asian republics of the former Soviet Union. Very likely, these efforts have already paid off. During the second half of 1992, there were persistent reports that Kazakhstan sold Iran at least several tactical nuclear warheads taken from the arsenals of the former Soviet Union.[6]

Iran's other nuclear benefactor is North Korea. Cut off from the subsidies it used to receive from the Soviet Union, abandoned and internationally isolated by the collapse of Communism, North Korea faces a grim and increasingly desperate future.

Famine is on the rise. Food and electricity are strictly rationed. Lacking hard currency, it cannot afford to import what it needs. But what it can do is barter ballistic missiles and nuclear expertise for Iranian oil.

One of the political lessons of the second Gulf War is that no nation has any hope of confronting the American-led coalition that defended Saudi Arabia in Desert Storm unless it has both weapons of mass destruction and the means to deliver them. Saddam's mistake was that he was too impatient. He refused to

106

wait until his nuclear program had produced any usable warheads. He refused to wait until his engineers figured out how to put an atomic bomb or a chemical warhead on top of a rocket without having it fall apart mid-flight.

Iran has no intention of repeating Saddam's mistake. Interestingly enough, once its nuclear and conventional buildup is complete, there may not even be any need to actually go to war.

It's hard to imagine America under President Clinton having the stomach to assemble an international coalition like that organized by former president George Bush. Especially against a nuclear armed adversary—that has already demonstrated its ability to carry out successful terrorist attacks inside the United States.

As a consequence, the Iranians may well be able to sufficiently intimidate Saudi Arabia and the other Gulf states that they will henceforth accept orders from Tehran. At that point, the Iranians will have certainly solved their oil pricing problem. They will also have achieved what Iraq did not—namely, the consolidation of the vast Mideast oil reserves under a single power.

Oil and war revisited

The military lessons of Desert Storm were obvious enough to be quickly learned—on all sides of the conflict. Saddam Hussein's tactical error was to try to fight the second Gulf War the same way he fought the first Gulf War against Iran—with World War I-style massed formations behind static defenses.

If all other things are equal, a strategy based on a doctrine of mobile warfare will always triumph against a static defense. That's because the defender has to defend everywhere, while the attacker is free to concentrate all his force against a single point of his adversary's line.

As a result, the weapons of the next Mideast war will not be delivered by massive formations of tanks and infantry, which are vulnerable to attack by precision guided weapons. Nor will they be delivered by massed artillery.

Allied computer-directed counterbattery fire made short work of Iraq's big guns. Against a technically sophisticated adversary, long-range guns will be able to survive only by quickly moving after each shot.

Instead, weapons of mass destruction will rain from the sky at supersonic speed, atop intermediate-range ballistic missiles of increasing accuracy. Irregular forces such as terrorists and urban guerrillas will play a much bigger role in the next war—for the simple reason that they cannot be spotted by reconnaissance satellites, or attacked by stealth bombers or Tomahawk cruise missiles.

As noted above, the reason chemical weapons were not used in Desert Storm is that the Iraqis still lacked the technical capability to effectively deliver a reliable chemical warhead by ballistic missile. This will not be the case in the next war.

As postwar inspections by U.N. investigators have revealed, the Iraqis were also within months of being able to explode their first nuclear device. Unlike the Iraqis, the belligerents in the next Mideast war will have already tested their ability to manufacture weapons of mass destruction—and their means of delivering them.

Despite large discoveries in Alaska, Mexico, and the North Sea, two thirds of the world oil reserves still lie in the Middle East. Sooner or later, another oil shock is inevitable.

Using conventional explosives, Saddam was able to put the Kuwaiti oil fields out of commission only for a few months. Had he been able to detonate a nuclear weapon, he could have taken Kuwaiti oil off the market for a thousand years.

---

1. "North Korea Alarms U.S. Over Mideast Missile Sales," *Asian Wall Street Journal*, July 19, 1993.

2. L. Spector, "Treaties Target China's Arms Trade," *Asian Wall Street Journal*, September 9, 1991, and K. R. Timmerman, "China's Comrades in Arms," April 3-4, 1992.

3. S. Emerson, "The Postwar Scud Boom," *Wall Street Journal*, July 10, 1991; R. W. Czeschin, "Cashing In on the Coming Oil Shock: How to Profit From North Korea's Military Mischief," *Taipan*, July 1993; "Korean Missile Near Completion," *South China Morning Post*, November 13, 1993.

4. J. J. Fialka, "Airliners Can Exploit U.S. Guidance System, but So Can Enemies: GPS Could Be Used to Direct Cheap, Accurate Missiles," *Wall Street Journal*, August 26, 1993.

5. "Weapons Rise Raises Concern," *South China Morning Post*, September 23, 1993.

6. K. R. Timmerman, "Time to Stop Russia's Nuclear Gangsters," *Wall Street Journal*, December 1, 1992.

Section II

Pearl Harbor II

Chapter 7

The Japanese Postwar Economic Miracle

From Ruins to Riches

I am inclined to think that our relations with Japan are going through the usual and unavoidable stages of the intercourse of strong and civilized nations with weaker and less civilized ones.
— Lord Palmerston, explaining the destruction of Kagoshima by the Royal Navy in 1864 —

For the Japanese, World War II came to an end on August 20, 1945, when Emperor Hirohito went on the radio to admit defeat. It was the first time the Japanese people had ever heard his voice. Later, he renounced his centuries-old claim to divinity and joined the ranks of mortal men.

This also marked the start of one of the most dramatic economic recoveries in recorded history. How Japan climbed from the devastation of World War II to the status of an economic powerhouse in the 1980s is a fascinating story. It is a story of superpower politics, of ham-fisted government intervention in the economy, and of the native ingenuity and adaptability of the Japanese people.

Without a doubt, the war was a catastrophe for the Japanese economy. Aerial bombardment by the U.S. Army Air Force—including atomic attacks on Hiroshima and Nagasaki—had utterly destroyed 119 major Japanese cities. About 2.2 million homes were reduced to rubble, and more than 9 million homeless civilians wandered the streets in search of shelter.

Unfortunately, even the figures in the following chart do not tell the whole story. Thousands more homes were lost to wartime confiscation and forced evacuations. If these losses are added in, more than 20% of the civilian housing stock was destroyed.

Number of Residences Damaged
During World War II[1]

	National Totals	Urban Area Totals
Total Damaged	2,362,000	2,264,000
Completely Burned	2,188,000	2,119,000
Partially Burned	49,000	39,000
Completely Demolished	64,000	55,000
Partially Demolished	61,000	51,000

In addition to residential housing, factories, roads, bridges, and port facilities were devastated as well.

Damage to Economic Assets
During World War II[2]

	% Damaged
Energy Utilities	11
Furniture and Household Goods	21
Production Goods	25
Commercial Buildings	25
Transportation Facilities	29
Industrial Machinery	34
Ships	81
Naval Vessels and Planes	100

As the above figures indicate, shipping suffered the most damage. Before the war, Japanese shipping capacity stood at 6.3 million tons. Afterward, only 1.53 million tons remained. To make matters worse, most of the surviving ships were unfit for long voyages. They had been hastily constructed during the war, when the military had first claim on the nation's output of raw materials.

Total wartime damage to the economy was estimated to be 99.2 billion yen—based on the prevailing price levels of 1945. At current price levels, that is equal to 32.7 trillion yen—or in today's dollars, about US$327 billion.[3]

When the war ended, 6 million demobilized soldiers returned to the civilian economy. At the same time, another 4 million civilian workers lost their jobs, as wartime industries shut down. Total unemployment reached 13.1 million.

War losses in 1944 alone accounted for 35% of Japanese national wealth—a number approximately equal to the nation's entire gross national product in 1946. The cost in human terms was also staggering. By the end of the war, military and civilian casualties numbered almost 3 million.

Loss of empire

Defeat also cost Japan her Asian conquests. The loss of territories in Manchuria, China, and Indochina reduced the size of the Japanese empire by more than 56% from its wartime peak. Consequently, the Japanese mainland was cut off from the vital flow of raw materials that formerly came from its overseas possessions.

Even the topography of the land had been laid to ruin. Entire forests had been stripped of timber. Pine forests were especially hard hit as a result of a failed scheme to make synthetic gasoline out of pine cones. (This was only one of many increasingly desperate efforts to cope with oil shortages in the last months of the war.)

Wartime neglect of reforestation resulted in widespread devastation from massive flooding in 1946. Over-cultivation during the war, when fertilizers were only haphazardly available, contributed to the rapid depletion of agricultural land. Crop failures in 1946 were the worst in decades, and famine further debilitated an already destitute population.

Economic Measures of Production and Consumption[4]

Production	1946 Levels as a % of Prewar Levels
Real G.N.P.	62
Per Capita G.N.P.	55
Coal Production	53
Steel Production	10
Textile Production	7
Per Capita Consumption	
Grams of Rice	70
Fish	65
Soy Sauce	53
Fruit	34
Sake	23
Eggs and Poultry	16
Sugar	6

With access to foreign markets cut off, the sudden increase in the domestic population (raised by returning soldiers) resulted in a demand for raw materials and basic daily necessities that far outstripped meager supplies. Massive shortages soon developed, and living standards dropped to unprecedented lows.

No strangers to adversity

In spite of these considerable hardships, there were early indications that the Japanese people would recover from the crushing burden of military defeat. Five days after the emperor's historic broadcast, blackout and curfew regulations were lifted. Soon Japanese children, who had been sent into the countryside to escape the heavy bombing of cities, were returning to their families. On October 9, 1945, professional baseball resumed in Japan.

Throughout their history, the Japanese have been well-acquainted with adversity. Living on a tiny chain of volcanic islands, they are perforce accustomed to picking up the pieces after the eruptions, earthquakes, typhoons, and tidal waves—the full range of natural disasters that have regularly devastated the Japanese archipelago.

Over the course of their 1,000-year history, they have also tasted the bitter medicine of military defeat many times. But always they have learned from their conquerors. For example, when the Portuguese first arrived with firearms in 1543, the Japanese copied their designs. Within a few short years they were making their own, which rivaled those of European manufacture.

It was no different in 1945. Displaying the same spirit of adaptability that has served them so well in the past, the Japanese set about learning English with a vengeance. Within weeks, English language texts topped the Japanese best-seller lists.

With the country's infrastructure destroyed, native ingenuity came to the rescue. Open-air markets appeared and flourished in bombed-out buildings that had once contained stores and shops. Portable stalls were set up in vacant lots alongside busy thoroughfares. Soon, items appeared for sale that had not been available during the war. Prices, however, zoomed toward the stratosphere.

Scourge of hyperinflation

Although the government pledged to provide food rations, surrender had impaired its ability to do so. During the war, farmers were easily compelled to provide produce at the low official prices. After the surrender, they found it easy to defy the central government—especially when black market sales brought 50 or 60 times the official price. With the crop failures of 1945 and 1946, prices rose even more. White rice traded at 150 times the official price as panic buying spread throughout the black market.

Other forces were at work as well. The value of redeemable Bank of Japan notes in circulation increased 40% in the last 15 days of April 1945. By February 1946, this measure of the Japanese money supply stood at exactly twice the level of the previous April—a 100% increase in only eight months.[5]

During the war, the Japanese government had raised the colossal sums necessary to support the armed forces by issuing bonds, for which there was no market. Some of these war bonds were bought by the Bank of Japan, which, in effect, printed the money to pay for them. This produced an immediate increase in the money supply.

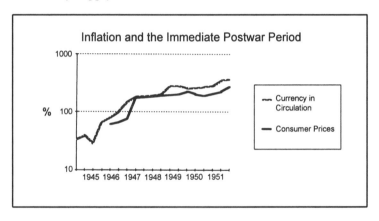

But other bonds were forced on the civilian population. Bonds bought by civilians were paid for out of savings. While the war was still being fought, strict economic controls prevented the bonds from being cashed in. Thus, an enormous reservoir of purchasing power built up in the civilian economy.

When the war ended, the government began to redeem the bonds. But this huge release of latent purchasing power came at a time when the war-torn civilian economy could scarcely produce any consumer goods.

To make matters worse, in the four months after the surrender, the government paid out millions to business owners as compensation for their contributions to the war effort. The government also offered business loans to finance the shift from military to consumer production, further increasing the amount of money in circulation.

True to one of the strictest canons of monetarist theory, which says that inflation is caused by overexpansion of the money supply, prices smartly followed suit. According to a Bank of Japan survey, black market prices rose 30% between September and December 1945. By February 1946, they had doubled.

As was the case in post World War I Germany, the roots of hyper-inflation lay in the familiar story of too much currency chasing too few goods.

Other hardships had to be dealt with as well. With communications in disarray, the average Japanese had little access to reliable information. Rumors of an impending war-profits tax or of a forced devaluation encouraged distrust of the nation's banks and created a climate of uncertainty and fear. Hoarding of scarce food and consumer goods was common.

Bungled economic policies

Influenced by American Keynesians, and under the thumb of occupation authorities headed by the Supreme Commander for Allied Forces (S.C.A.F.), the government tried several ham-fisted solutions. On February 16, 1946, the government announced the Emergency Economic Crisis Policy, which included: efforts to strengthen the food rationing system by vigorously prosecuting farmers who sold their produce illegally on the black market; a general crackdown on black market transactions involving consumer goods in short supply; a freeze on bank deposits; and the creation of a new currency.

As any student of free-market economics could have predicted, these measures only made things worse. Even beefed-up enforcement agencies were no match for the ingenuity of farmers and others who depended on black market sales to make ends meet.

Profitable enterprises, by their very nature, simply cannot be legislated out of existence. Making them illegal serves only to force them underground. The truth of this can be seen in the decades of futile efforts on the part of Western governments to stamp out gambling, prostitution, and narcotics trade. So it was with the black market in postwar Japan.

The monetary provisions of the Emergency Economic Crisis Policy had a dramatic, if short-lived, effect. As a result of the freeze on bank accounts, not only did the Japanese lose free access to their savings, but cash in circulation was effectively confiscated as well.

The government announced that the old yen notes would

cease to be legal tender as of March 2, 1946. They would, however, still be accepted for deposit in the otherwise frozen bank accounts until March 5. Thereafter, they would be worthless paper. Withdrawals from the frozen accounts were in new yen. They were strictly limited according to the family and income status of the depositor.

The aim, of course, was to shrink the money supply—usually defined as bank deposits plus currency in circulation. Confiscating currency and restricting access to bank accounts reduced the money supply by some 50 billion yen practically overnight. Inflation halted in its tracks—for a time.

These measures did nothing, however, to help expand production of food and other scarce consumer goods. Law-abiding urban dwellers suffered greatly as they tried to survive on the meager withdrawals of their own money that they were permitted under the government's program.

In rural areas, however, few people had bank accounts. And farmers who sold on the black market quickly accumulated cash balances in new yen. So the net effect of the monetary provisions of the Emergency Economic Crisis Policy was to increase the return on black marketeering—the very thing earlier provisions of the same policy were trying to stamp out!

By September 1946, inflation was again roaring out of control, and the danger of famine had become so acute that the occupation authorities had emergency relief sent from the United States.

Shifting American attitudes

Increasing volumes of aid coincided with a slow but profound shift in the attitude of the American government toward Japan. The United States, of course, had borne the brunt of the war in the Pacific. And in the early days of the occupation, the American high command was in no particular mood to be generous.

S.C.A.F.'s original proposals for postwar "democratization of Japan" were couched in the high-minded rhetoric of the United Nations Declaration on Human Rights. But to any neutral observer, it was clear that what S.C.A.F. had in mind was the complete disarming of Japan and the total destruction of the political, social, and economic systems that had made it possible for the country to wage war.

The first priority of the occupation authorities was the demobilization of the army and the demilitarization of the government. Former leaders were ordered to stand trial for war crimes. In spite of the increasingly desperate situation of the Japanese people, S.C.A.F. seemed in no hurry to repair the economic damage that the war had caused. For example, an early directive to General MacArthur from Washington stated, "You are not to assume any responsibility for the reconstruction or strengthening of the Japanese economy."[6]

Democratization of Japan included:
1) drafting a new constitution that
    a) gave women the right to vote and hold office,
    b) abolished all laws and state organs that restricted human rights,
    c) renounced war and the maintenance of armed forces;
2) giving workers the right to organize labor unions;
3) instituting universal education at state expense;
4) working on agricultural land reform; and
5) working toward economic democratization.

Something of the Allies' true intent could be seen in this economic democratization. This included the purging of more than 180,000 people in senior administrative and business posts who were thought to be right-wing, nationalistic, or militaristic. It also involved breaking up the *zaibatsu*,[7] the large financial and industrial holding companies that had dominated Japan's economy for 50 years.

In November 1945, the government froze all of the assets of the 15 largest *zaibatsu*. Other attacks on the *zaibatsu* came in the form of legislation. In April 1947, the Law Relating to the Prohibition of Private Monopoly and to Methods of Preserving Fair Trade, patterned after U.S. antitrust legislation, was enacted.

Eight months later, the Law for the Elimination of Excessive Economic Concentration was passed to provide the legal basis for the dissolution of any company deemed to be monopolistic. This was to be done by severing the holding company from its various parts and purging the prominent members of the founding *zaibatsu* families. Under this law, 325 *zaibatsu* were slated for dismemberment.

Pauley's plan for deindustrialization

If S.C.A.F. clothed its true intentions in the noble language of human rights, others were more candid. U.S. Ambassador to Japan Edwin W. Pauley helped produce a report outlining war

118

reparations that the Japanese would be forced to pay. It called for the physical removal of the existing plants and equipment of more than 1,000 factories from Japan.

Pauley's Final Reparations Report was a program for gutting what remained of Japanese industry—for returning Japan to the status of an underdeveloped agricultural country. A Brookings Institute report, prepared about the same time, urged that Japanese living standards not be allowed to rise above what they were in 1930—more than a decade before the war began.

As the 1940s drew to a close, however, events elsewhere in the world began to influence the U.S. attitude toward Japan. American relations with the Soviet Union began to sour. Britain, preoccupied with recovery from World War II, was no longer exerting the influence in Asia that it once had.

But most disturbing of all to U.S. President Truman and his advisors was the series of defeats suffered by another American ally, nationalist Chinese leader Chiang Kai-shek, at the hands of Mao Zedong's ragtag band of revolutionaries.

Against this backdrop of deepening geopolitical concern, punitive attitudes toward the Japanese began to give way. As the only industrialized country in Asia, Japan was increasingly seen by U.S. policy makers as the Western world's only opportunity to erect a bulwark against the rising tide of Asian Communism.

In due course, American policy began to tilt away from punishment and toward economic recovery. Before long, the Pauley Report was completely forgotten. Of the 325 *zaibatsu* slated for dissolution, only 30 were ever dissolved. Virtually all of Japan's big banks survived intact.

Soon the anti-monopoly laws of 1947 were being substantially rewritten to allow the new *zaibatsu* to dominate their old markets. Many were even allowed to re-establish themselves under their former names and trademarks.

Mitsui and Mitsubishi were among the first to take advantage of this newly relaxed attitude. Little did American policy makers realize that they were replanting the seeds of giant industrial monopolies that would plague American manufacturers 40 years later.

The Dodge Line
In February 1949, just six months before Communist victory in mainland China, Truman replaced Pauley. The new U.S. ambassador to Japan, former Detroit banker Joseph Dodge, arrived with specific instructions to contain inflation and get

Japanese industry moving as rapidly as possible.

In a famous press conference in Tokyo, the new ambassador first presented what later became known as the Dodge Line. The Japanese economy, according to Dodge, was like a man walking on stilts. One of the stilts was U.S. aid. The other was loans from the Japanese government's Reconstruction Finance Bank. Pursuing his metaphor, Dodge said that the economy was in danger of toppling over and falling on its head, that the stilts had to be removed, and that the economy had to learn to stand on its own two feet.

To accomplish this, Dodge called for: the government to pay off its debts; a slash in spending sufficient to produce a budget surplus—in essence a deflationary fiscal policy; an end to loans to business; the relaxation of rationing and price controls; and a devaluation of the yen to promote the growth of Japanese exports on world markets.

This last measure was especially important because it would affect the international competitiveness of every sector of the Japanese economy. Making export growth the engine of Japanese economic independence required a yen low enough to ensure that Japanese products could be attractively priced abroad.

Manipulating the yen to promote exports

As always, the Japanese learned from their conquerors. Manipulation of the yen to levels that permit Japanese exporters to undercut their competition has been a hallmark of Japanese economic policy until recent years.

The Dodge Line actually made more sense than earlier government efforts to manage the Japanese economy. Because of the strong deflationary measures it contained, spectacular progress was made in the fight against inflation. The Consumer Price Index declined 10% in 1949. On the black market, prices declined as much as 30%.

The Dodge Line also marked the beginning of the end of the black market as a major economic force in postwar Japan. With the end of rationing and price controls, a free market was officially re-established for the first time in nine years. The effect was immediate. For the first time since the end of the war, fresh bananas appeared on grocery shelves. In urban areas, beer halls began to reopen.

But the Dodge Line also had a darker side. Reduced government spending and an end to government loans left many businesses starved for capital. The sudden end of inflation also devastated profit margins. Many businesses were caught with expensive inventory that they could only sell at a loss as the general price level declined.

Bankruptcies swept over the country like a Pacific tidal wave. The daily newspapers were filled with articles on the suicides of presidents of smaller and medium-sized companies. Popular magazines carried stories of the suicides of entire families.

On July 5, 1949, three days before he was due to announce the first of more than 100,000 employee layoffs, the president of Japan National Railways was found dead on one of his company's tracks. All across the country, workers were dismissed on a massive scale. Labor disputes increased in both number and intensity. Reports of riots made the headlines on a daily basis. On top of all these miseries came the harshest winter since the end of the war. For most Japanese, 1949 was the darkest year in postwar history.

Dodge, a puritan at heart, refused to contemplate any reduced dosages of the deflationary medicine he had prescribed. And it is likely the country would have fallen into civil anarchy had geopolitical events not intruded.

In Peking on October 1, 1949, Mao Zedong proclaimed the People's Republic of China. In December, Chiang Kai-shek's forces fled across the Formosa Strait to the island of Taiwan. And on June 25, 1950, war broke out in Korea. On July 8, General Douglas MacArthur led the U.S. Army, formerly on occupation duty in Japan, in the first action in support of the beleaguered South Korean army.

Japan, of course, was the industrialized country nearest the war zone. Within weeks, enormous orders poured in for goods and services to support the troops in Korea. (Much the same thing happened again during the Vietnam War a decade and a half later.) In the early years of the conflict, these orders were mostly for military supplies—sandbags, barbed wire, army blankets, and ammunition. When the war ended, the demand shifted to goods and services needed for reconstruction in South Korea—the repair of trucks and aircraft, and the construction of military bases and communications and transportation services.

During the period from 1950 to 1955, foreign currency earnings of Japanese business climbed as high as US$3.6 billion.[8] War-related orders amounted to 60% to 70% of exports, reversing Japan's balance of payments in a single stroke.

Korean War boom

The Korean War boom also set off the explosive growth in Japanese exports that has continued for nearly 40 years. During one 12-month period alone (June 1950 to May 1951), Japanese exports increased 55%. The unsold inventories created by the Dodge Line deflation were sold almost overnight.

The war also set off an explosion in profits. One measure of Japanese business profits doubled twice between 1950 and 1951.[9] For the first time since the end of the war, the profitability of Japanese companies reached levels that permitted significant increases in equity capital accumulation. By October 1950, mining and manufacturing had surpassed prewar levels.

By the end of 1951, the Japanese gross national product exceeded its highest prewar peak. On the Tokyo Stock Exchange, the Nikkei Dow surged 81%. The postwar recovery had been achieved.

Seeds of conflict

By the time the Korean War boom wound down, the Japanese economy—in the words of Joseph Dodge—was back on its own two feet. But the seeds of future Japanese-American tension had already been planted. And nobody at the time foresaw the bitter harvest that would follow some three and a half decades later.

---

1. Economic Stabilization Board, *Taiheiyo senso ni youru waga kuni no higai sogo hokokusho,* 1949.

2. *ibid.*

3. *ibid.*

4. Tatsuro Uchino, *Japan's Postwar Economy: An Insider's View of Its History and Future,* p. 29.

5. Uchino, *op. cit.*

6. Uchino, *op. cit.,* p. 23.

7. From the Japanese roots *zai* (wealth) and *batsu* (clique).

8. Uchino, *op. cit.,* p. 57.

9. According to a Mitsubishi Institute study cited by Uchino, the profit rate on available capital rose from 2.2% in eary 1950 to 7.9% in late 1951.

Chapter 8

Buying Up the World

Orientals With Open Checkbooks

Japan, an abject loser in World War II, has achieved its pre-war goal of a Greater East Asia Co-Prosperity Sphere .... France, the Netherlands, and the United Kingdom have all gone home, and the United States itself is under siege from an expanding Japanese economy.
— General T. R. Milton, *Air Force Magazine* —

Deep in the American heartland lies the little town of Harrodsburg, Kentucky. On the outskirts of town sits an ominous-looking World War II tank, a memorial put up by local veterans in honor of the 29 Harrodsburg men who died at the hands of the Japanese during the infamous Bataan Death March in 1942. Just a few hundred yards east of the tank stands a brand-new Hitachi Ltd. factory.

In the last chapter, we examined how American influences on the Japanese recovery from the economic ruin of World War II sowed the seeds of future conflict—not only between Japan and the United States, but also between Japan and much of the rest of the world.

In this chapter, we will examine the growing dependence on Japan as a source of capital. The list of countries whose economic well-being increasingly depends on Japanese investment is long and varied. But rather than attempt a detailed analysis of each one, I shall focus on the United States. This is because the benefits and the risks to the United States of growing dependence on imported supplies of capital are emblematic of the benefits and risks elsewhere.

In addition, the United States is also a choice rich in irony. Few complain louder than Americans about the Japanese. Yet no nation is more directly responsible for bringing more of its ills entirely upon itself.

Capital surplus

One of the pillars of Ambassador Dodge's plan for Japanese economic recovery was export-led industrial growth. American orders for goods and services during the Korean War then touched off an explosion in the growth of Japanese exports that has continued to the present day.

Of course, the proceeds from all those sales abroad went back to Japan, where most of them were reinvested in new plants and equipment for the production of yet more exports. Relatively little was spent to purchase foreign goods. During the intervening decades, growth in exports consistently outpaced imports—with the inevitable result that money started to pile up in Japan.

The same thing happened to Mideast oil-producing countries in the late 1970s, when OPEC quadrupled the price of oil. Suddenly, a surplus of capital began to accumulate in countries with rather limited local opportunities for productive investment. Sooner or later that capital had to find a home abroad. At the zenith of OPEC's power, the countries had about US$385 billion invested abroad. But the Japanese have made that look like small potatoes.

Direct foreign investment in the United States has been increasing steadily for nearly a decade. And more and more Americans are divided in their reactions. In this respect, Harrodsburg is a metaphor for the entire nation. This profoundly ambivalent reaction—welcoming on the one hand, suspicious and resentful on the other—is one we shall see again and again.

The first wave of Japanese direct investment came when the big Japanese automakers—Nissan, Honda, Mazda, Mitsubishi, and Toyota—built assembly plants in the Midwest. Japanese car companies now account for about a quarter of all the automobiles manufactured in the United States. More than 350 Japanese auto parts companies have also built U.S. factories in order to supply both Japanese and American manufacturers.[1]

For the Japanese, this was one of the simplest ways to circumvent American import restrictions. U.S.-elected representatives might vote to limit importation of Hondas from Japan, but they are not likely to oppose the sale of Hondas manufactured in their districts—in factories employing hundreds of their constituents.

Indeed, some fret that substantial Japanese direct investment has lead to undue influence. Cutbacks in government funding for universities, museums, and public broadcast stations, have encouraged fund raisers to turn to Japan. At the Massachusetts Institute of Technology, for example, Japanese companies have endowed 16 chairs at about US$1.5 million each, and spent about US$4 million a year for access to research.[2]

About 80% of the funding for Japanese studies now comes from Japan. And, according to Patricia Steinhoff, director of the Center for Japanese Studies at the University of Hawaii, some of these Japanese scholars are very eager to express Japan's official point of view.[3]

The Japanese are also spending US$50 million a year on high-powered Washington, D.C. lobbyists. That is, in addition to millions more spent for consultants' advice, speeches, and background papers.[4]

As early as mid-1986, 63% of Americans in a *Business Week* Harris poll said that Japanese investments will result in "too much influence over U.S. governmental policies."[5] Two years later, the Washington consulting firm of Smick-Medley & Associates found 78% of those polled favored restrictions on foreign business and real estate investment.[6]

But while some worried, others welcomed foreign investment with open arms. All across the nation, local jurisdictions hired economic development directors whose job it was to bring in investment and industry. The governor of the state of Tennessee, for example, announced his goal was to "get the Tennessee economy integrated with the Japanese economy."

Real estate investments

After the factory building subsided, the Japanese turned to real estate. The first wave of Japanese purchases of American real estate peaked in 1988. As early as 1986, the Japanese surpassed the British to become the largest foreign owners of commercial real estate in the United States. About 40% of Japan's U.S. real estate holdings are in Hawaii. California accounts for about 31%, and New York for 18%.[7]

In most cases, the Japanese have been most interested in the bluest of the blue-chip properties and have often been willing to pay substantially more than market value for buildings in prime commercial locations. This can add up to a seller's dream. Shuwa's 1986 purchase of Arco Plaza in Los Angeles for US$620 million was at the time the largest all-cash real estate transaction in U.S. history. A year later, it bought the Washington, D.C., headquarters of *U.S. News & World Report* for about US$480 per square foot—at the time, the highest price ever paid for an office building in the U.S. capital.

Mike McCormack, head of a major Hawaiian realty firm, tells the story of a homeowner who thought his house was worth US$400,000, but sold it to a Japanese buyer for US$800,000. That buyer turned right around and sold it to another Japanese buyer for US$1.2 million.

Although sellers are delighted to have customers who pay top dollar in cash, not everyone is pleased to see the Japanese coming with open checkbooks. The mayor of Honolulu once sponsored legislation to limit foreign real estate purchases after a Japanese buying spree pushed residential prices up 32%. In an attempt to halt a 1989 sale of a Nebraska cattle ranch to Japanese investors, a local district attorney was forced to dust off a half-forgotten state law barring foreign ownership of farmland.

It is certainly ironic that citizens of the United States, which after all is a nation of immigrants, can work themselves into such a lather railing against the evils of foreign influence.

For example, the *Los Angeles Times* reported the bitter complaints of a Mr. Goldrich, a local real estate developer, about the "danger of being owned by foreigners."[8] A couple of paragraphs into the story, however, we discover that Mr. Goldrich is himself a Polish-born, naturalized American.

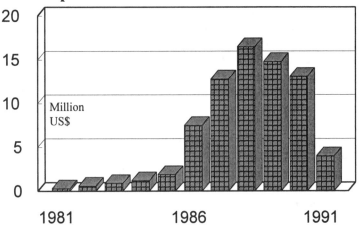

Japanese Purchases of U.S. Real Estate

Million US$

Commercial bank lending

While the Japanese push into U.S. real estate has been going on, yet another assault got under way in the financial sector. The world's seven biggest commercial banks (measured in terms of deposits) are all Japanese, and in recent years they've been making a big splash in the United States.

Almost a score of Japan's largest banks now have branches in the United States. That's an increase of nearly 100% from the number six years ago. In California, for example, Japanese bank assets rose 300% between 1982 and 1989. And in both New York and California, Japanese banks account for more than a quarter of all bank assets.

It is much the same story in investment banking as it is in commercial banking. Nomura, Daiwa, Nikko, and Yamaichi make up the big four of the Japanese securities industry. Along Wall Street, there have been worries that they hope to do what Toyota, Nissan, Honda, and Mitsubishi did in the automobile industry (the recent Japanese brokerage scandals notwithstanding).

Buyers of bonds

Nowhere is the theme of profound ambivalence stronger than in the securities markets themselves—where surplus Japanese capital is increasingly finding a home. The Japanese are major investors in U.S. government securities.

In 1985, net Japanese purchases of Treasuries totaled US$28.3 billion, nearly a threefold increase over the preceding year. And they have been steadily increasing. By some estimates, the Japanese account for more than 15% of all purchases of Treasury bills, bonds, and notes.

On the one hand, this inflow of Japanese capital is absolutely essential. In recent years, federal deficits have more than doubled the national debt. For the first time in many decades, the United States has become a debtor nation—that is, it owes more to foreign lenders than foreign borrowers owe to Americans. Total U.S. debt is now more than all that of Brazil, Mexico, and Peru combined!

When any government spends more than it takes in, it has only two choices for making up the shortfall. It can either print more money, or it can borrow it. Expanding the money supply enough to cover the budget shortfall every year would surely risk creating an inflationary nightmare worse than that of the 1970s.

The other alternative for making up the shortfall is to borrow.

(Most U.S. government borrowing amounts to the issuing of bonds. In effect, any owner of a T-bill, bond, or note is a lender to the U.S. Treasury.)

Without the inflow of Japanese capital, government borrowing would surely consume the lion's share of the capital available inside the United States—crowding out other borrowers, such as home and automobile buyers or businesses desiring to finance expansion. Interest rates would rise to the ruinous levels of the late 1970s—and perhaps beyond.

Today, double-digit interest rates would hit the fragile U.S. economy like the proverbial ton of bricks. And because the United States is the major export market for much of the rest of the world, the effects of a U.S. depression would hardly be confined to North America.

No control over monetary policy

You might say that the United States has effectively lost a measure of control over its own monetary policy. If the Japanese stopped buying, interest rates would spiral upward, and the Federal Reserve could do little about it. If the Japanese decided to cash in their chips, the results would be equally dramatic. Substantial selling could knock the bond market for a loop.

Much the same can also be said for exchange rates. If the Japanese ever decided to withdraw their investments from the United States, they would presumably want to convert the proceeds into yen. This selling of dollars for yen could weaken the already fragile U.S. dollar on the world's foreign exchange markets. Massive selling could knock it over the edge.

By 1990, American dependence on foreign capital had grown so acute that it began to be openly acknowledged at the highest levels of the federal government. As declining stock prices in Tokyo began to dampen the Japanese appetite for U.S. Treasury securities, then Secretary of State James Baker was dispatched to Saudi Arabia. His mission was to demand major Saudi purchases of U.S. government bonds in exchange for sending U.S. troops to defend the desert kingdom.

The extent to which U.S. investment markets are increasingly at the mercy of Japanese investors was frightfully confirmed in October 1987 when stocks crashed on Wall Street—and then crashed in every major world market shortly thereafter.

Several months later, the chairman of the commission appointed to investigate causes of the crash, Nicholas Brady, later to become U.S. Treasury Secretary, concluded the Japanese selling of U.S. bonds was one of the triggers of the worst debacle in world stock market history.[9]

International investment imperative

Thus far we have focused on Japanese investment in the United States (and, by extension, other countries as well) from the American point of view. But what about the Japanese point of view? What factors lie behind the wave of Japanese capital washing over countless foreign shores?

One of the most important factors is the chronic Japanese trade surplus. As long as Japan sells more abroad than it buys, the profits from those sales will continue to accumulate. In the 1980s, this rising tide of liquidity helped push Japanese stock and real estate prices to absurd levels. (See Chapter 10.)

Even so, this growing pool of capital could not stay bottled up inside Japan forever. Eventually, these capital surpluses flow into investments abroad. A familiar example of the same process occurred with OPEC countries after the oil shocks.

Desert sheikdoms—where there was almost nothing to buy—suddenly began receiving billions of dollars in income. In many of these countries, Islamic anti-usury laws effectively prohibited the development of a modern banking industry.

Where do you put a billion dollars, when there are no banks and nothing to buy? Not under your mattress—to be sure. The Arabs put their capital surplus into Western banks and investments, because there was really no other alternative. A decade or so later, the Japanese did the same thing.

A second factor that determines Japanese investment abroad is the level of the yen. This is because a high yen makes it expensive to pay business expenses—such as wages—in Japan relative to the costs in other countries.

In fact, the Japanese have moved so much manufacturing capacity out of Japan—to China, Korea, Thailand, Mexico, the United States, and elsewhere—that the official figures for the domestic Japanese economy now show some startling reversals. For example, in 1993, Japan became a net importer of color television sets. Today, TVs in Tokyo stores increasingly bear labels that say: "Made in China," or "Made in Korea," or even "Made in America."

Interestingly enough, production of all kinds of video equipment in Japan itself has now fallen to the lowest level since the

1980s. What a remarkable reversal for a country that built its reputation on supplying the world with low-cost, high-quality electronic goods.

Similar reversals have occurred in other industries. Also in 1993, for example, Korea overtook Japan as the world's largest shipbuilder.

What's more, the trend toward building new factories outside Japan appears to be accelerating. Matsushita Electric (owner of the Panasonic brand name) announced eight new factories in China in just the past year. Sony has announced plans to increase overseas production to 50% from the present 35%. Sanyo Electric, which presently makes 50% of its television sets outside Japan, plans to boost offshore production to 90%.

Today, Japan is investing abroad on such a scale, that the Japanese themselves worry that the industrial foundations of their country could be permanently eroded. A special term has been coined to describe the process: *kudoka.*

The pessimists point to the American lead in telecommunications, and note that Japan has lagged for years in the development of new service industries. If it loses its manufacturing base, what will be left?

In fact, the Japanese themselves are beginning to feel very much like the Americans described at the beginning of this chapter—when the sun seemed to have set on the U.S. manufacturing industry.

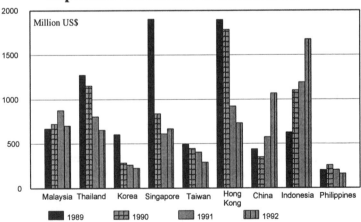

Japanese Direct Investment in Asia

Pension fund buying

Another important factor in Japanese investment abroad stems from the simple fact that Japan is aging faster than any developed country on earth. (See Chapter 13.)

By the year 2000, 16% of the population will be 65 or older—compared with 13% in the United States. An older population, unfortunately, generally is a less healthy one. At present, the costs of health and retirement benefits for one elderly person are divided among six working Japanese. By the year 2000, the burden will be divided among four workers.

One reaction to these trends has been an extraordinary increase in the amount of money flowing into Japanese pension funds. Assets of corporate pension funds, for example, tripled between 1981 and 1986. They will more than triple again by 2000. Many of these funds are charged with the task of investing these assets to be able to cover the staggering load of retirement benefit payments that lies ahead.

Where can all this money possibly go? Pension fund managers are notoriously conservative investors, and properly so.

When you hold the financial well-being of thousands of elderly people in your hands, you cannot afford to speculate. Consequently, the first concerns of any pension fund manager are liquidity and safety.

A suitable market for pension fund investments must be liquid enough so that it can absorb large blocks of buying and selling without difficulty. And as far as possible, it must be a market in a politically stable country—where the risk of revolution or wartime devastation is nearly zero.

Let's examine the liquidity issue first. The world's largest stock markets are:

Country Market Capitalization (US$ Billion)[10]

United States	4,050
Japan	3,500
Britain	1,100
Germany	405
France	349
Hong Kong	300
Australia	240

Note that after the United States and Japan, the next most liquid market is Britain. But it is only 31% the size of the Japanese stock market. Germany and France are only 10% to 12% as large. Hong Kong is only 8%.

In terms of size, liquidity, and political stability, the only possible destinations for Japanese savings outside Japan itself will continue to be the United States, and, to a lesser extent, Britain, and finally, Germany, France, Hong Kong, and Australia.

As a result, the flow of Japanese capital in and out of these markets will continue to have a major influence on whether the local index of stock prices rises or falls.

In the United States, foreign buying in general—and Japanese buying in particular—was a principal factor in the spectacular bull market of the late 1980s and early 1990s. Foreign selling also was a factor in both the crash of 1987 and the bear markets of 1990 and 1994. So it will continue to be in the future.

This is the heart of America's ambivalence toward foreign investment—it needs money from abroad to pay for its own government's overspending. Yet to the extent that it enjoys this benefit, it places itself increasingly at the mercy of events outside its borders—and outside its control.

And, as in the case of the unforeseen results of the American plan for the economic recovery of postwar Japan, it is a state of affairs that Americans have largely brought upon themselves.

---

1. Aron Viner, *The Emerging Power of Japanese Money,* p. 171.

2. *Business Week,* July 11, 1988, p. 70.

3. *ibid.,* p. 70.

4. *ibid.,* p. 67.

5. *Business Week,* July 14, 1986, p. 54.

6. E. Rubinfien, "Reverse Land Rush: Americans Pitch Property to Japanese, " *Wall Street Journal,* June 15, 1988, p. 1.

7. P. Apodaca, "Japanese Investors Fuel Resurgence," *Investor's Daily,* December 4, 1987.

8. *Los Angeles Times,* February 1, 1987, p. 5.

9. "Task Force's Brady Says Japanese Sales of U.S. Bonds Touched Off October 19 Crash," *Wall Street Journal,* April 22, 1988, p. 18.

10. *Asia Week,* May 11, 1994, p. 67; R. G. Ibbotson, and G. P. Brinson, *Global Investing,* Chapter 6.

Chapter 9

The Next Pearl Harbor

The Asian Tinderbox

Encouraging the Japanese to send troops abroad (even as part of U.N. peacekeeping operations) is like giving a chocolate liqueur to an alcoholic. Once the Japanese get off the wagon, it will be hard to stop them.
— Lee Kuan Yew, former prime minister, Singapore —

We will turn Seoul into a sea of fire.
— Pak Youg Su, North Korean delegate —

Kim Jong Il, the erratic 52-year-old son of North Korean dictator Kim Il Sung, wears elevator shoes and sports a bouffant hairdo in order to look taller. He stammers when he speaks. He also has his finger on a nuclear trigger.

Ballistic missiles and atomic weapons help bolster his claim to legitimacy. Otherwise, why would he be taken seriously by a world in which his country has become increasingly irrelevant?

In the aftermath of Deng Xioping's economic reforms, China has grown at double-digit rates for more than a dozen years. Measured in purchasing power parity terms, the International Monetary Fund recently ranked the Chinese economy among the five largest in the world.

At present growth rates, the Chinese economy will surpass the United States as the world's largest in less than a dozen years. Now Beijing is bent on acquiring military muscle to match its growing economic might.

Out of concern for their own self-defense against the Chinese dragon, neighboring countries have also jumped into a new arms race. The end of the Cold War may have signalled a period of military downsizing in Europe and North America. But not in Asia.

In December 1992, after much urging, Japanese troops were finally sent to join the United Nations peacekeeping mission in Cambodia. It was the first time Japan had sent combat battalions abroad since World War II.

But memories of Japanese atrocities in World War II still abound in Asia. During the rape of Nanking, for example, as many as 300,000 civilians were killed by Japanese occupation forces in a reign of terror as methodical and efficient as anything organized by the Nazis in Europe.

In mid-1994, a Japanese Justice Minister labeled the rape of Nanking a fabrication. That touched off such an explosion of international outrage, that he was sacked by his government despite statements of support by the Japanese Prime Minister.

Japan already has the third largest military budget in the world, and the largest Pacific fleet except for America's. It also leads even the United States in high-tech weaponry.

If the Japanese ever decided to pursue rearmament with a fraction of the skill and intensity they routinely display in conquering international markets, they would certainly stand the world's present military pecking order on its head.

During the last century, the world's economic center of gravity shifted westward—from Europe to North America. Now it is shifting westward again—this time, from North America to East Asia and the Pacific Rim. The first shift was accompanied by two world wars. It is almost inconceivable that the second will not also be accompanied by its share of military conflicts.

Some of them have already begun. As always, the security of strategic resources will be a central factor in any decision to go to war. And among them, none will be more important than oil in determining who wins and loses.

Flash points

Regrettably, there is no shortage of potential conflicts. In fact, among the Association of South East Asian Nations (ASEAN), there is scarcely a single country that hasn't been locked into a bitter border dispute with one or more neighbors sometime in the past few years.

For example, Thai navy boats recently fired on an armed Cambodian vessel alleged to have attacked a Thai fishing trawler. Myanmar sank more than 50 Thai fishing boats for allegedly encroaching on its territorial waters.

Indonesia deployed warships to protect fishermen after they reported clashes with foreign vessels. Vietnam has seized more than 100 foreign fishing boats at gunpoint in the past year.

In the South China Sea, piracy has emerged a major money-making enterprise for elements of the Chinese coastal navy. Military vessels flying the Chinese flag (sometimes with uniformed personnel aboard) routinely board passing ships and confiscate their cargos for sale on the black market. Hong Kong maritime officials say that the overwhelming majority of instances of reported piracy involved Chinese navy or coast guard equipment and personnel.

Chinese land forces have also tried to get in on the act. In March 1994, a group of 24 Taiwanese tourists visiting Qiandao Lake (together with eight guides) were robbed and stripped of their luggage. All were then locked below decks on a boat which was subsequently set afire and sunk, killing everyone aboard.

In what looked suspiciously like an attempt to get rid of potentially incriminating evidence, Beijing hastily imposed a news blackout and cremated all the bodies. Relatives of the deceased say the victims were assaulted by uniformed elements of the Chinese armed forces.

When a Japanese consortium struck oil 125 miles southwest of the Cambodian port of Sihanoukville in the Gulf of Thailand, it immediately triggered a territorial dispute between Cambodia and Thailand. Oil has also raised tensions in the Andaman Sea, where Myanmar has discovered gas.

Similarly, the Spratley and Parcel Islands in the South China Sea are believed to contain substantial oil and gas reserves. Not surprisingly, they are claimed in whole or in part by six separate nations. In 1975, and again in 1988, China used force to evict the Vietnamese from some of these islands.

Korean conundrum

In September 1993, Lee Jung Chul, a North Korean student sent to study in Nanking, defected. He brought with him chilling tales of famine. In his home province, he said, food rations hadn't arrived for more than three months, and people were starving.[1]

As early as 1988, students at North Korea's elite Kim Il Sung University sent an unsigned letter to the Great Leader, asking him to consider Chinese-style economic reforms. Despite the fact that they were hunted down and dispatched by the secret police for such heresy, discontent has continued to rise.

It will only get worse. Cut off from its subsidies from the former Soviet Union, the North Korean economy is going downhill fast. According to estimates by the South Korean Central Bank, the economy shrunk 3.7% in 1990, 5.2% in 1991, and 7.6% in 1992. Nor have things improved since then. Along with food, electricity is also strictly rationed. As a result, industry runs at 25% to 35% of capacity.

The commonsense advice for a country wanting to get out of a hole it has dug for itself is straightforward: Stop digging. But the North Koreans have thrown away the shovel. In its place, they have laid an explosive charge big enough to blow the house down.

I first publicly warned of the North Korean nuclear weapons program back in 1990.[2] Since then, of course, it has become the stuff of front-page headlines. Today, North Korea is dependent on transfers of nuclear (and missile) technology to Iran for about half its oil needs.

Unfortunately, atomic warheads are not the only weapons of mass destruction in Kim Jong Il's arsenal. According to reports from the Russian intelligence service, North Korea has ongoing development programs for both chemical and biological weapons. The latter is said to include anthrax, bubonic plague, cholera, and smallpox. Some of these have been tested on several small islands in the Sea of Japan.[3]

Although North Korea has only about 22 million people, it has the fifth largest standing army in the world—after China, India, the United States, and Russia. Two-thirds of its armed forces are deployed along the South Korea border.

In Chapter 6, we sketched the origins of North Korea's thriving exports of ballistic missiles. We also examined how they came to barter ballistic missiles and nuclear technology for Iranian oil.

In addition to upsetting the balance of forces in the Mideast, the North Korean weapons programs have also kept the lights burning late in the defense ministries of its Asian neighbors. One of them is China.

North Korea has already built several missile launch sites near its northwest border. From here much of China's northeastern industry base lies within Scud-C range. (See Chapter 6.) Using its Rodong-1, Pyongyang could hit Beijing. [4]

Chinese squeeze

China is North Korea's largest trading partner. Accordingly, it would seem an unlikely target. Nonetheless, Pyongyang's growing missile capability is one more factor that contributes to Chinese ambivalence about its onetime ally.

On the one hand, China's partnership with North Korea in exporting arms—especially to the Mideast—is part of its long-term oil strategy. (See Chapter 11.) On the other hand, it is not eager to see either nuclear weapons or an arms race on the Korean peninsula—particularly if Japan gets involved.

China will never cut off trade with Pyongyang, despite the urgings of the West to participate in economic sanctions. The reason is simple. North Korean refugees are already escaping across the border into both China and Russia. If North Korea were to completely collapse, this trickle could become a flood.

In addition, the Chinese don't want to be distracted from their own military buildup. Last year, the Chinese announced a 12.4% increase in military spending. It was the fourth substantial increase in a row.

In the aftermath of the American withdrawal from the Philippines and the Russian withdrawal from Vietnam, China is vigorously and aggressively acquiring the means to project power beyond its borders. Both nature and geopolitics abhor a vacuum.

There is also a domestic political factor in China's military buildup. Deng Xioping used an ingenious maneuver to secure military support for his economic reform. He convinced the generals that their only hope for building a credible force for the future lay in getting their hands on Western weaponry.

This was a compelling line of argument after Chinese forces were trounced by the Vietnamese in their brief border war. It was even more compelling after the virtuoso display of high-tech military prowess during the 1991 Persian Gulf War.

However, access to Western technology required accommodation with the West. Also required were drastic cuts in military spending—to support economic growth on a scale sufficient to ensure that China would one day be able to afford these expensive toys.

The Chinese military has not had an easy time during the reforms. In fact, that's why some units have turned to piracy and pillage—to supplement their income. But in recent years—and especially after the army came to the rescue of the central government during Tiananmen Square—the time came to pay back some old debts. Hence the increases in military budgets.

Like the North Korean buildup, the Chinese buildup has also alarmed its neighbors. As a result, military buildups are under way in Taiwan, Thailand, Myanmar, Indonesia, Malaysia, Singapore, South Korea—even Bangladesh. The Chinese, themselves, are the major arms suppliers to Pakistan.

At the same time, however, China is also a major destination for investment from many of these countries. Maintaining these investment flows is vital to the long-term future of the Chinese economy. Accordingly, China has few overtly territorial ambitions.

To be sure, Hong Kong will go back to Chinese rule in 1997. Macau will return in 1999. And China clearly hopes to reincorporate Taiwan as well someday. But apart from these and a handful of border disputes, Beijing seems uninterested in gobbling up any neighboring countries.

In a sense, China's strategy in Southeast Asia is like Iran's in the Persian Gulf. Both countries seek to fill a post-Cold War power vacuum. Both are counting on growing military might to intimidate their neighbors into accepting them as regional superpowers. If pursued with sufficient skill and persistence, such a policy could achieve its aim without ever firing a shot.

Japan rearmed

In Chapter 7, we observed how economic decisions made by American occupation authorities in 1945 set the stage for Japanese-American conflict 45 years later. History is full of the stories of unforeseen consequences. And ignorance of history results in repetition of old mistakes.

In the 1990s, American politicians find it easy to blame the problem of the U.S. trade deficit on Japan. Calls for protection of American industry from Japanese competition abound—from "voluntary restraint agreements" to import quotas to proposals for tough new rules on foreign takeovers of U.S. firms. Similar appeals for protection against foreign competition also echo in other capitals—from Europe to Australia.

But few of those clamoring for protection in the 1990s have read the history of the 1930s. And even fewer realize that they could be putting civilian rule at risk in Japan.

Japan has always been a natural-resource–poor nation, utterly dependent on access to raw materials and markets abroad. Denied access in the 1930s, the Japanese economy plunged into its deepest depression of the 20th century.

During the civil unrest that followed, new military rulers

came to power whose motto was: "A rich nation, strongly armed." Their efforts to secure by force what had been denied by protectionism is the story of events that culminated in the Pacific campaign of World War II.

Post-World War I protectionism

In the aftermath of World War I, formidable barriers to international trade were flung up all over the world. Some were wartime measures that were simply retained because governments sought to protect staple industries. Some governments found import duties an attractive source of additional revenues.

The rise of Nazism in Germany, for example, was accompanied by severe protectionist measures. France and Italy also imposed a round of new tariffs. Britain enacted the Import Duties Act of 1931. And in the United States, the infamous Smoot-Hawley Act was signed into law by President Hoover.

As Professor Bronfenbrenner has observed:

> *The Depression immediately accelerated protectionist attempts by the West—particularly the U.S.A. and the British Empire—to export unemployment and real-wage cuts to their trading partners. Protectionism was rationalized, as it affected Japan, by savage attacks on the Japanese wage level as "exploitive." ... The resulting tariffs, quotas and preferences were slanted, possibly for racist reasons, in an anti-Japanese direction. This leads both rapidly and naturally to Japanese trade paranoia.[5]*

The impact of these measures on Japan was devastating. As international trade plunged, the country quickly fell into depression. Bankruptcies soared. Farm prices dropped 30% to 40%. In urban areas, starvation was widespread. In rural areas, daughters were sold into prostitution.

These bitter developments quickly brought home to the Japanese the extent to which they were the captives of outside forces. China, Russia, the United States, and European powers either had critical natural resources within their borders or colonial empires to supply them. Japan, alone it seemed, had nothing.

Enactment of specifically anti-Japanese measures only further increased the nation's sense of being unfairly treated by the rest of the world. The 1924 Exclusion Act, for example, specifically prohibited Japanese people from living in the United States.

As the depression deepened, civil disorder increased, and Japanese politics lurched sharply to the right. Between 1930 and 1936, two prime ministers and two finance ministers were assassinated by right-wing militarists. In 1931, young army officers occupied part of Manchuria and declared the puppet state of Manchunokuo. Manchunokuo offered both territory and raw materials to the emerging Japanese imperial empire.

The new Japanese militarists took their inspiration from the 1887 *Ikensho* (Opinions) of the early Meiji General Viscount Tani Takeki:

> *Make our country secure by military preparedness—encourage and protect our people at home. Then wait for the time of confusion in Europe which must come eventually ... for such an event will agitate the nations of the Orient as well ... [then] we may become chief of the Orient.*[6]

Unlike European-style fascists, Japan's new military rulers were driven primarily by a sense of national frustration over the extent to which the nation always seemed to be at the mercy of foreign powers.

To restore the nation's independence, they set out to secure access to these critical raw materials—at the point of the bayonet if necessary. Announcing a plan for paternal domination of much of Southeast Asia, they sent troops into Thailand, Vietnam, and China.

Alliance with Axis powers

In 1940, Japan signed the Tripartite Axis Pact with Germany and Italy. This alliance helped contribute to the European disarray anticipated by Viscount Takeki. But more importantly, the Axis powers ratified Japanese ambitions in Southeast Asia. Article II of the Tripartite Pact read:

> *Germany and Italy recognize and respect the leadership of Japan in the establishment of a new order in Greater East Asia ....*

By 1941, Japan had acquired sufficient overseas possessions

to afford secure supplies of rubber, tin, bauxite, and most other strategic materials. Only in the case of oil was the country still dependent on a foreign supplier—in this case, the United States.

The story of how President Roosevelt's oil embargo against Japan led to the infamous attack on the American naval base at Pearl Harbor appears in Chapter 2, so I shall not repeat it here. But the lesson of the 1930s is clear.

If protectionist measures had not been directed against Japan, it is doubtful that Japanese militarists would have ever come to power. And without aggressive, acquisitive leadership in Japan, the war in the Pacific would probably never have occurred.

Article IX of the Japanese Constitution—essentially written by American occupation authorities—contains a formal commitment to official pacifism. But over the years, this commitment has been artfully reinterpreted. In the 1950s, at the behest of an American government concerned by Communist expansion in Asia, the Japanese then created the Self-Defense Forces (S.D.F.).

In 1952, the S.D.F. had 118,000 men under arms. Today, that number has nearly quadrupled. Defense spending has grown between 5% and 6% per year for a decade. As noted above, Japan has the third largest defense in the world and the largest Pacific fleet after the United States.

State-of-the-art technology

Japan's sophistication in electronics and computers has put it at the very forefront of new military technology. Japan today leads even the United States in state-of-the-art anti-submarine technology.[7] Japan also leads the world in advanced flat-screen display technology sought by the American Defense Department.

It should be noted, however, that much of this growth in the Japanese military establishment has been encouraged and applauded by the United States, which has been eager for Japan to shoulder a greater share of the defense burden in the Pacific.

But in Japanese postwar politics, military spending has always been a controversial matter. There are, however, indications that popular support for rearmament is on the rise.

In 1971, the well-known playwright Yukio Mishima committed *seppuku* (hara-kiri) at an S.D.F. rally to protest the lack of traditional values—among them, old-fashioned patriotism. History texts have been rewritten in such a way as to minimize Japanese atrocities during World War II.

Right-wing politicians today openly call for outright repudiation of Article IX. In addition, they also have sought to re-kindle popular awareness of the grandeur of Japan's imperial past.

Almost 50 years have passed since the end of World War II. As a result, less than half of the Japanese today have any memory of the horrors of war or the bitterness of defeat. Younger generations no longer carry a burden of wartime guilt.

Increasingly, they see little reason to apologize for Japanese economic success—or to automatically defer to U.S. leadership on foreign policy matters. Nor are they shy about suggesting that Japan adopt a more forceful foreign policy and act more aggressively in its own self-interest.

In the early 1970s, Yasuhiro Nakasone, then director general of the Defense Agency, produced a report entitled *Concerning Our Nation's Independent Defense and Its Potential Power* that recommended that Japan acquire tactical nuclear weapons.

In 1978, the government announced that the constitution would allow Japan to deploy nuclear weapons if it wished. With dozens of operating nuclear power plants and great technological sophistication, there can be no doubt that the Japanese could rapidly produce an arsenal of nuclear warheads. Perhaps they already have.

Oil vulnerability

Another temptation to rearmament stems from the nation's still painful dependence on imported oil. No industrialized nation was hit harder by OPEC's quadrupling of the price of oil in the 1970s than Japan. And no major country suffered more economic damage from the run-up in oil prices surrounding the 1991 Gulf War.

Today, nearly two-thirds of Japan's supplies come from the Persian Gulf. As in the 1930s, Japan is again being forced to consider what must be done to secure vital supplies of raw materials.

In recent years, the country has taken steps to extend its long-range bombing capability. Extra fuel tanks have been added to the Japanese fleet of American-built F-15 fighter-bombers, and airborne tankers that allow them to refuel in midair have been purchased. Such measures suggest that a military solution to the problem of protecting scarce resources has hardly been ruled out.

In the aftermath of the Cold War, fears of a Russian attack on Japan have greatly diminished. But at the same time, new fears are mounting on the Korean Peninsula and elsewhere in East Asia.

Of course, a new outbreak of protectionist fever that threatened to push the Japanese economy into depression could put all of these concerns on the back burner.

As the *Washington Times* has observed:

> *While most Japanese remain committed to their status as the world's only officially pacifist nation, it should not be forgotten that the spirit of 'bushido' still lurks in the depths of the Japanese psyche. It was not so long ago that the relentless drive which now sustains the world's most dynamic economy was channeled into an equally dynamic war machine. The fact that the genie has been back in the bottle for 40 years should not encourage complacency about the dangers of tampering with the cork.*[8]

Japan is as lacking in natural resources today as it was in 1930. Neither is the country any less dependent on access to foreign markets.

Mindless protectionism in the 1990s could do more than sabotage world economic growth and wipe out investors worldwide. It could also invite a fresh disaster on the scale of World War II.

---

1. "Pyongyang Food Crisis Fears Grow," *South China Morning Post,* September 24, 1993.

2. Robert W. Czeschin, "Nuclear weapons in North Korea," *Taipan*, April 1990, and "Apocalpyse Eclipsed," *Taipan*, May 1993.

3. *The Economist,* April 3, 1993, p.30.

4. "Missiles in North aimed at Beijing, report claims," *South China Morning Post*, April 8, 1993.

5. M. Bronfenbrenner, "Japan and Two World Economic Depressions," quoted in R. Dore and R. Sinha, *Japan and World Depression—Then and Now,* p. 33.

6. Viscount Tani Takeki, *Ikensho,* 1887 edition translated by R. K. Reischauer, included in *Meiji Bunka Zenshu*, cited by Bronfenbrenner, *op. cit.*

7. The following is a summary of the plot of a comic book called *Silent Fleet*, reportedly read by more than a quarter million young Japanese: The

American 7th fleet is in hot pursuit of a renegade Japanese nuclear submarine in the Western Pacific when suddenly the Japanese commander, Captain Umieda, decides to match his superior skill and technology against the Americans' greater numbers. After a series of brilliant tactical maneuvers resulting in the crippling of six American submarines, Captain Umieda declares his goal is "a war of independence from U.S. domination."

"Japan hasn't changed since Pearl Harbor," snarls the defeated commander of the American fleet ....

This story was quoted by A. Murray, and U. C. Lehner, "U.S. Japan Struggle to Redefine Relations as Resentment Grows," *Wall Street Journal,* June 13, 1990.

8. Smith, *Washington Times,* April 1984, p. 2.

Chapter 10

Japanese and Asian Investment Markets

Spectacular Profits, Extraordinary Risk

Panics, in some cases, have their uses .... Their duration is always short; the mind soon grows through them and acquires a firmer habit than before. But their peculiar advantage is that they are the touchstone of sincerity and hypocrisy, and bring things and men to light, which might otherwise have lain forever undiscovered.
— Thomas Paine —

In the 1960s and 1970s, both the Dow Jones Industrial Average and the Nikkei Dow in Tokyo stood at about 1,000. Since then, the Dow Jones Industrial Average has gone as high as 4,000. But in Japan, the Nikkei Dow went from 1,000 to 39,000!

Note, however, that this 39-fold gain is figured in local currency—that is, the Japanese yen. Against the U.S. dollar, the yen itself has more than tripled in value over the last 25 years. (See chart on next page.) In other words, the rising yen boosted that 39-fold gain another three-fold!

The bull market that ran from the late 1980s to the early 1990s on Wall Street may have been hot stuff—by U.S. standards. But it was nothing alongside what was going on in Tokyo.

Trees, however, don't grow to the sky. And stocks—even in Tokyo—don't go up forever. In the first edition of this book, which appeared in late 1987, I spent much of this chapter setting forth my forecast for a collapse in Japanese share prices.

That forecast has now been fulfilled. Between the fourth quarter of 1989 and the third quarter of 1992, the Nikkei Dow fell more than 67%.

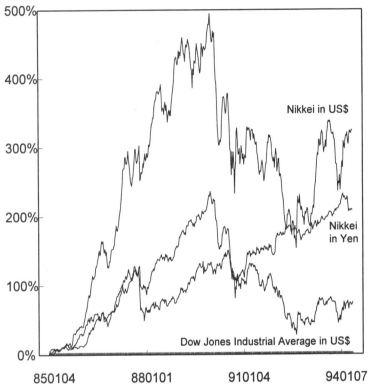

Japanese and U.S. Stock Market Performance
Since the end of 1984

Graph labels:
Nikkei in US$
Nikkei in Yen
Dow Jones Industrial Average in US$

Y-axis: 500%, 400%, 300%, 200%, 100%, 0%

X-axis: 850104, 880101, 910104, 940107

Anyone who took my advice and purchased one of the then popular American Stock Exchange-listed Nikkei Put Warrants easily chalked up gains in the 150% to 250% range.

In prior editions of this chapter, I also predicted a massive decline in Japanese real estate prices. Like the forecast decline in share prices, this prediction has also been vindicated by events. Japanese real estate prices are down 30% to 50% from their peak levels.

The rise and fall of Tokyo share prices is no less dramatic than that which has occurred in Hong Kong. During the first 15 years after Deng Xiaoping began China's economic reform program, Hong Kong share prices *rose more than 20-fold*.

The top line of the graph on the next page shows the percentage change in Hong Kong's Hang Seng Index since the end of 1978. The line second from the top shows the change in Japan's Topix Index.

Hong Kong, Japanese, U.S., and British
Stock Market Performance in US$ Terms
Since the end of 1978

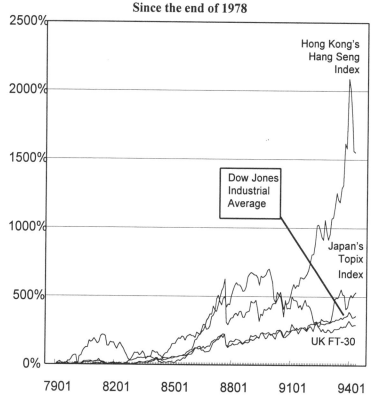

The bottom line shows the change in London's FT-30 Industrials. And the line second from the bottom shows the change in the Dow Jones Industrial Average. All performance measurements are in U.S. dollar terms.

Both Hong Kong and Tokyo illustrate the spectacular profits you can earn by investing in the world's fastest growing economies. But they also illustrate the extraordinary risks.

Take Hong Kong for example. The market crashed along with the whole world in 1987. (In fact, the market was closed for four full days.) It crashed in 1989 as blood flowed in the streets around Tiananmen Square.

It crashed in 1990, when Saddam Hussein invaded Kuwait. It crashed, recovered, and then crashed again in late 1992—when the controversy with China broke out over proposals for democratic reforms of local government.

In 1994, the Hang Seng crashed more than 30% when the U.S. Federal Reserve reversed the five-year decline in American interest rates.

It takes steady nerves to be a long-term investor in Hong Kong. However, where else but in Asia do you get a chance to buy in at the bottom of six stock market crashes in seven years?

Whether or not Hong Kong or Japanese stocks are a good investment today is a topic for Chapter 14. What I would like to draw your attention to here is the growing impact of Asian markets on your life and livelihood—no matter where in the world you live.

Much more is at stake than speculative stock market returns. Or the lack thereof.

Pacific Century

At the end of World War II, America emerged as the dominant commercial power in the world. Three out of every four barrels of oil that was pumped anywhere in the world was pumped in Texas, Oklahoma, and Pennsylvania.

America was also the world's leading exporter of funds for investment. U.S. funds financed the reconstruction of Europe, and American companies invested in productive capacity in dozens of countries around the world.

But a lot has happened since then. Now the world's economic center of gravity is shifting westward—from the American heartland to the Pacific Rim.

The United States has gone from being the world's largest exporter of oil to its largest importer. It has also gone from being the world's largest creditor nation to the world's largest debtor nation.

Today, the American government could not survive without a massive and continuous supply of capital from abroad. When a government spends more than it raises in revenues, it has only two choices for making up the shortfall. It can borrow what it needs. Or it can simply print enough currency to pay its bills.

In the 1970s, America preferred to print. As a result, U.S. dollar inflation eventually soared as high as 20%. Under presidents Reagan and Bush, America preferred to borrow the necessary amounts to cover its deficits. (The Clinton administration may prefer to borrow less and print more.)

However, the budget shortfall remains large. And Americans traditionally save very little. So if the government is to borrow, it has no choice but to borrow from abroad.

Who has money to lend? For the last decade or more, it has been the Germans and the Japanese.

But in the years ahead, I believe the lion's share of the world's surplus capital will increasingly come from Asia. The reason is simple. It's where the money is.

In the mid-1990s, for example, more new wealth is being created faster in China than in any other part of the world. Asia is also home of the world's highest savings rates.

Today, the world's second-largest stock market (after the United States) is in Tokyo. Japan is a major foreign investor in North America and throughout much of Asia.

In 1993, for example, the Japanese finally overtook the British and became the largest foreign owners of assets in America. As noted in Chapter 8, Japanese-built factories are increasingly a major source of employment for Americans (as well as for Australians, Asians, and others).

What would happen if America's supply of capital from abroad were suddenly interrupted? Or if capital already invested were suddenly withdrawn?

Interest rates would skyrocket. The dollar would get hammered. The stock market would collapse. Followed by the economy.

In the early 1970s, the first oil shock knocked the American economy into its worst downturn since the 1930s. It also knocked the U.S. stock market into its worst decline since the 1929-1930 bear market.

The first capital shock in the 1990s could be at least as devastating as the first oil shock of the 1970s. If the United States ever experiences another Great Depression, chances are an interruption in the supply of foreign capital—or foreign oil—will be one of the triggers.

I have focused on America because it provides the most dramatic example of a growing dependence on investors from and markets in Asia. But what is true of America in this respect is also true of dozens of other countries.

Not only is the world growing more interdependent than ever before. But this is occurring on the eve of what some have called the Pacific Century. Neither of these is a bad thing in itself. What it does mean is that your welfare and that of those you love will be increasingly at the mercy of obscure and unexpected events in far away places.

It is no longer enough to worry about what happens in

Washington or on Wall Street. Now you also have to worry about what could go wrong in Tokyo (and, increasingly, Beijing and Pyongyang as well). And what could go wrong in Tokyo is the subject of the balance of this chapter.

Triggers of collapse

One of the most profound threats to an increasingly interdependent world is the possibility of a return to protectionism by the United States and Europe.

Protectionism, of course, is always a bad idea. Contrary to what its proponents claim, it does not combat unemployment. It merely preserves present jobs at the expense of future jobs. And the damage it does is immense. The first casualty is trade. The second is the stock market. The third is economic growth.

As a result of a spate of protectionist measures enacted in the 1930s, foreign commerce plunged around the world. U.S. trade with the rest of the world fell 69% between 1929 and 1932. In the United Kingdom, France, Germany, and Japan, foreign trade declined between 54% and 71%.

This precipitous decline in commerce was a major factor in the worst stock market catastrophe on record. Between 1929 and 1932, the Dow Jones Industrial Average declined a staggering 89%. Much the same thing occurred in stock markets around the world.

In import-dependent Japan, the catastrophic plunge in world trade ushered in a recession so deep that widespread social unrest resulted. Eventually, a group of militarists came to power on a pledge to take by force what could no longer be obtained by peaceful trade. The rest, as they say, is history.

Today, the spectre of protectionism is no less frightening than it was in the 1930s. New protectionist measures continue to be introduced in both European legislatures and the U.S. Congress. And on both sides of the Atlantic, trade policy has become a perennial election issue.

Nuclear nightfall

If there ever were a doomsday trigger for world stock markets, and indeed the world economy, a nuclear crisis in Asia would have to be high on the list.

In Chapter 6, I told the story of North Korea's development of the Rodong-1 missile. With a range of about 600 miles, it is capable of striking Tokyo. Indeed, all of Japan is now within range, except the easternmost portion of the island of Hokkaido.

Japan has also been the historical enemy of Korea for generations. From 1910 to the end of World War II, the Japanese were colonizers of the Korean peninsula.

Japan's present 750,000 population of ethnic Koreans are in fact the descendants of slave laborers seized from their homes and sent to work in the Japanese home islands.

By all accounts, Japan's occupation of Korea was no less brutal than its occupation of Manchuria and Indochina. Memories of this period remain so painful that even in relatively democratic South Korea, various expressions of Japanese culture—such as books and films—are still banned by law. Clearly there is no love lost between the Koreans and the Japanese.

While it serves North Korean interests in the diplomatic cat-and-mouse game with the West over nuclear inspections to pretend it has not yet built its first atomic bomb, there has been no need to conceal who Pyongyang intends to target.

In 1994, North Korean ambassador to India Cha Song Ju told a Reuters correspondent in New Delhi, "Our nuclear arms, if developed, would be primarily designed to contain Japan." [1]

In the event the North Koreans do launch such an attack, look for the missiles to first rain down on the American military installations such as the U.S. Navy base at Sasebo in Kyushu, and the nearby Marine air base at Iwakuni.

This would not only be a blow against the hated Japanese, but also against the Americans, at whose hands the North Koreans were defeated in the Korean War.

Another nuclear attack on Japan would be at least as devastating to Japanese lives and property as the American atomic attacks on Hiroshima and Nagasaki at the end of World War II. But because Japan today is also one of the world's largest creditor nations, and the home of the world's second largest stock market, it would also be a catastrophe for financial markets everywhere.

Two minutes to noon

An average of four seismic disturbances occur somewhere in Japan every day. The last earthquake of truly devastating proportions, however, occurred about 71 years ago. At two minutes to noon on the morning of Saturday, September 1, 1923, an earthquake measuring in excess of 8.2 on the Richter scale occurred in the Kanto region of southern Japan.

About 150,000 people lost their lives as Tokyo and

Yokohama were both reduced to rubble. So were many smaller towns along the coast. Of those 150,000 dead, only about 50,000 were direct victims of the quake. The rest perished in the firestorm that followed.

Fires almost always occur in the aftermath of major earthquakes, especially because of the traditional Japanese fondness for paper and wood as building materials. In Tokyo alone, the combination of quake and fire reduced 7 square miles to rubble.[2] That's more than twice the area destroyed by the London, Chicago, and San Francisco fires combined!

In Yokohama, a 3-square-mile area was destroyed. Among the smaller towns, destruction ranged from 90% on Odawara—near the epicenter of the quake—to 10% in the coastal town of Ito, where a small tidal wave washed over the town and put out the fires before a conflagration could occur.

The official report of the Japanese Home Office (compiled by Viscount Goto and Rentaro Mizuno) estimated the total damage at 5 billion yen.[3] According to the *Japan Year Book 1923,* that amounted to 7% of the nation's total wealth. It would surely be many times that today.

Potential for greater damage

The great Kanto Earthquake released energy approximately equal to 27,000 atomic bombs of the size that devastated Hiroshima.[4] If such a quake occurred today, the damage would be much greater than it was in 1923. There are several reasons for this.

While fewer urban dwellings are made of wood today, gas utility lines now crisscross every town of any size. Widespread rupture of these lines would provide much more combustible material than was available 71 years ago.[5]

Second, while the supply of gas to Tokyo has increased many fold, the supply of water has not. In the event of a post-earthquake conflagration, the Tokyo fire department would run out of water before it ran out of hoses and trucks.

Today, *tsunami* (tidal wave) such as the one that engulfed Tokyo Bay in 1923 would also do enormous damage. For example, the huge construction projects on reclaimed land—such as Makuhari, Minato Mirai 21, and Tokyo Teleport Town—would find the loose soil on which they stand turned into muddy water.

In addition, since the oil crises of the 1970s, the Japanese have been building nuclear power plants at a rapid rate. Severe earthquake damage to the country's 33 operating reactors could cause a catastrophe many times worse than that suffered by the Russians at Chernobyl.

The Japanese National Land Agency conservatively estimates that a 1923-style quake would kill or injure 357,000 people today. Of course, much depends on what time of the day it strikes. There are 8.5 million inhabitants in Tokyo today—almost four times the number in 1923. However, during a typical workday, another 3 million commuters visit the city.

The worst moment for a quake to strike today would be in late afternoon on a winter weekday, with a 10-knot or more northerly wind—that is, of sufficient intensity to fan a firestorm.

Effect on the U.S. stock market

In 1923, it took nearly a week for news of the Japanese earthquake to reach New York. Today, the effect of any catastrophe of this magnitude would be instantaneous—leaving no time for investors to adjust.

To raise cash, Japanese insurance companies would have to dump assets wholesale. Because a large portion of the nation would simply vanish in a disaster of this magnitude, Japanese institutional investors—which include the Bank of Japan—would be forced to liquidate their overseas holdings.

The Japanese also could be expected to sell off their direct investments in the United States and elsewhere (for example, their real estate and factories). But these generally illiquid investments would take some time to dispose of. That's not true of stocks and bonds, however. And securities markets surely would plummet under the force of Japanese selling.

So would the U.S. dollar. Once Japanese investors cashed in their chips, they would have to convert them out of dollars and into yen. A fearsome round of dollar selling would inevitably ensue.

As capital fled, the full weight of the U.S. budget deficit would fall on the meager and depleted pool of U.S. savings, driving interest rates upward in a sickening spike. At that moment, the Board of Governors of the U.S. Federal Reserve Board would be faced with an awful dilemma.

The board could either permit spiraling interest rates to shove the economy into a depression worse than the one in the 1930s, or flood the system with freshly printed money to keep interest rates from rising to ruinous levels. In doing the latter, however, it would sow the seeds of another devastating period of inflation.

What is the likelihood of this terrible scenario actually coming to pass? The truth is that no one knows.

Although little understood by geologists and seismologists, major quakes have historically been preceded at intervals of five to 10 years by a major eruption of the Mihama volcano on Oshima. Mihama last blew its top in 1986. If history holds, "the big one" will hit Tokyo before 1996.

---

1. "Pyongyang says Tokyo is prime nuclear target," *Eastern Express*, March 10, 1994.

2. N. F. Busch, *Two Minutes to Noon,* p. 147.

3. "The Reconstruction of Tokyo," Tokyo Municipal Office.

4. "Waiting for the Big One," *Economist*, December 7, 1991, p. 97.

5. Peter Hadfield, *Sixty Seconds That Will Change the World,* Sidgwick & Jackson, London, England, 1991.

Section III

Preparing for Financial Upheaval

Chapter 11

Rough Sailing on Uncharted Seas

Riding the Wild Waves Ahead

Words ought to be a little wild, for they are the assault of thoughts on the unthinking.
— John Maynard Keynes —

When Saddam Hussein seized Kuwaiti oil fields in 1990, oil soared toward US$40 a barrel. As the Kuwaiti crisis deepened, a mass repatriation of Japanese capital ensued—not just from the U.S. stock market but from other world markets as well. Oil, war, and capital flight combined to create multibillion-dollar losses to investors worldwide.

Of course, it was not the first time. The first oil shock occurred in late 1973 when the Yom Kippur War broke out and OPEC imposed the now-famous oil embargo. Oil prices, which were US$3 a barrel in 1972, climbed to US$10 in 1974. World stock markets entered a vicious bear market as the global economy suffered its worst economic decline since the Great Depression of the 1930s.

The second shock coincided with the fall of the Shah of Iran in 1979. As the Ayatollah Khomeini swept into power, the Iraqi invasion of Iran ushered in the first Persian Gulf War. Oil prices, which were US$14 a barrel in 1978, climbed to US$35 in early 1980. In the United States, inflation soared above 15% as interest rates climbed to nearly 20%.

On land, the second Persian Gulf War lasted only 100 hours. And when it became clear that Saddam's army could not escape destruction at the hands of allied forces, stock prices everywhere except Japan rapidly reversed their downward slide. In the United

Crude Oil Prices
West Texas Intermediate (US$)

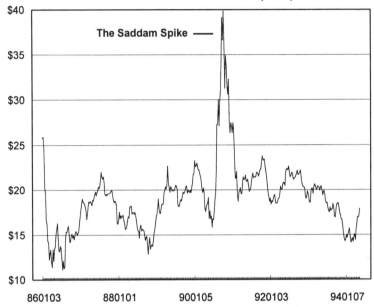

States, a bull market erupted that pushed the Dow Jones Industrial Average to a new series of all-time highs.

The crushing defeat of Iraq, in turn, helped open the door to a series of peace agreements between Israel and its Arab neighbors. The repair of the Kuwaiti oil fields, which were put to the torch by the retreating Iraqis, helped usher in an era of abundant supplies and falling prices.

Does all this portend an inflation-free era of stable oil prices and rising stock markets? Or is it merely a false dawn before some other yet unforeseen debacle pushes the world into a 1930s-style depression? What other hazards are likely to threaten your financial well-being in the waning days of the 20th century?

Above all, what sort of investment strategy promises the best chance of financial survival in light of what we have learned about oil and war and the rise of Japan?

Chapter 14 is devoted to answering the last question. I shall attempt to address the first three in the pages that follow.

Oil and war in the 21st century

Any forecast concerning the availability of future oil supplies is necessarily bounded by two important facts. First, most of the world's oil is in the Middle East. Second, after adjusting for inflation, oil prices in the 1990s are about as low as they were in the 1970s—before the first oil shock.

Examine the geographical distribution of the world's proven reserves and you find that two-thirds of the world's oil is in the Mideast. What are the chances this will change significantly? Very small indeed.

There are a couple of reasons for this. One is that low oil prices are discouraging exploration. In the North Sea, which accounts for about 7% of world production, oil companies are slashing their work forces. Chevron, for example, recently cut employment on its Ninian Platform by 25%. [1]

Low oil prices also discourage additional investment required to extend the life of North Sea fields presently in production. The same is true in the United States, where domestic oil production recently fell to a 35-year low. [2]

All this is not to say that there aren't plenty of major discoveries still waiting to be made. The biggest additions to world reserves outside the Mideast in the next 20 years will be made in Russia and the oil-rich states of the former Soviet Empire—particularly in Central Asia.

For example, Kazakhstan's Tengiz field is believed to be

Where the Oil Is
The World's Proven Reserves by Region

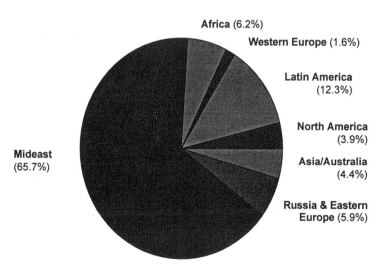

Africa (6.2%)

Western Europe (1.6%)

Latin America (12.3%)

North America (3.9%)

Asia/Australia (4.4%)

Russia & Eastern Europe (5.9%)

Mideast (65.7%)

twice the size of Alaska's Prudehoe Bay. The nearby Korolev reservoir may hold hundreds of trillions of cubic meters of natural gas. Turkmenistan, just North of the Iranian border, could turn out to have reserves approximately equal to that of Kuwait.

However, the mere fact that there are promising areas of the world in which to explore for oil does not mean these explorations will in fact take place. Difficult terrain and lousy weather make Central Asia an especially inhospitable and expensive region in which to operate. And as long as oil prices are below US$20 a barrel, fewer and fewer such efforts will be made.

As a result, the Mideast, which boasts the lowest finding and production costs in the world, is in no danger of losing its dominant position as the leading oil-rich region on earth.

Moreover, in the absence of another Gulf War-style crisis, oil prices are likely to remain generally weak for some time. There are two reasons for this: weak demand and abundant supply.

Demand has been weak because of sluggish world economic growth. Economic recoveries are under way in Australia, Britain, Canada, and the United States. And Southeast Asia is clearly booming. But Germany, most of Europe, and Japan are just as clearly still within the throes of recession. Only when all the world's major economies are again expanding at the same time, will the demand for oil reach its cyclical peak.

Supplies are abundant, in part because the two oil shocks of the 1970s stimulated an exploration boom that resulted in major discoveries in Alaska, Mexico, the North Sea, and elsewhere. As a result, the world has much higher production capacity than it did in the late 1970s. More producers pumping more oil—particularly in a period of weak demand—inevitably results in lower prices.

In addition, one day the United Nations will lift the remaining restrictions on sales of Iraqi oil that were imposed after its defeat in the second Gulf War. This will expand supplies even further.

Another effect of low oil prices is to undermine conservation efforts. It is hard to make the case for conservation when the world seems awash in oil. It also makes it difficult to create a political consensus to support measures intended to lessen dependence on imported supplies of oil.

The International Energy Authority (I.E.A.) has forecast that the 24-nation Organization of Economic Cooperation and Development (O.E.C.D.) will import 80% of its supplies of oil by the year 2010. This forecast is based on the assumption that oil prices remain steady at an inflation-adjusted US$20 per barrel.

The O.E.C.D. includes Australia, Austria, Belgium, Canada, Denmark, Finland, France, Germany, Greece, Iceland, Ireland, Italy, Japan, Luxembourg, the Netherlands, New Zealand, Norway, Portugal, Spain, Sweden, Switzerland, Turkey, the United Kingdom, and the United States.

Of these, the United States is the world's largest importer, and is presently dependent on imported supplies for about half its daily consumption. If present trends continue, this will rise to about two thirds by the year 2000.

Note that under such a scenario, not only does demand for imported oil continue to grow, but the world production balance shifts even farther in favor of the Mideast and Venezuela—because the relatively high cost of reserves elsewhere makes them increasingly uneconomic.

According to I.E.A. figures, the Mideast and Venezuela would wind up accounting for more than 56% of total world production. In other words, the world's developed nations will be more and more dependent for their energy needs on oil from some of the least stable regions of the world.

O.E.C.D. Oil Import Dependency
Actual and Forecast

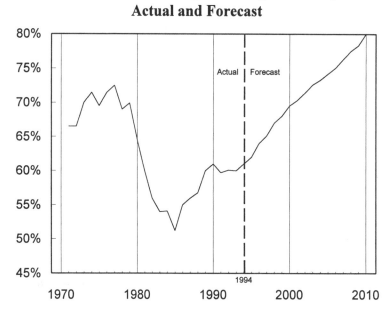

Source: *World Energy Outlook*

161

Persian oil tactic

Chapter 6 detailed Iran's ambition to become the dominant regional power in the oil-rich Persian Gulf. As we noted then, Iran's plans for achieving this include the development of both ballistic missiles and weapons of mass destruction.

In 1992, the head of the Yuzhmash ballistic-missile plant in the Ukraine confided to a visiting French parliamentarian that he was ready to sell Soviet-built SS-18 and SS-25 missiles to anyone with enough cash to pay for them. It is also known that the Iranians were among the first prospective customers to visit his plant. What kind of warheads may have been part of the deal has not been disclosed. [3]

Along with Syria, Iran has the most advanced chemical and biological weapons program in the Mideast. There have been credible reports that Iran plans to take delivery of 100 North Korean Rodong-1 missiles complete with nuclear warheads. [4]

Postwar U.N. inspections of Iraqi military facilities revealed that Saddam Hussein came very close indeed to producing a secret atomic arsenal. That, in turn, has cast doubt on whether the massive, multilateral military buildup of Operation Desert Storm would have been possible had it been known that Iraq was a nuclear-armed adversary.

For the Iranians, at least, the lesson of the second Gulf War is clear. Forget challenging the United States unless you can intimidate the Americans with an atomic arsenal. In the next Gulf War, *all* the combatants will have both the means and the will to use such weapons.

China syndrome

Ten years ago, the three things a typical urban Chinese dreamed of owning were a bicycle, a wristwatch, and a sewing machine. Five years ago, it was a television, a refrigerator, and a washing machine. Today, a new trio of status symbols has overtaken: a telephone, an air-conditioner, and a private automobile.

At 180,000 renminbi (US$20,500), an automobile costs about 18 years' average wages. However, new wealth is presently being created in China at a torrid pace. Accordingly, the Chinese government has already set a goal of one automobile per urban family by the year 2010.

With one quarter of the world's population, and the fastest growing economy on earth, China cannot fail to have a big impact on the world demand curve for petroleum.

China presently produces about 3 million barrels per day, making it the sixth largest producer in the world. But its appetite for oil has grown so fast that it became a net importer in 1993.

In fact, by the year 2000, China will have to import more than a million barrels per day. In other words, it will have been transformed from one of Asia's major oil exporting countries to a net importer, which, like Japan, will be dependent on Mideast oil to fuel its powerhouse economy.

To secure its future supply of oil, China's foreign policy is aimed at making friends in the Mideast today. For example, the Chinese have already sold missile technology to Saudi Arabia, Syria, and Iran. In the future, it will not shrink from providing nuclear technology in exchange for oil.

The demand for oil among developing nations has risen about two and a half times in the past 20 years. Today, the Asia Pacific region is the world's fastest growing oil market.

There are roughly two billion people in China and India alone who each consumes less than a barrel of oil per year. But consumption is rising along with living standards. How high will it go? Take Taiwan as an example of how much oil is necessary to support an Asian Tiger economy's standard of living. The Taiwanese consume about 11 barrels per person per year.

Suppose per capita consumption in China and India grows to only one-third Taiwanese levels in the next decade or so. That amounts to about 20 million barrels a day. To put this into perspective, that's *twice* Saudi Arabia's *maximum capacity*.

Already Asia consumes more than Europe, for example. Before the turn of the century, it will easily overtake the United States as the world's largest consumer. The United States— indeed the entire Western World—is also being overtaken in other ways as well.

In the nearly five decades since the end of World War II, both Western and Asian countries have been mesmerized by Japan's economic success. In the early 1950s, the Japanese G.N.P. was a third of Britain's and 1/20 of the United States'. Thirty years later, it was twice Britain's and half of the United States'.[5] (See Chapters 7 through 10.)

In the past 10 years, many have worried about growing Japanese economic dominance. With only 3% of the world's population and 0.3% of the world's habitable land, Japan has seen its stock market not only match that of the United States in size— but periodically overtake it.

Japanese capital and the stock market

Throughout most of this book, we have focused on oil shocks and capital shocks as the triggers of financial upheavals. Both were present in the second Gulf War. When oil prices soared to nearly US$40 a barrel, the Japanese, who are 100% dependent on supplies of imported oil, rushed to sell their overseas holdings.

Along with the oil price shock, the repatriation of Japanese capital pushed the United States into recession—and helped set off a devastating six-month bear market worldwide. This is not the first time a withdrawal of Japanese capital was linked to a stock market debacle.

For example, six months after the Wall Street crash of 1987, an investigation headed by Nicholas Brady, later to become U.S. Secretary of the Treasury, confirmed that foreign selling was indeed one of the major factors in the worst debacle in stock market history. On April 22, 1988, the page 18 headline in the *Wall Street Journal* read as follows: "Task Force's Brady Says Japanese Sales of U.S. Bonds Touched Off Oct. 19 Crash."

Since 1980, between 15% and 20% of the total marketable public debt in the United States has been foreign-owned. It is therefore no surprise that the U.S. Treasury worries about how well attended the next government auction may be by the Japanese (and, more recently, the Saudis). Twenty percent ownership of the total supply of government bonds is more than sufficient to have market-busting power.

In the early 1990s, however, Japan itself fell on hard times. Burdened by the aftereffects of the so-called bubble economy of the 1980s, it is now trying to dig out of recession. Meanwhile, it is being overtaken by greater China.

By greater China, I mean China, Hong Kong, Taiwan, and Chinese Singapore, as well as the Asian overseas Chinese communities in Indonesia, Malaysia, the Philippines, and Thailand. In these countries, companies owned or controlled by people of Chinese descent account for as much as 70% of the total private sector wealth.

In Asia, Chinese investment and trading might is now taking over from the previously ascendant Japanese. In China itself, growth rates in industry and agriculture have averaged 10% and 3% since the 1950s. Under the capitalist reforms of recent years, however, those numbers have risen to 12% and 8%.

As much as 80% of the investment that is powering this growth has come from Hong Kong, Singapore, Taiwan, and other

Chinese investors from southeast Asia.

In 1992, the exports of China, Hong Kong, Singapore, and Taiwan alone were approximately equal to Japan. I predict that by the year 2002, the gross domestic product (G.D.P.) of greater China will be larger than that of the United States. As former U.S. president Richard Nixon observed, [6]

> *Today, China's economic power makes U.S. lectures about human rights imprudent. Within a decade, it will make them irrelevant. Within two decades, it will make them laughable. By then the Chinese may threaten to withhold Most Favored Nation (M.F.N.) trading status from the U.S. unless we ... improve living conditions in Detroit, Harlem, and south-central Los Angeles.*

Imperial exhaustion

For the United States, dependency on imported capital dates only from the mid-1980s. Dependence on imported supplies of oil is also a relatively recent phenomenon.

Despite the conservation efforts that followed the oil shocks of the 1970s, imports have continued to grow. Today, they account for more than half of all the oil consumed in the United States—which means the U.S. economy is ironically far more vulnerable to an interruption of oil supplies than it was during the first oil shock back in 1973.

To the Japanese, who have always been 100% dependent on imported supplies, this may seem like no big deal. But countless Americans have yet to come to terms with the relative economic decline of the United States.

For them, dependence on foreign supplies of energy and capital has created an acute sense of distress, a yearning for the "good old days" when the United States could go its own way in the world pretty much as it pleased.

These sentiments have helped fuel the growing isolationist and protectionist currents in domestic American politics. As is often the case, it has become more tempting to blame one's troubles on foreigners than to clearly confront one's own short-comings. And since the Soviet Union no longer exists, the new focus of American xenophobia has inevitably become Japan.

In 1993, the Japanese overtook the British as the owners of the most assets inside the United States. In third place are the

Dutch. Yet British and Dutch investments were never controversial (at least not in the last 50 years) in the way Japanese investment has been.

One reason is that the British and the Dutch represent the European trading empires that were superseded by the rise of the United States. Japan represents the rising economic might of Asia, which has already begun to eclipse the United States.

In other words, the British and the Dutch symbolize American ascendance. The Japanese (and increasingly, the Chinese) symbolize American decline. That is why Asian investment has frightened so many Americans.

One response to growing fears of foreign domination has been to clamor for protection of domestic industry against foreign competition—and capital controls to restrict foreign investment.

Of course, America is scarcely the only country to indulge in this kind of thing. But because it accounts for such an important share of the world economy, American lunacies still have a disproportionate impact on the rest of the world.

Ironically, to the extent protectionist policies are actually adopted, they will only make things worse. That the collapse of international trade in the 1930s (following the widespread adoption of protectionist measures) prolonged and deepened the Great Depression has never been seriously disputed. Imagine what a fresh wave of protectionism could do for the weak economies of the 1990s!

Another forgotten lesson from the 1930s is the rise of the military in Japan. Without natural resources, and denied access to other sources of supply, Japan plunged into depression. And the depression made political careers possible for those who promised to take by force what had been denied by peaceful commerce. Ultimately, this new generation of militarist leaders brought Japan into World War II.

Could it happen again? You bet. Only this time, Japan would be an even more formidable adversary than she was in 1941.

Capital controls

A round of 1930s-style protectionism will be a growing threat to international investors in the 1990s. And not just because barriers to trade create economic losses that are rapidly reflected in lower stock prices.

You can't halt the cross-border flow of goods and services without also obstructing the flow of money to pay for them.

166

(Conversely, you can't impose controls on the free movement of capital without obstructing the sale of the goods and services that would have otherwise been purchased with that capital.)

Capital controls and protectionism are two sides of the same worthless coin. In South Africa, for example, exchange controls were used to make sure that anyone who left the country did so practically penniless. Prior to World War II, German capital controls were intended to make sure anyone who wanted to escape the Nazis suffered a similar fate.

In the United States, capital controls have taken several familiar forms. In the 1960s, the so-called interest equalization tax was enacted to discourage the flow of U.S. capital abroad.

Capital controls also appear in other guises, such as efforts to outlaw investment in certain countries—South Africa used to be an example—or to restrict the movement of funds thought to be associated with the drug trade. (Notice that you don't have to be for apartheid or drug use to be against capital controls. All you have to be is concerned about freedom of international investment.)

Even more alarming is that a host of laws have already been enacted that permit federal officials to prohibit the transfer of capital inside or outside the country. For example, the so-called International Economic Emergency Powers Act, gives the president the authority to halt all private trading in currency and gold. Other measures extend and reinforce executive authority to instantly outlaw virtually any kind of investment transaction. [7]

This can all be legally done by executive order. All it requires is a declaration of an economic emergency. And what constitutes an emergency could be anything. A bad day on Wall Street. A plunging U.S. dollar. Or more likely, a failed government auction—at which the U.S. Treasury discovers that foreigners are no longer willing to pay hard currency for government notes and bonds.

Because none of this requires an act of Congress, it can happen literally overnight. Investors are likely to have virtually no warning—which, after all, is exactly the point.

So if you have money inside the United States, you could quite literally wake up one morning to find that you cannot get it out. If you are an American resident, you may wake up to find that you can no longer transfer assets to safety abroad.

And if you think America would never confiscate the assets of its citizens, remember that a historical precedent already exists. In the 1930s, President Roosevelt issued an executive order that confiscated all the privately owned gold in America.

Tides of history

Dependence on imported supplies of energy and capital may be a relatively new experience for Americans. But for many Europeans, this is not the case. Nonetheless, the importance of Asian capital to the global economy will only increase in the decade ahead. That's because the world's economic center of gravity has been steadily moving westward for some time.

Nowhere has economic growth been more robust than in Asia. In 1960, the gross domestic product of the Asian Pacific countries accounted for 7.8% of the world's total. By 1982, that had risen to 16%. Before the year 2000, these countries will account for more than half the world's total output of goods and services.

Earlier this century, the world's economic center of gravity moved from Great Britain to the United States. Now it has continued westward, first to Japan, and then beyond, to China.

To be sure, these great currents of world history move slowly—so slowly that most people don't even notice until a hiccup in world capital flows helps push a stock market over the edge somewhere. That, of course, gets everybody's attention.

No doubt the next upheaval, like the last, will also take most investors by surprise. But they scarcely will be able to complain about being washed away when the tide has been plainly rising for a long time.

Zones of turmoil

In their recent book, *The Real World Order*, authors Singer and Wildavsky argue that the key to understanding the post-Cold War world order is to divide the world into two parts: 1) zones of peace and democracy—North America, Western Europe, Japan, and Australia/New Zealand, and 2) zones of turmoil and development—which comprise the rest of the world.

The zones of peace are characterized by high living standards and a lack of military competition between nations. But in the zones of turmoil, life is often solitary, poor, nasty, brutish, and short. Poverty, tyranny, and tribal slaughter will continue to devastate millions of lives.

Bosnia, Somalia, Rwanda, Yemen—not to mention Angola, East Timor, Burma, Kashmir, Cambodia, and Tibet—are unfortunately not exceptions. Unhappily, they are the rule. And they are even more dangerous because they are so little understood in the West.

During the second Gulf War, U.S. President George Bush suggested that Saddam Hussein was a power-mad dictator in the mold of Adolf Hitler or Josef Stalin. In reality, Western notions of political leadership simply have little application in the zones of turmoil.

Tribal passions

Figures such as Saddam Hussein and Syria's Assad are best understood as ambitious patriarchs of an archaic tribal society. Unlike Western politics, which is driven by special interests, tribal politics are often driven by blood feuds. As a result, a political setback is frequently tantamount to execution.

Consider the leadership succession in Iraq. In 1958, when Iraqi King Faisal II was deposed, he was machine-gunned to death. His fate, however, was mild alongside that of his minister, who was dismembered. The minister's body parts were then dragged by his killers through the streets of Baghdad.

Faisal was deposed by Abdul Karim Kassim, who himself perished in a second coup 11 years later. To consolidate their power, the new Iraqi rulers showed Kassim's bullet-ridden body on TV night after night.

As author Samir al Khalil recounts in *Republic of Fear*: [8]

> *The body was propped upon a chair in the studio. A soldier sauntered around, handling its parts. The camera would cut to scenes of devastation at the Ministry of Defence where Kassim had made his last stand. There, on location, it lingered on the mutilated corpses of his entourage. Back to the studio and close-ups of the entry and exit points of each bullet hole. The whole macabre sequence closed ... [when] the soldier grabbed the lolling head by the hair... and spat full face into it.*

Such a degree of ferocity, however shocking to Western sensibilities, is often characteristic of how societies resolve disputes in the zones of turmoil. Witness the remarkable brutality of the civil wars in Liberia, Ethiopia, or Mozambique. Or the clash between the Inkatha and the followers of the African National Congress in South Africa.

Or in Cambodia. A Cambodian army officer recently described to Agence France-Presse his preferred form of execution: "If we catch a Khmer Rouge, we cut their head off and send it back to them .... To show them that we were angry with them, we took a long time to kill them. We used an old rusty hacksaw to cut their heads off slowly." [9]

As the Marquis de Custine observed after a visit to Czarist Russia, "Oppressed people always deserve their fate; tyranny is achieved by a whole nation; it is not the accomplishment of a single individual."

Another characteristic of tribal society is a powerful propensity to vilify anyone outside the tribal group. Iraqi racism, for example, is frequently breathtaking in its crudity. One essay written by a former mayor of Baghdad and widely distributed by the Iraqi government printing office, Dar al Hurriyya, is titled "Three Whom God Should Not Have Created: Persians, Jews, and Flies."[10]

(In it, Iranians are described as "animals God created in the shape of humans." Jews, on the other hand, were made from a "mixture of the dirt and leftovers of diverse peoples." And flies are that which "we do not understand God's purpose in creating.")

The world's largest oil reserves are all located in the zones of turmoil. Nearly two dozen countries in the zones of turmoil have developed or are developing weapons of mass destruction. They also conduct research into chemical weapons or stockpile them. About a dozen countries own ballistic missiles capable of carrying nuclear or chemical warheads far beyond their borders. [11]

It is one of the ironies of history that the zones of turmoil in the Mideast are also where Western civilization began. The ancient Sumerians, whose capital lay just south of modern Baghdad, developed the world's first alphabet as well as its first urban culture. The ancient Babylonian king Hammurabi was the first to establish a legal code for the governing of society.

But Arabic, the language that gave the Western World "algebra" and "logarithm," also bequeathed us the term "assassin." In my view, any realistic analysis of the region will conclude that the threat to the West's oil lifeline is far from ended.

We will not see the last of either oil shocks or energy crises this century. Tribal passion plus regional proliferation of ballistic missiles and chemical and nuclear weapons guarantee an explosive future in the zones of turmoil—and many chapters yet unwritten in the living epic of oil and war.

And even if you live on some distant continent, chances are you will be unable to escape the fallout from the next explosion. Trillion-dollar losses rocked world investment markets after Iraq's invasion of Kuwait. What will happen to your portfolio when the next armed clash over oil begins?

Terror in the 1990s

Another powerful force in the zones of turmoil is militant, fundamentalist Islam. Much has been written about the violent potential of the Shi'ite revolution in earlier editions of this book and elsewhere. (See Chapter 5 for a brief account of the militant origins of Shi'ism.)

Suffice it to say that restless Shi'ite minorities abound in the zones of turmoil. And in many nations, they are potentially as powerful a force for overthrowing governments as they were in Iran.

In the aftermath of the second Gulf War, fundamentalist Shi'ite Iran has been among the most aggressive in courting the Muslim populations of the Central Asian republics of the former Soviet Union. For example, a 1991 Iranian trade mission to the area produced more than US$1 billion in business.

Discreet support is also being offered to groups seeking to create an Iranian-style regime (called Turkestan) out of the Muslim remnants of the former Russian empire. In other capitals, Muslim leaders have begun to speak openly of an Islamic crescent—an economic zone similar to the European Community—that would stretch from the Middle East to the Indian Ocean.

With the collapse of the Soviet Union and the defeat of Iraq, the primary focus of support for international terrorism has shifted to Syria and Iran. Clearly, legions of fanatics eager for martyrdom could be as economically destructive to the developed nations of the West as Communism ever was. [12]

Investment upheavals and long-wave theories

In October 1929, the upheaval that took investors by surprise ushered in both the worst bear market and the worst depression in modern times. When it comes to stock market crashes, the nearest relative to the crash of 1987 is the crash of 1929.

In truth, a simple plot of the Dow Jones Industrial Average for the two periods reveals some striking similarities. In fact, the resemblance is so remarkable that it inspired a minor boom in apocalyptic literature about the stock market even before the crash.

Numerous authors dusted off various long-wave theories that purport to show that crashes and/or depressions tend to occur at 50- or 60-year intervals. The best known of the long-wave theories is the Kondratieff.

Nikolai Kondratieff was a Russian economist who, in the 1920s, published a theory that capitalist economies move in broad cycles of 45 to 60 years. While his theories and those of others who have built upon his work make interesting reading, it is hard to derive any definite conclusions as to when the next crash will occur.

For one thing, there is disagreement among the followers of Kondratieff on exactly when the first cycle began. Another problem is that the number of cycles is too small to permit testing for statistical reliability. Indeed, Kondratieff himself conceded that "the period that was studied, covering a maximum of 140 years, is too short to permit definitive conclusions." [13]

Finally, numerous studies have shown that while long-term fluctuations in prices appear to give some support to the long-wave hypothesis, other important economic time series do not. [14] Long-wave theories, for example, do not appear to be able to predict fluctuations in industrial production or changes in the G.N.P.—the true measures of recession and depression.

Another long-wave theory that made specific predictions belonged to Dr. Ravi Batra.[15] Professor Batra claimed to have identified a 30-year cycle of inflation, money-supply growth, and degrees of government intervention in the economy.

Batra's book, *The Depression of 1990*, was the best-selling financial book of 1989. Fortunately, however, 1990 came and went without a depression. So did 1991, 1992, and 1993.

One of the undeniably appealing aspects of long-wave theories is that they make possible simple interpretations of what might otherwise be complex, bewildering, even frightening phenomena. (An exception to this is the Elliott wave theory, developed by Ralph N. Elliott, an accountant who, it is said, lost his savings in the stock market crash of 1929. Elliott waves are so complicated that making sense of them is rather like Talmudic exegesis. It requires years of study, and sometimes even then it escapes the ken of mere mortals.)

On the other hand, long-wave theories often explain very little. Kondratieff, for example, never gives a satisfactory explanation as to why capitalism should undergo a convulsion every 50 years, and Batra never adequately explains why his cycles should be 30 years in length.

Imaginary waves

One of the privileges of authorship is a forum for one's own opinions. I have an idea why long-wave theories are so frequently silent both on the specific question of what determines cycle length and on the more general nature of the causes underlying wave phenomena. My idea is this: There are no underlying causes. As phenomena, most long waves are far more psychological than economic.

Totally random processes are capable of generating a series of results that, in retrospect, may appear to be cyclical. In fact, they are not. A random series is, by definition, patternless. If this all seems a trifle unconvincing, I invite you to try the following experiment.

What we will do is use a random process to generate an imaginary price history. Take three fair coins and toss them all at once. Each toss will determine the next day's closing price. Let's say we start with an opening price of 100.

Now throw the coins. If two of the three turn up heads, the closing price will be one point above the previous day's close. If two of the three coins turn up tails, the new closing price will be one point lower. If all three turn up the same, the price will be unchanged.

Do this for several hundred trials and plot the results on a piece of graph paper. Chances are you will wind up with something that looks rather like a chart of stock prices. Moreover, if you look closely, you may also see something that looks like rising and falling cycles of price movements.

You should, however, resist the temptation to conclude that an analysis of these apparent cycles would enable you to predict the outcome of future tosses of the coins. If you are tossing fair coins, the outcome is, by definition, random.

Patterns awry

Pattern recognition is a highly developed faculty of the human species. No doubt it proved its survival value again and again during our long evolutionary history. In some of us, perhaps, the tendency to see patterns is so strong that sometimes we see them even when they aren't there.

If you think no economist or stock market analyst could be fooled into mistaking a random series for the real thing (or imagining patterns and waves where none exist), I would like to call your attention to an ingenious experiment conducted by Arditti and McCollough and reported in the *Financial Analysts Journal*. [16]

Among those who make their living forecasting the stock market, so-called technical analysts generally are among the most devoted to wave theories. Specifically, technical analysts generally devote themselves to painstaking study of price histories in an attempt to define patterns that will help them forecast future price movements.

To test their ability to distinguish real waves from the merely imaginary variety, the experimenters asked a panel of analysts to examine a bunch of anonymous stock charts. Some were real stock charts, but others were drawn by a computer following a random process not unlike the one used in the coin-toss experiment. Their task was simple: Identify the real charts.

Want to guess what happened? They all flunked! These results suggest that people whose business it is to see waves will see them whether they are there or not. For this reason, I am inclined to regard most of the wave theories as interesting but generally uninformative curiosities.

Apocalypse postponed

Another reason to be skeptical of long-wave theories and, for that matter, much of what has been written about parallels to 1929, is their frankly apocalyptic character.

In America, as perhaps befits a nation founded by Puritans, it is quite common to feel some kind of vague sense of guilt—especially if you are relatively well-off. A feeling that you invite some kind of divine retribution whenever you enjoy yourself a little too much.

If an economic expansion lasts an extraordinary length of time, then an especially deep depression must lie around the corner. If the stock market sets too many new record highs, then malignant forces must be building up somewhere for a titanic crash.

Not surprising, there always seems to be someone around to exploit these fears. Somewhere, in virtually every age, you can find the doomsday preacher. And chances are he's probably making a pretty good living at it.

Even when disaster fails to occur on schedule, the prophet of gloom and doom is rarely disconcerted. Usually, he just goes back and recalculates. And then, lo and behold, he discovers that the date of the true apocalypse is still some months or years hence. [17]

Millennium fever

By the way, we are likely to see a drastic increase in the volume of gloom-and-doom forecasts as we near the end of the century. Something about years ending in zero seems to act as a lightning rod for people's anxieties about the future.

Of course, the ultimate in years ending in zero is the end of a millennium—in this case, the year 2000. And nowhere is this phenomenon more dramatically illustrated than in what happened just prior to the year 1000. If popular accounts of the period can be believed, nearly half the people of Europe abandoned their jobs and homes to prepare for the second coming of Jesus Christ.

As Charles Mackay recounts in his 1841 book, *Extraordinary Popular Delusions and the Madness of Crowds*:

> *Numerous fanatics appeared in France, Germany, and Italy at that time .... The scene of the Last Judgment was expected to take place in Jerusalem in the year 999. The number of pilgrims proceeding eastward to await the coming of the Lord in that city was so great they were compared to a desolating army .... Buildings of every sort were suffered to fall into ruins. It was thought useless to repair them, when the end of the world was so near.*

Brace yourself—it's already beginning to happen again. Experts estimate there are as many as 900 apocalyptic cults proclaiming the end of the world in a cataclysm of earthquakes, floods, and war.

Consider the case of Harold Camping, the head of California-based Family Stations, Inc., a chain of 38 Christian radio stations. For years, he attracted a growing audience by proclaiming that the world would end between September 15 and September 27, 1994.

David Koresh, who perished along with fellow cultists in a fiery shootout with federal authorities in Texas in 1993, claimed apocalpytic prophecy. He also claimed that his unique biblical knowledge gave him the power to unleash earthshaking catastrophes.

As many as 2,000 followers of Elizabeth Clare Prophet's Church Universal and Triumphant trekked to a remote region of the American state of Montana. There they built concrete underground bomb shelters in which to await the end of the world.

Of course, when the end of the world failed to arrive on schedule, the group claimed that 1) its prophecy had been misinterpreted, 2) that its round-the-clock prayer vigils had won a reprieve for mankind, or 3) that God, in his mercy, simply postponed the date.

In Japan, a man calling himself Okawa has made a very good business out of claiming to be the reincarnation of Buddha and Hermes, the Greek god of science and commerce. He has reportedly sold 30 million copies of books and tapes predicting the apocalpyse. One of his best-sellers is *Nostradamus: Fearful Prophecies*. During the final days, he predicts the destruction of the United States and Russia, and the salvation of Japan. [18]

South Korea's most controversial doomsday church, the Dami Mission, predicted the end of the world on October 28, 1992. When bleary-eyed members stumbled out of their all-night prayer vigil to find the world still there, they were greeted by the glare of television cameras, as reporters jostled for the comments of the disillusioned. [19]

Several critics of the cult were attacked and beaten, and one was knifed in the frenzied buildup to the final day. Attacks by individual fanatics are also said to be increasing in America. In Arizona, a man fascinated with the Book of Revelation, hijacked a bus and died in a shoot-out with police. A California survivalist, arrested for bank robbery, claimed he needed the money to build a bunker in which to wait for the end of the world. [20]

One reason, end-of-the-world fears have been such a timeless theme in human history is that they are encouraged and supported by all of the world's leading religious traditions. For Judaism, the apocalypse coincides with the coming of the Messiah. In Islam, it is a day of judgment. In Christianity, it is the second coming of Jesus Christ.

More violence on the scale of the Branch Davidians—who perished in a fiery, televised 1993 shootout with U.S. authorities in Texas—looms as the millennium approaches. Very likely lesser forms of craziness will also increase. One of the most difficult tasks investors will have as the 1990s wind down will be keeping their heads during this crescendo of hysteria.

George Santayana once observed that those who are ignorant

of history are condemned to repeat it. Czeschin's corollary to Santayana's axiom is this: Those who are mindful of the cycles of popular delirium can profit from them.

* * * * *

So where does all this leave us? Preparing to profit from the next oil crisis? Perhaps. Determined to oppose the twin lunacies of protectionism and capital controls? I hope. Skeptical of long-wave theories and gloom-and-doom merchants. Certainly. And fully cognizant that the folly of governments can transform even the most modest crisis into an enduring calamity.

It is worth noting, however, that just about anything that happens in the world is bad news for someone—and good news for someone else. One man's misfortune is another's opportunity. The secret to investment success is knowing how to find the opportunity even when you must dig beneath the surface of seemingly unhappy events to find it.

But as long as free investment markets exist, individuals are never powerless. For those armed with an informed analysis of what likely lies ahead and the courage to act, the future is never dark.

---

1. "Cheap Oil Makes North Sea Waves," *International Herald Tribune*, April 13, 1994.

2. "Oil Output Fell to 35-Year Low in U.S. in First Half," *Wall Street Journal*, July 15, 1993.

3. B. W. Nelan, "Fighting Off Doomsday," *Time*, June 28, 1993.

4. *Ibid.*

5. Paul Kennedy, *The Rise and Fall of the Great Powers: Economic Change and Military Conflict From 1500 to 2000*, p. 451.

6. Richard Nixon, *Beyond Peace*, pp. 127-128.

7. For a superb piece of research on the body of laws that enables the American government to virtually confiscate your U.S. assets, see the report titled "Government Emergency Financial Controls," published by Globacor, Ltd., P.O. Box 41, Gainesville, GA, 30503; telephone 404-531-2030, or toll-free in the U.S. 800-542-9221.

8. Samir al-Khalil, *Republic of Fear*, p. 59.

9. "Decapitation 'Widespread,'" *Eastern Express*, May 20, 1994.

10. Khairallah Tulfah, "Three Whom God Should Not Have Created: Persians, Jews, and Flies," Dar al-Hurriyya, 1981. In addition to being a former governor of Baghdad, Tulfah is also foster-father, uncle, and father-in-law of Saddam Hussein. Clearly his views reflected official attitudes of the Iraqi regime.

11. B. W. Nelan, *Op. cit.*

12. Far from being a relic of bygone centuries, a yearning for martyrdom remains very much a part of Islam today. Consider the following letter from the front lines, written by Mohsen Naeemi, an Iranian soldier during the Iran-Iraq war:

> *My wedding is at the front and my bride is martyrdom.*
> *The sermon will be uttered by the roar of guns. I shall attire*
> *myself in my blood for this ceremony. My bride, martyr-*
> *dom, shall give birth to my son, freedom. I leave this son in*
> *your safekeeping. Keep him well.*

From "The Devil's War Against Islamic Iran," published by the Revolutionary Guard Corps, 1982.

13. Nickolai Kondratieff, *The Long Wave Cycle.*

14. M. N. Cleary, and G.D. Hobbs, "The 50 Year Cycle: A Look at the Empirical Evidence," in *Long Waves in the World Economy* by C. Freeman.

15. R. Batra, *The Great Depression of 1990.*

16. F. D. Arditti, and W. A. McCollough, "Can Analysts Distinguish Between Real and Randomly Generated Stock Prices," *Financial Analysts Journal*, November to December 1978.

17. For an excellent study of apocalyptic behavior, see Leon Festinger, *When Prophecy Fails.* See also P. Boyer, *When Time Shall Be No More: Prophecy Belief in Modern American Culture*, Belknap/Harvard University Press, 1992.

18. G. Niebuhr, "On the Horizon, Apocalypse Dates Still Being Set by Prophets of Doom," *Washington Post*, March 4, 1993; "Church of doom meets bitter end," *South China Morning Post*, November 2, 1992.

19. M. Yamaguchi, "Dateline Tokyo: Fears Grow Over 'Messiah,'" *South China Morning Post*, October 18, 1992.

20. J. Bone, "Experts predicting repeat of tragedy," *South China Morning Post*, April 22, 1993.

Chapter 12

The Coming
Mutual Fund Debacle

If making money is a slow process, losing it is quickly done.
— Ihara Saikaku —

One of the central themes of this book is the danger to your financial well-being created by oil and war, and various prospective upheavals in world investment markets. But there are other dangers as well. Some of them have nothing to do with the financial fallout from events in far away places. Some of them are, in fact, unique to a particular investment vehicle.

For example, most investors are aware of the risks associated with futures contracts—where you can actually lose more than 100% of your initial investment. What you may not be aware of are the hidden risks of the most popular investment vehicles of the 1990s: unit trusts and mutual funds.

In the crash of 1929 and in the U.S. bear market of 1973-74, people who bought mutual funds and unit trusts were hurt worse than just about any other class of stock market investor. Much the same thing also happened during the two-year period ending in December after the crash of 1987.

Ironically, one of the original aims of the modern fund industry was to lower investment risk through diversification. By pooling the capital of many like-minded investors, mutual funds could offer individuals a share of a portfolio larger and better diversified than they could ever hope to amass on their own.

But mere diversification is yesterday's mutual fund product. Today's crop of speculative new funds—the industry funds, the sector funds, the funds that invest only in certain geographical areas—are all selling something else and have abandoned mere diversification to distinguish themselves from the competition.

179

At one time, mutual funds may properly have been regarded as safe "buy-'em-and-forget-'em" investments. But that time is long gone—if indeed it ever existed. The crash of 1987 may be past, but the danger lingers. Now, more than ever, it is important to know how to steer clear of the quicksand.

For the sake of clarification, I will identify five threats to mutual fund profits that are widely unrecognized by the investing public. Two of them are never mentioned in any mutual fund prospectus.

One of them hangs over the entire stock market like the proverbial Sword of Damocles. Although the fund industry itself is not eager to discuss this, the truth is that there is a growing possibility that the funds themselves could easily trigger the next stock market crash.

I will also show you how you can use these insights to protect yourself and your investments. The analysis that follows focuses mainly on the American mutual fund industry as an example. But what's true of American funds also applies in varying degrees to funds registered in other financial centers—such as London and Hong Kong.

Bull market in mutual funds

With all the attention focused on the stock market, it's easy to lose sight of the fact that the world mutual fund industry has been in a bull market all its own. Take the United States, for example.

From the mid-1980s to the early 1990s, mutual fund assets grew faster than at any other time in American stock market history. The formation of new mutual funds also hit a near-record pace.

This extraordinary growth is a fairly recent phenomenon. During the first three-and-a-half decades following World War II, the increase in the number of funds was very modest. But all that changed with the surging inflation and sky-high interest rates of the late 1970s.

Prior to this time, the major savings vehicle for most Americans was the passbook savings account. But the rate of return on passbook accounts was fixed by law at 5.25%. With inflation roaring along at 15%, passbook savers weren't saving at all. In real terms, they were losing 10% a year!

Fortunately, the mutual fund industry came to the rescue. In the early 1980s, money market funds appeared. By pooling the assets of hundreds of small investors, they allowed each to earn the going rate of return in the nation's inter-bank money markets.

In a few years, money-market mutual funds were selling like hotcakes. Hundreds of new funds were created to meet investor demand. And the growth in the number of funds began its long acceleration through the present day.

The fund debacle of 1929

By any reckoning, 1929 was an epic year for investment funds as well as the U.S. stock market. The Dow opened at 300 on the morning of January 2 and rose 17 points on the first trading day of the year. The market remained essentially confined to a fairly narrow trading range between 300 and 320 until summer.

But in the midst of what should have been the summer doldrums, when brokers go on vacation and investors go to the beach, the market suddenly exploded. Soon every morning paper was full of stories on the previous day's record close.

Investors discovered that lazy days in the summer sun could scarcely compare with the excitement of following the market. The words of noted stock market observer Robert Nicholson aptly describe the character of those incredible months before the crash: "It was a time when every barber shop had a ticker ... and a flapper with a broker was the cat's meow."[1]

Black Thursday

On the morning of October 24, 1929, the New York Stock Exchange mustered its newly expanded corps of employees to handle the heavy margin and sell orders that had been placed overnight. Prices at the opening bell were steady, but then the backlog of sell orders hit.

By 10:30 a.m., there was pandemonium on the floor, and the tape was running 16 minutes late. Prices dropped $5 and $10 at a clip, and there were no bids at all for many less actively traded issues.

As news of the disaster spread outside the exchange, the streets of the financial district were in an uproar. With reports from the trading floor lagging farther and farther behind events, anxious investors descended on the exchange to see for themselves. For the vast majority of investors, it was the beginning of a financial nightmare.

The headline in the *New York Times* the following Monday read, "Stock Prices Slump $14,000,000 in Nationwide Stampede to Unload." Three weeks later, the Dow stood at 198.69—down 49% from its 1929 high. However, the worst was still to come. In July of 1932, the Dow hit 41.22.

Carnage among the funds

No company or industry was spared the devastation of the crash or the stomach-churning decline that followed in the next several years. Financial stocks suffered the worst, and among them, investment trusts were hardest hit.

Leading U.S. Investment Trusts 1929-1932[2]

Trust	Market Price as % of Book Value at 1929 High	1929 Low as % of 1929 High	Market Price as % of Book Value at 1932 Low	1932 Low as % of 1929 High
Goldman Sachs	295	2	17	1
Lehman Corp.	149	46	53	23
Tri-Continental	356	18	na	3
United Corp.	205	25	11	3
United Founders	245	33	42	na

The funds of the 1920s and 1930s were closed-end funds. Unlike open-end funds, which appeared later, a closed-end fund does not stand by ready to redeem shares on investor demand. Instead, a fixed number of shares is issued. Thereafter, shares in the fund trade on an exchange just like any other stock.

Approximately 1,200 investment companies were created in the 1920s and early 1930s. By 1936, approximately 600 had disappeared as a result of dissolution, merger, or bankruptcy—a failure rate of 50%.

While a bear market imposes losses on all stockholders, too often fund investors seem to get hurt worse than anyone else. This is an investment risk you will never read about in any investment company prospectus.

Let's examine why this has been the case. One reason for the fund debacle of 1929 was that fund managers embraced an ancient temptation: reckless use of leverage. Leverage is the first of the five threats to your fund investments.

Greasing the skids with borrowed money

Most investors today are familiar with the practice of buying stocks on margin. That simply means you borrow money from your broker to buy stocks for your portfolio. Let's take a quick look at a hypothetical example to see how this exaggerates both gains and losses.

Suppose you are interested in 100 shares of an alpine grain producer, Ethereal Cereals, which currently sells for US$20 a share. A 100-share investment would cost you US$2,000. If

182

the stock moves US$1, the change in the value of your portfolio is US$100 (100 shares x US$1). On a US$2,000 investment, that amounts to a 5% (US$100/US$2,000) gain or loss.

Now suppose you buy the stock on margin. Let's say you put up US$1,000 and borrow US$1,000 from your broker. If the stock moves US$1, you still have a US$100 change in the value of your portfolio. But on the basis of only a US$1,000 initial investment, that means a gain or loss of 10% (US$100/US$1,000).

Double your margin, double your fun

In this case, borrowing half your initial investment effectively doubled your rate of return. But if the stock had moved down, it also would have doubled the rate of your loss. Many investment companies of 1929 did exactly the same thing. They raised money from the public to buy stocks, and then they borrowed money to buy more.

Leverage was also achieved in other ways. Goldman, Sachs & Company, for example, created its first investment company, Goldman Sachs Trading Corp., in 1928. During the height of the new-issues craze in July 1929, the company created a second investment company, the Shenandoah Corporation.

Goldman Sachs Trading Corp. (along with Central States Electric Co.) sponsored the new issue and retained 80% of its common stock. Having discovered a good thing, they tried it again a month later.

In August 1929, they created a third investment trust, Blue Ridge Corp. This time, Shenandoah retained 80% of the common stock issued.

Here is a case in which one investment company issued stock in a second, which in turn issued stock in a third. Blue Ridge raised approximately US$100 million in both common and preference stock. Guess what stock the fund bought with the public's money? One of their largest holdings was Central States Electric, co-sponsor of the previous new issue!

The net result of these practices was to create a corporate pyramid as highly leveraged as if it had all been bought with borrowed money (which, in a sense, it had been!).

In 1929, the president of Goldman Sachs, Waddill Catchings, wrote a book called *The Road to Plenty*, in which he explained to the public his method for achieving and preserving prosperity. Anyone who took his advice soon found out that this particular road was a two-way street.

The lure of larceny

Another reason for the 1929 investment company debacle was flagrant conflicts of interest. Fund managers frequently "borrowed" fund assets for their personal use. After the 1937 bankruptcy of the Continental Securities Co., several officers were tried for larceny—they had plundered US$3.25 million from the investment company portfolio.

Other fraudulent practices included using the fund's money as a vehicle for stock market manipulation and dumping (buying the leftover stock from failed public offerings at inflated prices). In effect, the fund was used as a dumping ground for issues that could not be sold to anyone else.

Alarmed by the growing number of complaints received by his fraud division, the Attorney General of New York, John J. Bennet Jr., ordered an investigation of investment companies within his jurisdiction. In a report to the state legislature, he revealed that half the 100 companies examined had engaged in dumping.[3]

Further public indignation fell on the aggressive promoters of investment trusts, many of whom made fortunes despite the funds' dismal performances. Larceny, fraud, and questionable promotion tactics constitute the second major threat to your mutual fund investments.

Birth of regulation

In due course, U.S. congressional investigations led to new securities legislation. The Securities Act of 1933 established the S.E.C. It also required "full and fair" disclosure of all information relevant to newly issued securities. The Revenue Act of 1936 established the special tax status of investment companies that distribute 90% of their dividends and capital gains to shareholders.

Seven years later, the Investment Company Act of 1940 codified standards for formation, capital structure, management, and underwriting of "regulated investment companies." This is the legislation that, along with its several amendments, established the modern American mutual fund industry.

How much has changed since 1929?

To be sure, a half-century's worth of securities legislation has left its mark upon the mutual fund industry. Since World War II, most new investment companies have been organized as open-end funds. In fact, the term "mutual fund" has become practically synonymous with open-end funds. Only in the last few years have their closed-end cousins started to emerge from relative obscurity.

Funds today still find ways to leverage their returns. Some are permitted to buy on margin, others indulge in the newest highly leveraged instruments of the present era: futures and options. The important difference today is not that leverage is less widely used than it was in 1929. Rather, it is that the use of leverage is more openly disclosed.

Whether or not a fund may use these techniques must now be clearly stated in the prospectus. At least theoretically, any changes to the investment rules as declared in the prospectus require the approval of a majority of the fund's shareholders. Clearly this is a step forward. But it means that the burden is on the individual investor to take responsibility for keeping up with what fund managers are doing.

Lower incidence of fraud

By just about any measure, the incidence of U.S. investment fraud is lower now than it was in 1929. This is not because mutual fund managers are more virtuous than they used to be, but only because stringent disclosure requirements have made it more difficult to conceal fraudulent acts.

For a clearer picture of just how much things have changed since 1929 (and how much they have not!), let's look at another more recent cycle of stock market boom and bust.

Debacle of 1968–1974

One common characteristic of speculative stock market bubbles is a simple vision of instant wealth. In 1929, everyone was going to get rich on steel and utility stocks. In 1961, everyone was going to get rich on electronics stocks. Like 1929, 1961 saw a flood of new issues.

The 1960s mania started innocently enough when a number of technology issues began to do spectacularly well. For example, investors who bought shares in Control Data when it was first issued in 1958 watched their holdings appreciate 120% by 1961. Shares in Litton Industries, to cite another example, increased fiftyfold during nearly the same period.

Intoxicated by the prospect of profit on such a scale, investors began to seize anything that sounded electronic or scientific. Soon a flock of new issues appeared to satisfy the public's demand for companies with names ending in "onics" or "tron."

Underwriting new securities suddenly became a land-office

business. "Why go broke? Go public!" became the joke along the corridors of Wall Street.

New-issue orgy

A company named Dynatronics issued its first stock offering at US$7 a share. Within days it was trading at US$25. Simulmatics, a company with a *negative* net worth of US$21,000, went public at US$2 and rose almost instantly to US$9.

The boom in electronics and technology companies cooled off in late 1961. But by 1967, it was back again in force. This time the highflyers included a number of now familiar names—IBM, Texas Instruments, Xerox, and Polaroid.

Mutual fund managers were now ready to get in on the act. By the mid-1960s, a generation of mutual fund managers had appeared with no real memory of 1929. Dubbed "gunslingers" by the financial press, these were members of a new breed of financial swashbucklers—men such as Fred Carr, Gerald Tsai, Fred Mates, and Fred Alger.

Go-go funds

Tsai was one of the earliest pioneers of what later became known as the "go-go" style of mutual fund investing. Go-go investing simply meant an aggressive, short-term-oriented trading strategy. At the time, this kind of fast, in-and-out trading was new to mutual funds. Using these methods, Tsai achieved annual returns of more than 65% for the Fidelity Growth Fund in the mid-1960s—three to five times the gain of the Standard & Poor's 500 Stock Index.

Sensing that he was on to a good thing, Tsai quit Fidelity to go into business for himself. In 1967 he started the Manhattan Fund, which more than doubled the 20% rise in market averages that year. Despite this superb record, within less than a year, more money was flowing out of the Manhattan Fund than was coming in.

The reason was simple. It didn't require any special genius to pick stock market winners in the overheated stock market climate of the late 1960s. Virtually any company with a story to tell and a technical-sounding name was enthusiastically bid up by investors.

Even the executives of these corporations were themselves bewildered when their company's stock soared for no apparent reason. One company president, when asked to explain the surge in the company's stock at the annual shareholders meeting, simply shrugged and said, "God has been good to Solitron Devices."[4]

186

Managers of rival funds quickly caught on and were soon beating Tsai at his own game. Fred Carr's Enterprise Fund was up 116% in 1967. Fred Mates' Mates Fund was up an astounding 158%. Why should anyone be satisfied with the Manhattan Fund's paltry 40% when gains such as those were available?

Amid the speculative fervor of the times, big money flowed to mutual fund managers who could post higher quarterly performance figures than their rivals. Before long, many were unable to resist the temptation of financial chicanery.

One favorite tactic was to cash in on new issues. Because go-go investing meant turning over every stock in the portfolio several times a year, the gunslingers generated enormous brokerage commissions. Some clever fund managers dangled their sizable commission business before the underwriters of new issues.

A typical arrangement worked something like this. In exchange for the fund's commission business, the underwriter would agree to sell large blocks of hot new issues to the fund at the issue price. As soon as the initial public offering was completed, many of these new issues immediately went to substantial premiums in the secondary market—thus generating instant profits for the fund.

Market price manipulation

Another tactic was to pour money into thinly traded issues. In many cases, the weight of the fund's buying power alone was sufficient to raise the stock 20%, 30%, or more. These holdings were then listed on the fund's books at the most recent—and higher—market price. This is the third threat to your mutual fund investments.

Profits such as these amounted to little more than accounting fiction. If the fund attempted to actually realize the trading gains listed on its quarterly report, it would find almost no one else to sell to. This is because the fund's selling would drive the price down as fast or faster than buying the stock had pushed it up.

Letter stock roulette

Finally, there was a whole new game going on with restricted securities, or so-called "letter stock" purchased directly from the company by a major investor according to the terms of a private agreement. Because such stock is never publicly offered, it allows both buyer and seller to circumvent the disclosure of all new public issues required by the S.E.C. This is the fourth threat to your mutual fund investments.

A typical arrangement works like this. A company in need of some quick capital issues letter stock to a mutual fund at a substantial discount (usually 30% to 50%) to the market value of the firm's comparable publicly traded securities. The fund agrees to hold the stock for some minimum period—usually two or three years.

This amounts to a very cozy arrangement. The company gets fresh capital on better terms than it could get from banks or bondholders. The mutual fund gets a discounted security, which it immediately revalues on its books at the market price for the firm's comparable publicly traded securities. Another source of instant profit!

World Cup of restricted securities

Testimony before the U.S. House of Representatives Committee on Interstate and Foreign Commerce detailed Fred Carr's mastery of this particular technique:

On March 27, 1967, the Enterprise Fund paid US$316,000 for Bell Electronics convertible debentures. Its March 31 report listed the value of those debentures at US$444,744—a 40% gain in four days.

On May 1, the fund bought 100,000 shares of Texas American Oil Co. at US$5.52 per share. The fund's June 30 report up-valued the shares 38%, to US$7.63 each.

On June 28, Enterprise paid US$743,000 for 50,000 shares of Wellington Electronics and up-valued them to US$1,263,938 in its June 30 report—an appreciation of 59%, one-third of a million dollars, in 48 hours.

On Dec. 22, the fund bought 80,000 shares of AITS for US$2,081,000 and put a value of US$2,718,000 on those shares in its Dec. 31 report six business days later—an increase of 30.6%.

On Dec. 22, Enterprise bought 21,000 shares of Larsen Industries for US$2,101,000 and valued them five days later at US$2,473,000—an 18% increase.[5]

Every time a quarterly report came due, Mr. Carr added a little something extra to boost his performance figures. It's no wonder the Enterprise Fund had a good year—at least according to the numbers!

In 1969 the S.E.C. filed charges against Fred Mates for representing to shareholders that the Mates Fund would not deal in restricted securities, when in fact the fund had substantial letter-stock holdings in its portfolio.

What happened to the high flyers when the bulls ran out of steam and the market turned south? Well, the Enterprise Fund went from a net asset value of US$11.88 in 1968 to US$3.84 in 1974—a decline of 68%. The Mates Investment Fund went from a net asset value of US$15.51 in 1968 to US$1.12 in 1974—a 93% decline.

In fact, the glory of 1968 was short-lived indeed. Only three of the top 20 funds in 1968 managed to finish in the top 20 again in any of the following five years. Only one of the 20—the Templeton Growth Fund—managed to post an increase in net asset value (N.A.V.).

The 19 Top Performing Mutual Funds of 1968[6]

Fund	1968 Rank	1969 Rank	1970 Rank	1971 Rank	1972 Rank	1973 Rank	1974 Rank	1968 NAV	1974 NAV	Change in NAV
Mates Investment	1	312	424	512	465	531	400	15.51	1.12	-93%
Neuwirth Fund	2	263	360	104	477	397	232	15.29	6.24	-59%
Gibralter Growth	3	172	456	481	na	na	na	17.27	na	na
Insurance Investors	4	77	106	317	417	224	na	7.45	na	na
Pennsylvania Mutual	5	333	459	480	486	519	521	11.92	1.09	-91%
Puerto Rican Invest.	6	30	308	387	435	na	na	19.32	na	na
Crown Western-Dallas	7	283	438	207	244	330	133	13.86	4.66	-66%
Franklin Dynatech	8	342	363	112	120	453	453	14.47	4.56	-68%
First Participating	9	49	283	106	27	220	310	19.25	13.47	-30%
Connecticut Western	10	5	202	na	na	na	na	127.27	na	na
Enterprise Fund	11	334	397	133	364	250	416	11.88	3.84	-68%
Ivy Fund	12	357	293	233	161	312	443	12.37	4.58	-63%
Century Shares	13	120	55	62	62	127	428	13.09	8.48	-35%
Mutual Shares	14	284	272	152	452	62	4	22.18	15.44	-30%
Putnam Equities	15	376	384	45	54	354	211	17.05	6.42	-62%
Fin. Indust. Income	16	244	222	277	231	35	90	8.40	4.73	-44%
Consumers Invest.	17	354	na	na	na	na	na	6.21	na	na
Columbia Growth	18	33	322	27	370	332	253	14.23	9.05	-36%
Templeton Growth	19	1	241	163	1	81	84	4.00	6.23	56%
Shuster Fund	20	129	231	253	425	445	434	12.29	4.86	60%

Fund investors clobbered again

Consecutive annual declines of 15% and 26% in the stock market[7] made the bear market of 1973-74 the worst two-year period since 1930-31. And just like the 1929-32 period, mutual fund investors got hurt worse than just about anyone else.

The Investment Company Institute (I.C.I.), the Washington, D.C.–based trade association, has compiled industry-wide performance figures from 1970 to the present. According to the I.C.I.'s weighted equity mutual fund index, the average fund lost 19.2% between 1970 and 1974. That's significantly worse than the 14.6% decline in the stock market as a whole.

Performance this poor did not go unnoticed by the investment public. After years of pouring more money into mutual funds, the public abruptly began pulling its money out. I.C.I. figures reveal that the money started pouring out of mutual funds in 1972 and continued without interruption for a record seven consecutive years.

Trigger of a coming crash

One long-time market observer, noted U.S. money manager Charles Allmon, has suggested that the mutual fund industry was responsible for making the bear market of 1973-74 deeper and more prolonged than it would have been otherwise.

The first premise of this school of thought is that investors are often stampeded by emotions—usually fear or greed. This is often the case among inexperienced investors who have never been through a market downturn before.

That is one reason why the recent surge in fund growth is so worrisome. It suggests that the universe of first-time investors is getting larger with every passing year.

Because open-end mutual funds now compose such a large segment of the market, they cannot hope to escape any sudden wave of selling. Open-end funds, remember, are required to redeem shares on demand.

So unless fund managers keep large amounts of cash on hand to meet them, they have no practical alternative but to sell off some of their holdings to raise cash.

Whenever the stock market takes a tumble, a run on the funds can easily develop, as investors scramble to get their money out. This leads to a round of forced selling, as hard-pressed fund managers scramble to raise cash to pay off panicky shareholders.

If fund mangers are forced to sell into a declining market, the net asset values of the funds themselves will also take a beating. And falling net asset values could easily worsen investor panic—and trigger additional waves of redemption demands.

In the right circumstances, this could easily result in a self-intensifying rush to convert securities into cash. And that, of course, is a textbook definition of a stock market crash. This is the fifth and final threat to the mutual fund investor.

The graph below shows the net inflow of funds to American mutual funds. Note how closely it tracks the Dow Jones Industrial Average. It doesn't take much imagination to guess what might happen to stock prices if this flow suddenly reversed.

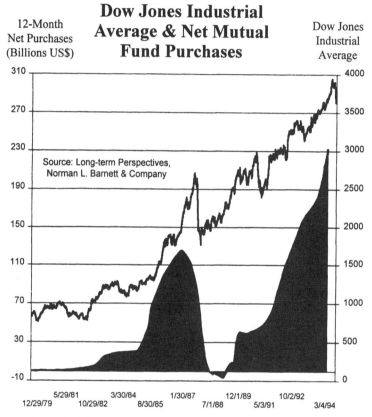

Dow Jones Industrial Average & Net Mutual Fund Purchases

12-Month Net Purchases (Billions US$)

Dow Jones Industrial Average

Source: Long-term Perspectives, Norman L. Barnett & Company

Fund holdings have grown so large that if something happened to spook a significant fraction of first-time investors, they could easily touch off the worst self-intensifying rush to catastrophe in stock market history.

In truth, the market-moving power of funds is not new. As far back as 1967, S.E.C. Commissioner Hugh F. Owens noted two instances in which fund selling had contributed to extraordinary declines in individual securities.[8] In both instances, stocks that had suddenly fallen out of favor with the funds declined 8% and

191

16% in a single trading session. In the first instance, mutual funds accounted for 44.7% of the selling volume; in the second instance, they accounted for 43.5%.

In both 1987 and 1994, the price-bashing power of mutual fund redemptions was felt in a minor way in the bond market. In both cases, U.S. interest rates reversed a multi-year downtrend and abruptly turned up. Among the first to get burned were investors in fixed-income or bond funds. (Remember, as interest rates rise, the value of bonds declines, and vice versa.)

In both cases, lots of bond-fund shareholders were inexperienced, first-time investors. They remembered with great fondness the double-digit yields they had earned on their money-market funds in the late 1970s and early 1980s.

And they were naive enough to be persuaded by aggressive brokers and mutual fund promoters that bond funds were a "safe" alternative to recently disappointing money-market and fixed-deposit yields.

As long as interest rates kept going down, of course, they did fine. But when rates suddenly began to rise, they saw the net asset values of their funds plunge. And a bunch of them all wanted to cash out at the same time.

When enough disappointed shareholders start calling their funds and demanding their money, managers of open-end funds have no practical choice but to start liquidating their portfolios. Most bonds are traded over the counter in markets that are rather thin even in less chaotic times.

So it usually doesn't take too much selling before the spread between bid and ask prices hits new highs. For some issues there may be no bids at all. Factors such as these helped make the decline in the net asset values worse than they would otherwise be.

In 1987, this bond fund debacle helped set the stage for the crash of 1987 a few months later. Whether something similar lies ahead sometime in 1994 or 1995, of course, remains to be seen.

Defending against financial catastrophe

I hope by now I have been able to convince you that mutual fund investments are not as safe as commonly thought. If there is a lesson to be learned from the last 60 years of mutual fund history, it is that failure to look beyond mere appearances can easily lead to financial ruin. Let's re-examine each of the five threats to mutual fund investments to see what you can do to head off any unhappy surprises.

Leverage

As mentioned earlier, a fund's use of margin, or leveraged instruments such as futures and options, must be disclosed in the fund's prospectus. Be sure to read all the fine print before you invest. In addition to the prospectus, the fund's statement of additional information should also be required reading.

Once you understand what the fund's investment rules are, be alert for any effort on the part of management to change them. This may mean going to the annual meeting to speak against any changes that increase the risk to shareholders. It certainly means taking the time to read your proxy materials carefully and voting accordingly. If all else fails, you can always sell your shares.

Fraud

Without a doubt, regulation and surveillance by the S.E.C. has decreased the incidence of mutual fund fraud. Nonetheless, there is never any shortage of rogues and rascals out to make a quick killing for themselves with your money. And occasionally one will slip through the cracks.

Perhaps the best defense against mutual fund fraud is to deal only with well-established, reputable investment companies. Or as the title of a frequently requested S.E.C. publication urges: "Investigate Before You Invest."

Thinly traded issues

Whether or not a fund is trying to inflate its paper profits by dealing in thinly traded securities is an especially difficult matter to evaluate. Sometimes the investment rules stated in the prospectus limit the fund's investment in any one company to a certain percentage of that company's market capitalization. Such a provision may make price manipulation of thinly traded securities more difficult, but it is scarcely any guarantee.

There is no law that prohibits a fund from buying obscure or thinly traded stocks. Furthermore, there are whole classes of funds with legitimate interests in such stocks. Small-company funds and emerging-growth funds, for example, regularly comb the universe of obscure stocks in their search for the next IBM or the next McDonald's.

If you're in such a fund, you'll just have to trust the investment manager. Make sure the fund is reputable and well-established, and limit your investment to 20% or less of your total portfolio. That way, even if you make a bad choice, you will still survive.

Restricted issues and letter stock

There is no law against a fund's participation in restricted issues. But there is a law against failing to disclose the practice in the prospectus. So read the fine print and be alert.

Redemptions and bear markets

The last and perhaps most insidious threat to your mutual fund investment is the possibility that mutual fund redemptions might set off another self-intensifying wave of liquidations.

Of course, one way to avoid such a debacle is to sell your shares before the next bear market hits. But as any experienced investor can attest, this is easier said than done.

You can, however, do a couple of things on your own. One is to stay abreast of mutual fund redemptions. These figures are reported monthly in *Barron's,* the American financial weekly. They are also available from the Investment Company Institute, 1600 M Street N.W., Washington, D.C. 20036.

Similar figures are gathered by the Hong Kong Investment Funds Association, 25/F Jardine House, 1 Connaught Place, Hong Kong, and the British Association of Unit Trusts and Investment Funds, 65 Kingsway, London, WC2B 6TD, UK.

The American mutual fund industry as a whole hasn't had a year of net redemptions since 1979. But sooner or later, this explosive period of expansion in mutual fund assets will come to an end.

When you start to see more money flowing out than is flowing in, it's time to be on your guard. A sustained period of net redemptions will eventually force fund managers to begin liquidating their portfolios.

Closed-end protection

One way to reduce the danger of being caught up in a mutual fund bear market is to avoid open-end funds entirely and to limit yourself to closed-end funds. Closed-end funds, remember, have no obligation to redeem shares on demand and therefore are immune to the danger of forced liquidation. The universe of closed-end funds is much smaller than that of open-end funds, and selection is somewhat limited. But this is starting to change. More and more closed-end funds are now being launched as investors become increasingly aware of the risks associated with conventional open-end funds.

Before you go plunging into closed-end funds in a big way, however, let me add a word of caution.

Never buy a closed-end fund at an initial public offering. Usually the underwriter takes his fee out of the money raised from the public in such an offering. That means that only a portion of the money you put up is actually ever invested. If you wait until the fund starts trading in the secondary market—and then buy it—you avoid having to contribute to the underwriter's profits.

If you wait a little longer, you may get an even better deal. History shows that almost all closed-end funds sell at a discount to net asset value sometime in the first year or so after they are issued. (Unlike open-end funds, closed-end funds may trade at prices either above or below net asset value.)

By buying them at a discount, you can effectively purchase shares at 85 cents or 90 cents on the dollar (assuming a 15% or 10% discount to net asset value). That's a lot better than the US$1.10 or US$1.15 you'd pay for a dollar's worth of stock if you bought at the initial public offering.

False security and toll-free busy signals

Many mutual fund families offer telephone-switching facilities that promise that you can cash in your chips on a moment's notice. Beware of the false sense of security that sometimes comes with telephone-switch privileges. Some of the worst horror stories from the crash of 1987 concerned toll-free numbers that suddenly turned into toll-free busy signals.

The sheer human dimension of the stock market tragedy that unfolded in October 1987 came home to me in the hundreds of telephone conversations I had with readers of my newsletter. One called me late at night three or four days after the crash and told me how he had stayed home from work to telephone sell orders to his mutual funds. All day he had sat by the phone, dialing. And not once did he get through. Meanwhile, the market was falling farther with every passing minute. "It was like being caught in a burning building," he said, "with no way out."

There are a couple of things you can do to avoid a catastrophe such as this the next time the market goes into a tailspin. One is to let a broker handle your mutual fund trades. Most U.S. brokers are accustomed to handling load fund transactions for their clients. More recently, Charles Schwab Discount Brokers has begun handling no-load fund transactions.

Chances are, your broker can get through to your mutual funds even if you can't. But there may still be a catch: During the panic that followed Black Monday in 1987, a lot of people had trouble even getting through to their brokers.

To guard against this possibility, I recommend you find out the location of your broker's nearest office. If you can't get through on the phone, you can always show up in person. Another possibility is to arrange for your broker to accept instructions by telegram. Whatever you do, don't rely on a facsimile number. If you can't get through by phone, chances are you won't be able to get through by fax either.

You can also take steps to ensure that you can deal directly with your fund. Find out the location of the nearest office. Some of the larger fund families maintain branch offices in several major cities. Assemble in advance all the necessary documents (including signature guarantees and whatever else your fund may require) to liquidate your holdings. Then you can deliver them yourself. Or if all else fails, you can dispatch them by overnight express mail.

Of course, the ideal solution would be to arrange redemption by telegram. If your fund offers such privileges, be sure to make arrangements in advance.

Remember, a crash is a crash because very few people are able to see it coming, and once it hits even fewer are able to react quickly enough to escape without damage. But with proper planning, attention to detail, and a healthy regard for the risks, you need not be among those caught up in the next mutual fund debacle.

---

1. Robert Nicholson in a speech delivered before a meeting of Investment Seminars International Inc. in Fort Lauderdale, FL, January 1984.

2. B. A. Wigmore, *The Crash and Its Aftermath: A History of Securities Markets in the United States 1929-1933.*

3. D. Palance, *Mutual Funds...Legal Pickpockets?*, p. 53.

4. Quoted by D. A. Dreman, "Psychology and Markets" in *Readings in Investment Management.*

5. Testimony before the House Committee on Interstate and Foreign Commerce, quoted by J. L. Springer, *The Mutual Fund Trap*, p. 141.

6. Lipper Analytical Division, Lipper Analytical Services Inc., quoted by B. G. Malkiel, *A Random Walk Down Wall Street*, p. 166-167.

7. Declines calculated on the basis of the "Total Return on Common Stocks Series," part of the *Index of Year-End Cumulative Wealth 1925-1986* compiled by R. G. Ibbotson and R. A. Singuefield, *Dow Jones-Irwin Business and Investment Almanac 1987.*

8. Speech by SEC Commissioner Hugh F. Owens delivered before a group of investment bankers in 1967, quoted by D. Palance, *op. cit.*, p. 132.

Chapter 13

Age War 2011

A Survivor's Handbook

Youth loves honor and victory more than money ... for it has not yet learned what the lack of money means.
— Aristotle, *Rhetoric, Book II* —

I feel the earth move under my feet. I see the sky come tumbling down.
— Carole King —

Despite the many upheavals since the story of oil and war began in the early years of this century, one thing has remained constant: the age-related composition of the countries we now regard as the developed world.

Throughout history, the young have always outnumbered the old by a vast margin. That this would always be true was taken as a commonplace of human existence.

Today, however, we stand on the threshold of a demographic revolution unprecedented in human affairs. Much of the future will forever remain mysterious, but this much is already written: More of us are growing old together than ever before.

In Chapter 8, we observed that the aging of Japan virtually guaranteed that Japanese pension fund investments would be a market-moving force in world bourses throughout the 1990s. By the year 2000, Japan will have the largest percentage of elderly among all developed nations. But other places are also aging rapidly, including all of North America and most of Western Europe.

The following chart shows countries in order of the largest percentage of elderly by the year 2000.[1]

	Over 65 1991	Over 65 2000
Japan	17.2%	23.7%
Greece	14.3%	18.0%
Italy	15.0%	17.6%
Sweden	17.9%	17.4%
Belgium	15.1%	17.0%
Germany	15.1%	16.7%
Spain	13.7%	16.5%
Switzerland	14.7%	16.0%
U.K.	15.7%	16.0%
France	14.3%	15.9%
Norway	16.3%	15.4%
Portugal	13.4%	15.3%
Finland	13.6%	15.1%
Netherlands	13.0%	14.3%
Canada	11.7%	13.1%
United States	12.7%	13.0%
New Zealand	11.3%	12.5%
Ireland	11.6%	12.3%
Australia	11.3%	12.1%
Singapore	5.8%	7.4%
South Korea	5.0%	6.8%

It would be hard to imagine a more profound shift in the ground upon which modern society has been built. One result will be that those who are not alert enough to prepare for the increasingly obvious will suffer serious financial losses.

Another will be civil strife on such a scale that it will threaten the very existence of the welfare state—if not democratic society itself. I predict an age war in 2011.

Note that 2011 is 1946 plus 65. In other words, it is the year that the first members of the more than 100 million strong post-World War II generation will reach retirement age. It is also the year in which the same retirement benefits they helped fund for their parents' generation are likely to be abruptly withdrawn from them.

When a few thousand people share an opinion or buy a product, it may amount to a curiosity or even a trend. But when

100 million do so, it's a revolution. This time, the revolution will shake the developed world to its foundations—as an age war breaks out between the generations.

The issue will be who will benefit and who will pay, and the early battle lines are already being drawn. And in some countries, the opening skirmishes are already being fought.

If you were born between 1946 and 1964 and aspire to a comfortable and leisurely retirement, chances are you are a member of a doomed generation. But even if you are already in your 50s or 60s, you will still be the victim of reduced benefits.

Retirement will be neither comfortable nor leisurely. In fact, it may not even be possible.

But unlike the typical disaster, which strikes without warning, this one is absolutely predictable. It is a crisis on a timetable. That is because it is the inescapable result of three demographic trends with precedents in modern times.

Three demographic trends

The first of these trends, as we have noted, is the aging of the baby-boom generation, the numbers of which account for fully one-third of the population of North America, and large proportions of the populations of Western Europe and Japan. The sheer size of the postwar generation has made it a society-transforming influence at every turn.

The second trend is the rapidly increasing number of senior citizens. Since 1900, the average life expectancy has increased by 28 years. *Two-thirds of all the men and women who have lived beyond the age of 65 in the entire history of the human race are alive today.*

Because of continuing advances in health care, older folks are also healthier and more active than any other older generation in history. Japan is perhaps the most dramatic example of this phenomenon. As the Japanese have grown richer, their life expectancy overtook that of Americans in 1982. Even today, it continues to lengthen.

As recently as 1990, 11% of the Japanese were 65 and above. On this basis, Japan was younger than either the United States or Western Europe. But by 2010, the fraction of Japanese 65 or older will be 18%—making Japan the oldest developed country on earth.

There have been many baby booms throughout the course of human events. But never before has there been an elder boom.

The third trend is the so-called "birth dearth." In 1986, for example, the fertility of American women (defined as the number of children each woman would have in her life if the present rate of birth continued) declined to 1.8.

That's less than half the rate of their mothers, 27% lower than the rate in 1970, and less than one-fourth the rate in 1900. In fact, it's the lowest fertility rate ever recorded in the United States.

The replacement fertility rate is approximately 2.1. So for every country after Ireland in the listing below, the rising number of elderly is not being offset by increasing numbers of children. Moreover, this is likely to continue to be the case through the year 2000.[2]

Forecast	Fertility 1991	Fertility 2000
Cambodia	4.7	4.4
Philippines	4.3	3.9
Vietnam	4.1	3.7
Myanmar	4.0	3.7
Malaysia	4.0	3.6
Indonesia	3.5	3.1
Thailand	2.6	2.2
China	2.5	2.3
Ireland	2.1	1.8
Singapore	2.0	1.8
New Zealand	1.9	1.8
Sweden	1.9	1.8
Norway	1.8	1.8
U.K.	1.8	1.8
France	1.8	1.8
Australia	1.8	1.8
U.S.	1.8	1.8
Finland	1.7	1.7
Canada	1.7	1.7
Netherlands	1.6	1.6
Belgium	1.6	1.6
S. Korea	1.6	1.5
Japan	1.6	1.6
Switzerland	1.6	1.6
Portugal	1.5	1.5
Greece	1.5	1.6
Spain	1.5	1.5
Italy	1.4	1.5
Hong Kong	1.4	1.4
Germany	1.4	1.6

Explosive effects

These three demographic trends will have a number of profound consequences. Taken together, they add up to an extremely explosive mix.[3]

1) An aging society. Lengthening life expectancy and the birth of fewer children add up to an increasingly aging society. The South Korean government, for example, has publicly expressed alarm that the ratio of elderly (over 65) to juveniles (under 14) increased from 7.2% in the 1970s to 11.2% in 1980. By the late 1990s, it will be 19.4%.[4]

In Singapore, the fertility rate dropped from 4.7 in 1975 to 2.1 in the mid-1990s. If nothing were done, by 2030, there would be only two young persons for every senior citizen. As a consequence, the government completely reversed its previous emphasis on birth control. The old slogan "Stop at Two" has been officially replaced with "Go for Three."

In order to leave nothing to chance, the government also organized what may be the world's first taxpayer supported matchmaking and dating service: the ingenuously titled "Social Development Unit."

In the United States, the number of citizens over 65 surpassed the number of teenagers for the first time in July 1983. By 2025, seniors over 65 will outnumber teenagers by a ratio of 2 to 1.

In countries that are aging even faster than the United States,

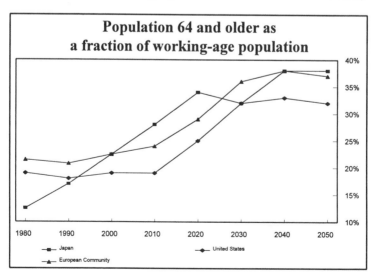

Population 64 and older as a fraction of working-age population

- ■ Japan
- ◆ United States
- ▲ European Community

the rise of seniors relative to younger citizens is even more dramatic.

2) Social Security bust. The fact of an aging society completely undermines the basic assumption of pay-as-you-go, government-sponsored retirement schemes—namely, that there would always be a relatively large working-age population to support a relatively small number of retirees.[5]

In the United States, for example, for every worker who retired in 1940, there were more than 40 workers to support his Social Security benefits through their payroll taxes. But by 1950, there were only 17. In 1990, only 3.4. By 2020, there will be only 1.78. In the more rapidly aging countries of Japan and Europe, these dependency ratios will be even more lopsided.

Living longer while having fewer children means boomers will be the first seniors unable to draw on the financial support of a much larger number of younger taxpayers. With fewer than two workers for every retiree, merely maintaining the present level of benefits will create a crushing burden for those still employed.

The workers who suffer most will be the ones in countries that depend most heavily on government-sponsored retirement schemes. For example, Spain, Italy, and France pay pensions directly to the old directly out of money earned by the young. A recent French government study concluded that if present benefits are maintained, the cost will climb from the present 19% of payrolls to as high as 42% by 2040.[6]

In the broadest macroeconomic sense, countries in which private pension schemes account for a major fraction of total

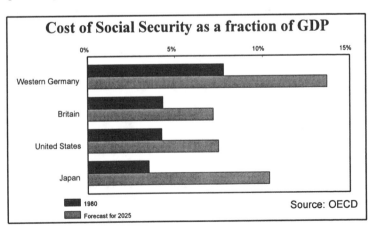

Cost of Social Security as a fraction of GDP

Source: OECD
1980
Forecast for 2025

retirement benefits—such as America, Britain, Canada, and Holland—may be somewhat better off. Relatively speaking, that is.

But just because most people receive a private pension in addition to government-sponsored Social Security doesn't mean Social Security will not suffer the same funding crisis as it does elsewhere. Nor does it mean that people who for generations have been promised Social Security benefits as an entitlement will voluntarily give them up—just because they may have recently become more expensive for the government to provide.

3) Age war in the 21st century. The inability to pay Social Security benefits will set the stage for an age war the likes of which no one has ever seen. Boomers today are paying record portions of their incomes to support today's retirees. After having made these sacrifices, they will scarcely relinquish similar benefits for themselves without a fight.

In Japan, which is legendary for its consensus politics, the population has already begun engaging in intergenerational conflicts that up to now never existed. At issue are clashes over money, living space, and, of course, status.[7]

Singapore is considering enactment of a so-called "sue-your-son-for-money" law. The measure would legally guarantee a parent's right to financial support from his or her children.[8] Imagine the controversy that would ensue if similar measures were eventually proposed in Europe, North America, or Australia.

Of course, controversies are nothing new to democratic political systems. But what will make this one especially nasty is that the debate is increasingly likely to become polarized along ethnic and racial lines.

One interesting demographic side effect of the birth dearth is the fact that children today are increasingly members of various minority groups. In the United States, for example, almost 20% of the population under age 15 is Hispanic—compared to only 11% of those over 65.

As a consequence, seniors by the year 2011 will have almost no blood relationship to the younger working-age population on the other side of the retirement debate. Worse, there will be an unavoidable tendency to equate age and ethnicity.

For example, U.S. concerns about infant mortality or pediatric health will be labeled a Hispanic problem, retirement issues an Anglo problem, etc.

Nowhere have the reactions to the demographics of an aging

nation been more forcefully expressed in terms or racial or ethnic hatred than in Europe. In a number of countries, the increase in relatively young immigrants and guest workers—often with much higher fertility rates—has raised the uncomfortable possibility that native citizens could someday become a minority in their own countries.

Non-European Community Population in 1989 As a Fraction of Total Population By Country[9]

Germany	5.7%
France	4.4%
Belgium	3.3%
Netherlands	3.1%
U.K.	1.8%
Greece	1.2%
Portugal	0.7%
Ireland	0.5%
Italy	0.4%
Spain	0.4%

A foretaste of the increasing civil strife to come is clearly visible in the new prominence of neo-Nazi skinheads and the rise of Ultranationalist and Fascist parties in Germany, France, Belgium, Italy, and Russia.

Across Europe, expressions of racial hatred and attacks on foreigners have become a routine occurrence. To the extent that age conflicts wind up being defined along already polarized ethnic and racial lines, these will only get worse.

As a result, the impending battle over who will pay for retirement benefits will make today's bitter conflicts over immigration policy seem genteel by comparison.

As members of the post-World War II generation age, they will unite in a powerful organized defense of their entitlements.

For example, the leading U.S. lobby for the aged, the American Association of Retired Persons (A.A.R.P.), already numbers 30 million strong. And unlike young people, most all seniors vote.

On the other side of the issue, early battle lines are also being drawn. In North America, a group called Americans for Generational Equity was established in 1985. According to its literature, one of its missions is to "prevent young families from being sold into financial slavery."

4) Investment consequences: boom and bust. As the post-World War II generation moves into its peak earning and savings

204

years, large supplies of capital are being created. The median baby boomer is now in his mid-30s. He will steadily increase his savings for perhaps another two decades. As a result, private-sector pension funds will grow rapidly.

Generally speaking, each percentage-point rise in the fraction of the population over 45 tends to produce about a percentage-point rise in the ratio of total institutionalized savings to gross domestic product (G.D.P.). In 1990, pension funds in America, Japan, and the European Community totaled some US$4.2 trillion. By 2000, this amount will top US$11 trillion.

This rapidly rising pool of capital formation has to be invested somewhere. When it flows into the stock market, it inevitably pushes up share prices. Booming stock markets encourage new share issues, and thereby reduce companies' costs of capital.

But this entire process will also work in reverse once the boomers retire and start drawing down their savings. Then, capital will become increasingly expensive.

Interestingly enough, this will happen just as there will be fewer people entering the labor force. Often companies' first response to a shrinking work force is to replace labor with capital. In other words, they automate instead of hire. This implies further demands on a diminishing pool of available capital.

As capital dries up, interest rates will tend to rise. Economic growth will slow down. And share prices will tend to fall.

What to do

Despite their numbers and their political clout, today's boomers will not be able to avoid being cruelly shortchanged by today's government-sponsored retirement schemes. That is, they cannot hope to get back in benefits what they paid in along the way.

That makes it absolutely imperative that they begin early to take steps to fund their own retirement. That means putting away the maximum amount possible in various tax-advantaged pension schemes.

One pitfall to avoid is counting on the appreciated value of suburban real estate to finance your retirement. Another consequence of the birth dearth is falling demand for housing—which merely follows the birth rate with a lag of about 20 to 30 years. Postwar birth rates peaked in most developed countries in the late 1950s and early 1960s—and have been declining ever since.

205

That suggests falling demand for housing well past the turn of the century. In other words, a generally bear market for residential real estate.

Because time is short and retirement is expensive, you will have to seek the highest return on your savings that a reasonable level of risk will allow. Happily, this is the subject of the next chapter.

However, the single most important thing you can do is get started early. As Ralph Waldo Emerson once observed, "Tobacco, coffee, alcohol, hashish, prussic acid, strychnine, all these are weak dilutions. The surest poison is time."

1. Source: U.S. Bureau of the Census, International Data Base.

2. "Grey Clouds on the Horizon," *Asia Magazine*, October 1, 1993; U.S. Bureau of the Census, International Data Base.

3. For a largely optimistic treatment of the implications of these trends from a U.S. point of view, see K. Dychtwald, and J. Flower, *Age Wave*, Bantam Books, New York, NY, 1990.

4. *This is Korea*, Vol. 5, No. 6, December 25, 1991.

5. See P. R. Mason and R. W. Tryon, "Macroeconomic effects of projected population aging in industrial countries," International Monetary Fund Staff Papers, Vol. 37, No. 3, September 1990, pp. 453-485.

6. "Tomorrow's Pensions," *The Economist*, June 20, 1992, pp. 17-19.

7. McConatha-Douglas, "Japan's Coming Crisis: Problems for the Honorable Elders," *Journal of Applied Gerontology*, Vol. 10, No.2, June 1991, pp. 224-235.

8. "Singapore Mulls Sue-a-Son Bill," *Eastern Express*, May 30, 1994.

9. Source: Eurostat, 1985 OECD estimate cited by *The Economist*, February 15, 1992, p. 20.

Chapter 14

Riding the Last Wave

Investment Success in a World
of Accelerating Events

Our wasted oil unprofitably burns,
Like hidden lamps in old sepulchral urns.
— William Cowper —

A wise man once said that one should open the door when opportunity knocks. However, he neglected to say precisely what this "opportunity" looked like. All too often, the caller comes disguised and appears either all too obvious or too improbable to be recognized.

It is normal to feel a bit overwhelmed by events when the air is filled with echoes of distant thunder or of the clash of arms. As individuals, there may be little we can do to influence the course of events set in motion in Teheran—or Tokyo or Washington, D.C. But what we can do is take investment advantage of human folly.

As long as free investment markets exist, when upheavals threaten, opportunities also abound for those farsighted enough to anticipate what takes everyone else by surprise.

Every economic change is good news for some—and bad news for others. The secret to successful investing is knowing how to find the good news—even when you must dig beneath the surface of seemingly forbidding events.

The most elementary analysis of who gains and who loses from oil and war in the 1990s begins with producers and consumers.

Any uncertainty or interruption in Mideast supplies increases the relative value of oil elsewhere in the world. Higher oil prices, for example, will help Russia, which depends on oil sales for a major portion of its hard-currency earnings. Unfortunately, there are as yet few opportunities for non-Russian stock market investors inside what was the Soviet Union.

Although the United States is a major producer, it is also the world's largest consumer. As long as consumption continues to outstrip production, the United States will be a net loser in any oil-related energy crisis.

World's 8 largest oil-producing nations	World's 8 largest oil-consuming nations
Russia/C.I.S.	United States
United States	Russia/C.I.S.
Saudi Arabia	Japan
Mexico	China
Iran	Germany
Iraq	Italy
China	France
Venezuela	United Kingdom

United States

In all likelihood, the United States will continue to grow more dependent on foreign supplies. The last time an effort was made to create a political consensus in favor of reducing dependency on foreign supplies of oil was in the late 1970s. Around the time of the second oil shock, then president Jimmy Carter declared energy independence the moral equivalent of war.

To find the reasons for the failure of the "moral equivalent of war," you need look no further than its acronym—MEOW. Even more debilitating than the timidity of its approach, however, was its reliance on regulatory rather than market means to achieve its ends.

Among the best examples of this are the demanding fuel efficiency standards imposed on American automobile manufacturers. To meet the new standards, U.S. automakers were forced to spend billions to re-engineer products and re-tool production lines. The results were impressive. Today, even big cars have achieved mileage standards that were once expected only of a Volkswagen beetle.

However, this contributed neither to conservation nor to energy independence. What it did do was slash the real per-mile cost of driving by about half in the past 15 years.

The enormous reduction in the cost of driving encouraged a vast increase in car ownership. And along with increased ownership came accompanying increases in miles driven and traffic congestion. Of course, congestion only drives efficiency down again. In bumper-to-bumper traffic, even the most fuel-efficient vehicles turn into gas-guzzlers.

As a result of government-imposed fuel efficiency standards, the United States now has an enormous fleet of expensively redesigned, fuel-efficient vehicles. But fuel consumption never declined as predicted. Instead, it has continued to rise. And today, nearly two-thirds of all the oil consumed in the United States goes for transportation.

In government, however, failure rarely leads to a reversal of misguided policies. Accordingly, it is by no means likely that future efforts to further the goal of U.S. energy independence will be any less lunatic than those of the past.

In Chapters 6 and 11, I made the case that the next war would destroy far more of the Mideast's oil supplies than either of the two Persian Gulf wars. Any interruption in Mideast supplies makes oil elsewhere proportionately more valuable. Two favorite oil companies which are also major non-Mideast producers are Royal Dutch Petroleum and Total Francaise Petroles.

Royal Dutch Petroleum owns 60% interests in Shell Petroleum N.V., and the Shell Petroleum Company Limited, owner of Shell Oil Company. These companies, in turn, have ownership interests in numerous other companies in the oil, natural gas, metal, coal, and chemical businesses worldwide.

This collection of enterprises is known collectively as the Royal Dutch Shell Group (30 Carel van Bylandtlaan, 2596 HR, The Hague, Netherlands, phone: 31-70-377-4540).

One of the most general measures of the quality of an oil company's management is its ability to increase the liquidation values of its asset base. According to this yardstick, Royal Dutch Shell is the best major oil company in the world.

Over the past five years, its asset base, which includes filling stations, refineries, tankers, and reserves, has increased by more than 50%. This is especially remarkable in light of the fact that oil prices have dropped more than 50% from their 1990-1991 high.

The group earns about 10% of its operating profit in North and South America, 40% in Europe, and 50% in the East. For example, it is very well positioned to benefit from the booming Asian market, where the demand for refined petroleum products is growing more than 6% annually.

Shares in Royal Dutch Shell Group companies trade on Europe's major markets. In addition, Royal Dutch is also listed on the New York Stock Exchange (RD-NYSE).

Like Royal Dutch Shell, **Total Francaise Petroles** (Tour Total, 24 cours Michelet, Puteau, France 92800, phone: 33-1-42-92-4000) has interests in virtually all aspects of the petroleum industry worldwide. In addition to its Mideast production, the company also has major oil production in the North Sea, North

America, Africa, and the Far East.

The company operates in 80 countries—which include both so-called upstream and downstream operations. (Upstream operations include exploration, development, and production. Downstream operations include transport, trading, refining, and marketing.)

In 1992, the French government effectively privatized the bulk of its one-third ownership of Total, and retained a residual interest of only 5.4%. In 1991, Total began trading on the New York Stock Exchange (TOT-NYSE) in addition to its listing on the Paris Bourse.

Total has also made a major commitment to the natural gas industry, particularly the fast-growing Asian market where the demand for liquified natural gas (LNG) will nearly double over the next six to nine years. Japan is presently the largest user of LNG. Both South Korea and Taiwan will increase consumption by about 50% in the next three to five years.

Not long ago, natural gas was burned off at the wellhead as a nuisance by-product of oil production. Today, it is in growing demand as one of the world's major energy sources. There are several reasons for this. First, it generally burns cleaner than refined petroleum products—such as fuel oil and gasoline. That alone increasingly makes it the fuel of choice in environmentally sensitive applications.

In addition, developments in gas turbine technology have made natural gas competitive with coal for electric power generation. For example, a decade ago, the peak efficiency of gas turbines was about 35%. Today, modern equipment—such as the Siemens/Kraftwerk Union V.64.3 turbine and its successors—routinely achieve peak efficiency levels in excess of 52%.

The growing popularity of natural gas will benefit gas utility companies. So also will any interruption (or threatened interruption) in Mideast oil supplies—which raise doubts about the reliability of oil supplies. My two favorite gas utility companies are North America's Consolidated Natural Gas Company, and Equitable Resources.

Listed on the New York Stock Exchange, **Consolidated Natural Gas Company** (CNG-NYSE) is a holding company for a group of subsidiaries that operate in all phases of the natural gas business—including exploration, production, trading, transmission, storage, and distribution.

The company's distribution area includes the U.S. states of

Ohio, Pennsylvania, Virginia, and West Virginia. CNG (CNG Tower, 625 Liberty Ave., Pittsburgh, PA 15222-3199, phone: 412-227-1000) produces between a quarter and a third of the gas it sells to residential and commercial customers. It buys the rest from independent producers or on the spot market.

Not only does CNG give your portfolio excellent exposure to the natural gas industry, but it is a substantial income producer as well. Its current dividend yield is well above what you can earn on U.S. dollar money funds and time deposits.

Like CNG, high-yielding **Equitable Resources Inc.** (EQT-NYSE) also trades on the New York Stock Exchange and has subsidiaries engaged in all aspects of the natural gas industry. In addition, it has a number of oil interests.

EQT (420 Boulevard of the Allies, Pittsburgh, PA 15219, phone: 412-261-3000) produces between a fifth and a quarter of the gas it sells, and buys the rest from other producers. In addition to operations in parts of Pennsylvania, West Virginia and Kentucky, the company has interests in Louisiana, Utah, and Canada.

Like CNG, EQT provides an attractive current return to shareholders. It has paid cash dividends continuously since 1944.

Energy real estate in America

Another way to profit from the next oil crisis is to position yourself to benefit from a real estate rebound in energy-producing regions of the United States. Interestingly enough, these were the regions where the decline in American real estate values struck earliest—and, in some cases, hardest.

That's because real estate values closely followed the boom in oil exploration in the late 1970s and early 1980s. The leading energy-producing states in America are Texas, Alaska, California, Oklahoma, and Louisiana. Except for California, real estate prices in each of these states crashed and burned when the bottom fell out of oil prices in the mid-1980s. (See chart of oil prices in Chapter 11.)

In part because real estate in energy producing regions of the United States were the first to decline, they have also been among the first to recover. And if oil prices return to the levels we saw in the early years of the 1980s—which could easily happen as a result of a future conflagration in the Mideast—property values could easily double or triple from today's levels.

One of the easiest ways to position yourself to benefit from rising real estate values in these energy-rich regions is to buy

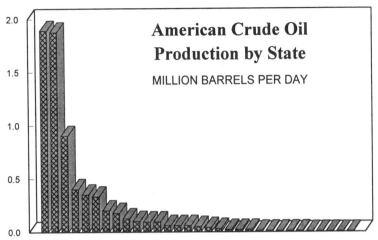

American Crude Oil
Production by State

MILLION BARRELS PER DAY

shares in **Weingarten Realty, Inc**. (2600 Citadel Plaza Dr., P.O. Box 924133, Houston, TX 77292-4133, phone: 713-866-6000). Listed on the New York Stock Exchange, Weingarten (WRI-NYSE) is a real estate investment trust with major holdings in Texas, Oklahoma, and Louisiana.

WRI either owns or has interests in 123 community shopping centers, 11 industrial properties, three multi-family residential projects, and one office building. In recent years, the company has been adding to its holdings at the rate of about one million square feet of building space per year.

It also pays an attractive dividend yield—substantially in excess of what you can earn on U.S. dollar money funds and time deposits.

Inflation's return

In February 1994, there occurred a virtual sea change in world investment markets. After five consecutive years of falling interest rates, American interest rate policy made an abrupt U-turn, as the U.S. Federal Reserve began pushing short-term interest rates up once again.

According to Fed Chairman Alan Greenspan, the Fed hiked rates in order to rein in future inflation. But if that were true, long-term interest rates (which include expectations of future inflation) should have dropped after the Fed's announcement. Instead, they soared. That, in turn, sent both bond and share prices plunging. (And not just in America.)

For both investors and the Fed's board of governors alike, this has been a bit of a puzzle. After all, as measured by the American Consumer Price Index (C.P.I.), inflation has generally been very well behaved. In fact, there is no sign at all of any acceleration in inflation. So what were the investment markets so worried about?

Contrary to the Fed's claim, the rise in short-term rates will not reduce future inflation at all. In fact, it will actually make inflation even worse. I believe this is what the market is really afraid of—although it has yet to be widely understood by individual investors. Here's why.

U.S. interest rates have been so low for so long that money has poured out of time deposits (such as Certificates of Deposit) and into so-called demand deposits (such as checking accounts). From demand deposits, much of this money subsequently wound up in stock market mutual funds. (See Chapter 12.)

After all, the exodus of funds from low-yielding, interest-bearing deposits, and the subsequent flow of funds into the stock market has been one of the forces that propelled the Dow Jones Industrial Average to its series of all-time highs.

The key point I want to make here is that falling interest rates have caused a massive shift of funds inside the banking system: from time deposits to demand deposits. Now that interest rates are rising again, that money will start to flow back the other way: from demand deposits back into time deposits.

Why is this important? Because there is a vast difference in the reserve requirement between demand and time deposits. A reserve requirement is the fraction of customer deposits that a commercial bank must hold "in reserve" in the form of a deposit at the Federal Reserve. Amounts held in such a reserve cannot be used to fund loans.

The Fed imposes an average reserve requirement of about 10% on demand deposits. But on time deposits, reserve requirements are effectively zero. So this movement of funds effectively creates a massive reduction in the nominal value of banks' reserve requirements.

Consider the impact of such a development on the U.S. money supply. In a fractional reserve banking system, two things are capable of producing a massive increase in the money supply: more loans and smaller reserve requirements.

Loan demand is already increasing as businesses raise funds for expansion. The danger is that this is occurring just as the

213

effective reserve requirement is about to plummet. Such a development could easily ignite an explosion in the broad money supply.

Properly understood, inflation is purely a monetary phenomenon. Simply put, it is merely a case of too many dollars chasing too few goods. If the effective reserve requirement is 10% (and banks lend as much as they can), then an extra dollar's increase in bank reserves results in a US$10 increase in the money supply. (In other words, the money supply increases by the reciprocal of the reserve requirement.)

But if the effective reserve requirement is 1%, then *one extra dollar results in a US$100 increase in the money supply*!

So far, this has been slow to occur. The broad money supply in America has been about as well-behaved as the Consumer Price Index. But when the explosion in broad money occurs, inflation could well climb to levels undreamed of by even alarmists of today.

This is why the yields on 30-year U.S. Treasury bonds soared when Greenspan hiked the Fed funds rate (the rate charged on overnight loans). Fearing a big increase in inflation in the months to come, bond buyers as a group suddenly began to demand a much higher yield.

Remember, buying a bond is really the same thing as making a loan. As lenders, bond buyers are simply demanding compensation for the growing likelihood that they will be repaid with dollars that are vastly cheaper than the ones they originally lent.

What do you do when the market has a bad case of inflation jitters? In inflationary times, tangible assets tend to outperform financial assets. So the return of American inflation will benefit the share prices of oil and gas producers we have already examined. It should also benefit the shares of Weingarten, the real estate investment trust we examined above.

Of course, the classical inflation hedge is gold.

Bull market bullion bonanza

I know there have been some people forecasting that gold would go to US$2,000 an ounce since 1980. Up to now, I have never been among them. But times change. For the first time in years, it is possible to make a bullish forecast purely on a demand and supply basis. Add to that the chances of an inflationary shock, and the stage is clearly set for a big increase in metals prices.

Let me explain the supply and demand picture. Mine output

accounts for the lion's share of the gold supply—about 59%. The melting down of old scrap accounts for a further 14%. Mine supply is still increasing, but at a shrinking rate.

Since 1990, the average annual increase has been about 3%. That's far below 1989's 8% increase.

In addition, the level of mine production clearly responds to price—but with several years' lag. Just as the rally to US$800 an ounce in 1980 encouraged exploration and development of massive new supplies, so also has the post-1980 bear market discouraged new exploration and development.

The chart below shows how the seven big annual increases in mine output followed the 1980 price rise—after a lag of about four years.[1] This interval merely reflects the time required to locate new deposits and build the necessary infrastructures to extract them.

But gold prices have been basically declining since 1980. And as expensive exploration programs are cut back, those big annual rises in output have come to an end.

Interestingly enough, this is occurring just as the demand for gold is starting to take off. For example, fabrication demand is

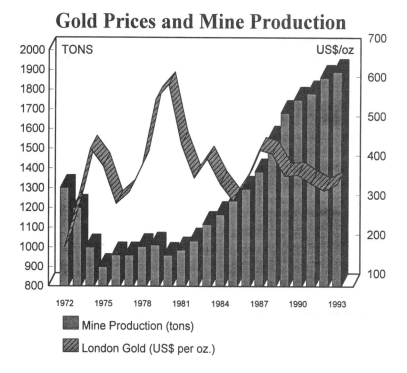

Gold Prices and Mine Production

■ Mine Production (tons)

▨ London Gold (US$ per oz.)

rapidly increasing. And nowhere is it growing faster than in Asia. Jewelry alone accounts for 71% of total demand. Other industries—such as dentistry and electronics—take up a further 14%. (Hoarding by investors plus gold loans account for the remaining 15%.)

In Asia, the demand for jewelry and gold bars (so-called bar hoarding) is rising at several times the rate of developed countries. There are several reasons for this. First of all, Asian economies have been growing 7% to 9% in recent years. That's more than twice the growth rates of the industrialized world. (In 1993, the Chinese economy grew 13%. After inflation.)

As a consequence, many more Asians have much more money to spend. What's more, Asians traditionally save 25% to 40% of their income—far more than Westerners.

Now consider this. If you live in a country without a well-developed investment market—or banking system—where you cannot legally buy real estate, or own Deutschemarks or dollars, exactly where do you put your savings? Chances are, your only real alternative is to accumulate the local currency.

Yet many Asians have good reason to be skeptical of paper currencies. The hyper-inflation of 1948-1949 in Shanghai, for example, rivaled that in Germany of the 1920s. You had to have a whole trunk full of money to buy a newspaper.

In fact, the Chinese hyper-inflation was a major factor in the collapse of the Nationalist government and the subsequent victory of Mao Zedong. That's one reason why China's present rulers are so terrified at the prospect that inflation might get out of hand. Even today, worries about the local paper currency make gold the most preferred store-of-value asset inside China.

This is a key aspect of the bullish case for gold. In the wake of the collapse of Communism and the end of the Cold War, the world has broken up into what some have called "zones of peace" (North American, Western Europe, Australia, and New Zealand) and "zones of turmoil" (everywhere else).[2]

From Somalia and Rwanda to Bosnia and Yemen, the upheavals in the world's zones of turmoil appear to be intensifying. Apart from inflation, nothing undermines confidence in government paper money like the threat of revolution. Or civil war.

The chart on the next page lists the countries outside Europe and North America that have made the largest additions to their hoards of gold bars since 1990. [3]

Apart from Japan and possibly Taiwan and South Korea, are there any countries on this list to whose currency you would

Country	Tons	Country	Tons
Japan	209.0	Cambodia	21.5
Thailand	177.6	Soviet Union/C.I.S.	21.0
India	103.0	Kuwait	20.0
China	98.0	South Korea	19.5
Taiwan	91.0	Burma	18.0
Saudi Arabia and Yemen	84.0	Arabian Gulf State	16.3
Vietnam	71.5	Colombia	13.2
Iran	34.0	Turkey	12.3

entrust your life savings? I suspect not. Moreover, most of the citizens and residents of these countries agree with you. That's why they hold so much gold.

At present, world fabrication demand plus bar hoarding already exceeds mine and scrap supply by a substantial margin. Add to that the likelihood of increasing instability in the zones of turmoil, plus the threat of U.S. dollar inflation, and you have all the ingredients of a new bull market.

What shares should you buy to cash in on this potentially explosive forecast? Well, my favorite gold share is the Australian mining company, **Kidston Gold** (LVL 16 1 Alfred Street, Sydney 2000, Australia, phone: 61-2-256-3800). The company (which is 76% owned by Placer Pacific Ltd.) operates the Kidston Mine in North Queensland.

In addition to its Sydney listing, Kidston also trades in the United States in the form of an American Deposit Receipt (A.D.R.). An A.D.R. is a U.S.-registered security that trades as a proxy for the underlying non-U.S. stock inside North America.

(The cusip of Kidston's A.D.R. is 49392120. A cusip is a kind of identification number assigned to all U.S.-listed securities. Any broker familiar with U.S. securities should be able to use the cusip to punch up Kidston on his computer terminal.)

One reason I like Kidston is its high dividend yield. The U.S. A.D.R. paid US$0.257 over the past 12 months. That amounts to a current yield in excess of 5%. Despite the Fed's interest rate hikes, that's more than you get on your C.D. or money market fund.

So even if I'm wrong on the timing of the next bull market, you still earn a competitive return on your money. That's really important. As I noted above, I know people who've been waiting a decade-and-a-half for the next bull market in bullion. *I like to get paid for waiting.*

Of course, a gold mine, like an oil well, is a wasting asset. The day will inevitably come when it is totally exhausted. Kidston's

217

main mine is expected to last only until the turn of the century. Accordingly, the company budgeted A$3 million this year to explore for new reserves. In early 1994, this effort began to pay off.

Two new ore bodies were found very near the present mine. One is expected to yield about 2.95 ounces of gold per ton, the other 6.16. If this estimate proves correct, this is even higher grade ore than what the company presently exploits.

In 1993, Kidston produced 223,728 ounces of gold—an 18% increase over 1992. Its average cost of production ran US$248 per ounce. With gold above US$375, this is a very good business. Above US$400, it's wildly profitable.

If you are a speculator at heart—and high current dividends are unimportant to you—there are vast profits to be made in gold mining in the former Soviet Union. Of course, there are also vast risks.

London-listed **Bakyrchik Gold** (165 Queen Victoria Street, London EC4V 4D U.K., phone: 44-71-240-6140) is a British company whose main business is a 40% share of the joint venture to work the Bakyrchik mine in northeastern Kazakhstan, the former Soviet Union's third largest republic. The remaining shares are held by Altynalmas, a Kazakhstan state-owned company. Formally, Bakyrchik Gold is entitled to 75% of net operating income until it recovers its investment, and 40% thereafter.

Proven reserves are 2.23 million tons at 9.13 gm/ton gold; probable reserves are 18.45 million tons at 9.46 gm/ton; and possible reserves are 7.30 million tons at 8.20 gm/ton. Divide Bakyrchik's proven reserves by its market capitalization, and you find that it is selling for a 70% to 90% discount to the market price of reserves of blue chip mining companies in North America and Australia.

Of course, that's because of investors' perception of the risks of doing business in the former U.S.S.R. Without a doubt, those risks are substantial and growing. But if I can buy at a 90% discount, chances are it's worth a punt, nonetheless.

Finally, for conservative investors, there is one more share I'd like to recommend. This is the closed-end **Central Fund of Canada** (#805, Hallmark Estates, 1323 15th Avenue S.W., Calgary, Alberta T3C OX8 Canada, phone: 408-228-5861).

Central Fund of Canada (CEF-AMEX) trades on the American Stock Exchange and on the Toronto Stock Exchange. Its major asset is simply a pile of bullion. In fact, the fund's policy is to have not less than 90% of net assets invested in either gold or silver bullion. Like most closed-end funds, CEF sometimes trades at a discount to its net asset value. This is the only way I know to effectively buy bullion at 96 or 98 cents on the dollar.

Market cycle theory

One of the most useful investment tools I've discovered is what I call market cycle theory. In a sense, it underlies much of what we've been discussing thus far.

The basic idea is very simple. In the long run, share prices go up when the companies that issued those shares make lots of money. Not surprisingly, corporate profits tend to ebb and flow along with the business cycle. So does the stock market. Because profits rise during the initial stages of an economic recovery, so too does the stock market. But only for the first couple of years.

The chart below shows what happened in the stock market after every recession since the end of World War II. Note that the market goes up on average about 31% for approximately 21 months before a correction sets in. The average bear market lasts about 13 months and takes the market down about 25%.

Recession ending in year	Length of market advance	Size of rise	Length of market decline	Size of drop
1982	15 months	21%	5 months	17%
1980	9 months	6%	16 months	25%
1975	20 months	33%	18 months	28%
1970	27 months	32%	21 months	52%
1960	10 months	9%	7 months	27%
1958	22 months	50%	8 months	15%
1954	21 months	43%	18 months	22%
1949	40 months	55%	8 months	10%
Average:	**21 months**	**31%**	**13 months**	**25%**

In the United States, the most recent recession officially ended in mid-1991. It was about 31 months from the time the recession ended until the Fed began hiking interest rates. During this time, the Dow rose from just under 2,960 to just under 4,000—about a 34% advance.

If what follows is an average bear market, it will probably last until sometime in early 1995. And before it's all over, we'll see the Dow at around 3,000.

How do you make money in a bear market? Well, if my forecast for oil prices and inflation is correct, you will do well in the natural resource and gold mining shares already recommended. But the truth is that market cycle theory doesn't only tell when to sell. It also tells you when to buy. Generally speaking, the

219

best time to buy stocks is in the late stages of a recession.

Now, it's too far along in the cycle to do that in the United States. But it's not too late in Switzerland and Japan—both of which are just coming out of a recession. In both countries, interest rates are still coming down. And generally speaking, nothing makes the stock market happier than lower interest rates.

Alpine harvest

My favorite Swiss stock is the closed-end, New York Stock Exchange-listed **Swiss Helvetia Fund.** (The trading symbol is SWZ.) Like Swiss real estate, Swiss stocks normally come in two varieties. The first is a modestly priced version reserved exclusively for the Swiss themselves. The second is an outrageously expensive variety that foreigners are allowed to purchase.

One of the great things about the Swiss Helvetia Fund is that it somehow wrangled permission to buy the class of stock normally restricted to the Swiss themselves.

SWZ (521 5th Avenue, New York, NY 10175, phone: 212-867-7660) presently has 26% of its assets in Swiss banks, 22% in pharmaceuticals, 14% in insurance, and 12% in food and beverage industries. The top four holdings are Nestle, 17%; Roche Holdings, 16%; Union Bank of Switzerland, 13%; and Sandoz, 7%.

Shogun shootout

Like Switzerland, Japan is also emerging from recession. In Tokyo, like Zurich, interest rates are falling. My favorite Japan fund is appropriately titled, the **Japan Fund** (175 Federal Street, Boston, MA 02110, phone: 617-439-4640, or toll-free in the U.S. 800-535-2726).

This is a no-load fund, (with no hidden charges—such as redemption fees and 12(b)1 fees—as well). Managed by Asia Management (a division of Scudder), its annual expense ratio runs about 1.25% per year. Because this is an open-end fund, you can buy shares directly from the fund itself at no charge.

Not only is Japan about to emerge from recession, but its stock market has already suffered a fearful decline. From approximately 39,000 in 1989, it fell to under 15,000 in 1992.

Despite this more than 60% decline in the Nikkei Dow, the Japan Fund still managed to post a 3.2% gain over the past five years. If there ever were a test of fund management skill, I'd have to say avoiding a loss during a 60% stock market debacle would have to be it. Imagine how well these managers might do once a new bull market finally gets under way in Tokyo.

Giant profits in third world telecoms

As an investment advisor, I am constantly looking for ways to improve investment performance. And when a particular investment does especially well, I'm always trying to find out the underlying reasons for it. Success understood is often success that can be repeated.

It was in this connection that I started to wonder about telecommunications companies. For example, during Thailand's bloody pro-democracy riots of 1992, I urged readers of my market letter, WORLD MONEY ANALYST, to buy shares in Shinawatra Communications—which doubled over the next seven months. In the January 1993 issue of WORLD MONEY ANALYST—in the midst of Brazil's constitutional crisis—I urged my readers to buy Telecomunicoes Brásileiras (Telebrás). Within a year, the stock climbed as much as 200%!

In the six months after privatization, Syariket Telecom Malaysia climbed more than 100%. After the newly privatized Compañia de Teléfonos de Chile was listed on the New York Stock Exchange, it climbed from US$16.75 to US$48.38 in just 14 months.

In my managed account program, I bought Teléfonas de México on behalf of some of my clients in July 1990. Since then, this investment has risen nearly fourfold.

In the mid-1980s, as former Philippine president Marcos was deposed, I urged my subscribers to buy Philippine Long Distance Telephone. Those who followed that advice have chalked up an investment return of approximately 79% *every year since*.

After a while, I started to wonder what accounted for the spectacular performance of these telephone and communications stocks. Perhaps they have certain distinctive characteristics in common. If such characteristics could be identified, then perhaps I could use them to identify other stock market winners.

As it happens, four such characteristics do exist. And we can use them to pick future winners. I'll explain each of them shortly. I'll also tell which stocks I think you should buy—including one I think could be the next Philippine Long Distance.

And if you prefer investing in funds to individual shares, I'll introduce one fund that's already homing in on the world's most profitable communications stocks.

Emerging market origin

The first of the four characteristics common to all of the examples above is that each of these companies is based in one of the world's so-called emerging stock markets. Strange as it may seem, merely to be based in the Third World is often an advantage all by itself. That's because emerging markets tend to outperform New York, Tokyo, and London—as well as the rest of the world's major stock markets.

The graph below shows the performance of most of the world's emerging stock markets (as defined by Morgan Stanley Capital International) relative to the United States, Japan, and the U.K.

Over this period beginning in 1988 and ending in mid-1994, Argentina and Mexico outperformed the U.S. stock market by almost seven to one. And that's after adjusting for currency fluctuations. (And among the top four emerging markets, three are Latin American.)

Of course, emerging markets are a little like high-flying growth stocks. When times are good, there is almost no faster way on earth to make money. But when times are bad, these stock markets will drop like a stone. Worse, emerging markets also tend to be uncommonly vulnerable to various mishaps. A massive fraud or business failure, a sharp rise in interest rates, or even some external shock, can easily trigger a crash.

Crashes in Thailand in 1992 (shooting of pro-democracy

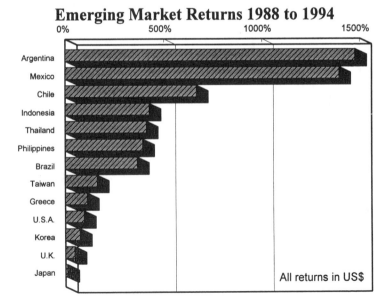

Emerging Market Returns 1988 to 1994

demonstrators), Taiwan in 1990 (government crackdown ends stock market boom), and Hong Kong in 1989 (Tiananmen Square) all fit this pattern. (You might argue that Hong Kong isn't really an emerging market—which is true. But Hong Kong is also a proxy for the Chinese market, which is.)

However, telephone companies—even in the Third World— usually tend to be relatively conservative investments. That's one reason why emerging market phone companies often make such attractive investment candidates.

If you're going to invest in some crash-prone market halfway around the world, one of the best ways to do it is to pick the safest, most conservative stocks in that market. Often these turn out to be the local communications stocks.

Moreover, you can often use the inevitable upheavals that occur to your investment advantage. The big profits in Philippine Long Distance and Shinawatra that I mentioned earlier are partly the result of buying in the midst of a government crisis.

Recently privatized

If one characteristic of extraordinary performance is an emerging market location, another one is to have been recently privatized. To get a grip on this, I compared the investment performance of 10 telecom stocks:

Country	Company
Brazil	Telecomunicoes Brásileiras (Telebrás)
Chile	Compañia de Teléfonos
Hong Kong	Hong Kong Telecom
Japan	Nippon Telephone & Telegraph (NTT)
Malaysia	Syariket Telecom Malaysia
Mexico	Teléfonas de México (Telmex)
New Zealand	Telecom Corp
Philippines	Philippine Long Distance (PLDT)
Spain	Telefonica de España
U.K.	British Telecom

For the purpose of simplification, I defined privatization as a recent public offering of shares formerly held by the government. The effective date of privatization we defined as the date price histories of secondary market trading in these shares began being reported by Reuters.

(For Telmex, I used the date the L-shares began trading on the New York Stock Exchange. For Telebrás, I used the date the A.D.R. began trading over the counter. For PLDT, I used a starting date in mid-1985.)

Next, I obtained post-privatization weekly price histories of these shares and converted them to U.S. dollars. Then, I divided them into two groups:

1) Emerging markets: Brazil, Chile, Malaysia, Mexico, and the Philippines, and

2) Industrialized markets: Hong Kong, Japan, New Zealand, Spain, and the U.K.

Finally, I plotted the average weekly post-privatization percentage change of both the emerging market and industrialized market telecoms.

The result could not have been more striking. As you can see from the graph on the next page, the developed country telecoms barely broke even three years or so after privatization.

But the emerging market telecoms climbed more than 700%.

To be sure, this is a very small statistical sample from which to draw very sweeping conclusions. For example, our industrialized market index was heavily influenced by the disastrous

First and Third World Telecom Stocks
Return Since Privatization

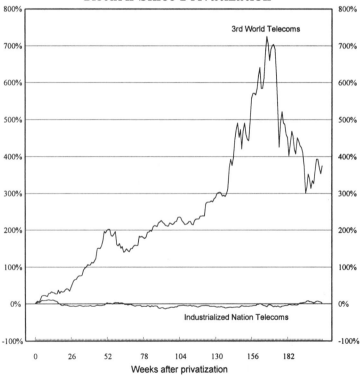

privatization of Nippon Telephone and Telegraph (NTT). NTT became a public company in the late 1980s—just as the Japanese market was nearing its peak.

Likewise, the emerging market index is heavily influenced by the spectacular performance of Philippine Long Distance. This is especially true in later periods, because many of the other emerging market privatizations are too new to have price histories longer than a year or two.

For example, you might be tempted to conclude from the shape of the emerging market index that the optimum time to unload your shares would be about three years after privatization. However, the thinness of the data in these later periods is a slender reed upon which to base such a profound conclusion.

What we can conclude, however, is that buying Third World telecom stocks after privatization has been a fantastically profitable investment strategy. And in my opinion, so it will remain.

Lousy service

One of the most surprising things about Third World telecoms is that terrible service is absolutely no obstacle to spectacular investment performance. In fact, the very best performing stocks often belong to the companies that give the *worst* telephone service to local customers.

Certainly this has been the case in Mexico. Since the beginning of 1988, Telmex so-called A-shares (listed over the counter in the United States) have climbed more than 850%. Yet in many parts of Mexico, you still have to bribe someone to get a line installed. And even then, chances are you will still have to wait months for service.

In the Philippines, the poor service of Philippine Long Distance is legendary—as anyone who has ever tried to do business in Manila can attest.

Former Singapore prime minister Lee Kwan Yew once joked that 90% of the people in the Philippines are on the waiting list for a telephone. Meanwhile, the other 10% are waiting for a dial tone.

Under former president Ferdinand Marcos, everyone in the Philippines with a telephone was once forced to buy shares of a special non-voting stock issue—or else be denied service.

One reason why mistreating customers is no barrier to investment success is that these phone companies are all former government monopolies. (And after privatization, most of them remain de facto private monopolies.)

In most cases, the government permits the newly privatized company to raise local rates as part of the privatization plan. So even if service remains poor while prices go up, all the local customers can do is complain. Most of the time, they have little or no prospect for lining up alternate service.

International profits
However, local service is not where the big profits are anyway. The big money is in international calls. Here's why.

Outside the United States—where government deregulation of the telecom industry is farthest along—the usual government pricing policy is to gouge international callers to subsidize local service. As a result, the profit margins on international calls are enormous.

In addition, international service is relatively easy to provide. Unlike extending the local telephone network—which is slow and capital-intensive—expanding international capacity is often merely a matter of renting a few more satellite circuits.

Not only can this be done at relatively low cost, but it can easily result in a doubling or tripling of international call revenue.

Not surprisingly, telephone use tends to be generally correlated with the overall rate of economic growth. The more business there is going on, the greater the demand for communications services.

But the leverage on demand for international communications services is often much greater than on domestic services. Even relatively sluggish economic growth can result in an explosive rise in demand for overseas calls.

This particularly tends to be the case when foreign investment interest is high. For example, if the Americans or the Japanese are busy building factories in some small country, you can bet on a big increase in the demand for international communications.

For all these reasons, it's surprisingly easy for newly privatized Third World phone companies to show big post-privatization profit increases. And nothing makes investors happier than sharply rising profits.

Preaching to the choir
In religion, you usually find the truest believers among the ranks of the recently converted. So it is with beliefs about economic policy as well.

In the developed world, the notion of the free market is so old and familiar that lots of people barely believe in it any more. Consequently, the most enthusiastic boosters of genuinely market-oriented policies tend to be in Third World countries—where capitalism is still news.

Nowhere is the difference between a genuine and a merely lukewarm commitment to capitalism more striking than in the privatization policies of developed and developing countries. To see this more clearly, compare the privatizations of Telmex with that of the Spanish telecom, Telefonica de España.

After privatization, the Mexican government approved increases in domestic rates and line charges. It rescinded a telecom tax, and weighed in on the side of the company in negotiating a cost-cutting agreement with powerful local unions.

But in Spain, the government capped the profits of the newly privatized telecom at 5% return on equity. It also retained a big equity stake in the company to ensure that it could still be run for political purposes.

For example, local phone rates figure prominently in the Spanish inflation index. And the government is more concerned about holding down phone rates to look good on inflation than about maximizing returns to Telefonica's shareholders. So it refused to guarantee Telefonica's ability to raise local rates in line with increases in inflation.

Even so, Spain has enjoyed one of the faster economic growth rates in Europe. And since privatization in mid-1987, Telefonica's share price has risen about 50%. But over the same period, Telmex soared more than 600%.

Who's calling where

The fourth and final characteristic common to the most promising telecom stocks is a particular international calling pattern. Most of the international traffic tends to go to countries that are a major source of funds for local investment—such as the United States, Japan, and Germany.

Meanwhile, the countries in second and third place tend to be emerging markets nearby—and particularly those with market-oriented economic reform policies. Virtually all of the stocks in our emerging market index come from countries that fit this pattern.

To summarize, we've thus far identified four characteristics common to the world's most profitable telecom stocks:

227

1) Emerging market location,
2) Newly privatized,
3) Poor service no barrier to big investment gains, and
4) A specific international traffic pattern.

There will be a host of telecom privatizations to choose from in the months ahead. You can now use these four criteria to help select the best of the lot. But if you'd rather not do all the homework yourself, don't despair. There is at least one fund that will do it for you: the Emerging Market Telecommunications Fund.

Third World telecom funds

The **Emerging Market Telecom Fund** (ETF-NYSE) is a closed-end fund listed on the New York Stock Exchange. Its investment objective is long-term capital appreciation primarily by investing in the stocks of telecommunications companies in emerging markets.

ETF (One Citicorp Center, 58th floor, 153 E. 53rd Street, New York, NY 10022, phone: 212-832-2626) defines emerging markets as any country in the International Finance Corporation's emerging market composite index with a total stock market capitalization of no more than US$150 billion.

I strongly recommend the Emerging Market Telecommunications Fund as an excellent vehicle to cash in on the big profits that will be earned in Third World telecom stocks.

Big bucks beckon in Brazil

But if you find fund investing a little too tame, let me recommend to you my single favorite Third World telecom stock. This is a stock that could easily be another Telmex or Philippine Long Distance all over again. The company is Telecomunicoes Brásileiras–**Telebrás** for short.

Incorporated in November 1972, Telebrás (Sector de Autarquias Sul, Quadra 6, Bloco E 10 andar, Brazil 70313) is Brazil's major supplier of telephone, cellular mobile telephone, telex, telegraph, and data transmission services. It clearly meets all of the characteristics identified above.

There is no question that Brazil is an emerging market. The first public shares began trading in the United States in November 1992. Local service is poor. And the lion's share of Brazil's international telecommunications traffic goes to the United States, a major foreign investor, and Argentina, a neighboring emerging market with a vigorous market-oriented economic reform program.

Crisis and opportunity

One thing to keep in mind is that Brazil is always more or less in a political crisis. For example, several years go, Fernando Collor won the presidency on a pledge to contain the country's chronic inflation.

He appointed Zelia Cardoso as finance minister. She devised a plan for halting the runaway growth of the money supply that was as unique as it was radical: She froze all the bank accounts in the country.

Despite an inauspicious beginning, the Collor regime did many good things for the Brazilian economy. Tariffs were slashed, subsidies reduced, and the economy slowly began to open to foreign investment and competition. A program to privatize state-owned industries was set in motion. Inflation even declined somewhat.

But then disaster struck. Zelia was caught dancing cheek to cheek with a married member of the Collor cabinet—and was forced to resign by the ensuing scandal. Then Collor's brother came forward to accuse him of looting the treasury for personal gain. The evidence he brought was so damaging that Collor was impeached and forced out of office.

In Brazil, the office of vice president is much like it is in the United States—a political afterthought. No one ever really expects the vice president to become president.

Collor's V.P. was a man named Itmar Franco. And Franco proved to be at least as gaffe prone as his predecessor. For example, as part of the run-up to the 1994 presidential elections, his political advisers suggested that he attend *Carnivale* in his shirtsleeves. The aim was to enhance his reputation as a "man of the people."

Unfortunately, all Franco managed to do was get himself photographed dancing with a woman who, according to press reports, was naked from the waist down. In Brazil, the scandals never end.

For this reason, Telebrás will always be somewhat more volatile then the average Latin American stock. My recommendation, however, is to get a good grip and hang on for the ride. Do that, and in three or four years, you'll probably find you've made more money in Telebrás than in all the rest of your portfolio combined!

Telebrás trades in A.D.R. form in the United States. Telebrás is listed "over the counter" in the so-called pink sheets. The cusip

229

is 87928710. Each A.D.R. is the equivalent of 1,000 Brazilian shares of the company's non-voting preferred stock.

---

1. "Gold 1994," Gold Fields Mineral Services, Ltd., London, 1994.
2. Max Singer and Aaron Wildavsky, *The Real World Order: Zones of Peace/Zones of Turmoil.*
3. "Gold 1994," *op. cit.*
4. Doug Casey, *Crisis Investing for the Rest of the '90s.*

* * * * *

Epilogue

"Money," said Scipion de Gramont—no doubt quoting someone else—"is the blood and soul of men. He who has none wanders as one dead among the living."

I hope that having taken you this far, I have left you fortified with some full-blooded investment ideas for making the most of both the last wave of investment prosperity, and the troubled times ahead. And even if I have not, I hope I have at least spun a compelling tale.

If you would like to continue the financial adventure begun in these chapters, here are a pair of publications you should know about. First, Czeschin's **World Investor** (824 East Baltimore Street, Baltimore, MD 21202; fax: 410-539-7348) provides international stock recommendations tailored specifically to North American investors.

By contrast, I write WORLD MONEY ANALYST (#11C, Casey Building, 38 Lok Ku Road, Hong Kong; phone: 852-541-6110; fax: 852-854-1695) for international investors worldwide—and it is presently read in 114 countries.

Both publications are monthlies, and both reflect the investment point of view I've tried to set forth in these pages—namely, that wherever crises loom, opportunities abound. As an individual, you may not be able to alter the course of events in distant capitals—or, for that matter, even in your own home town. But what you *can* do is arrange your affairs to profit from the march of human folly. As long as free markets exist, *you* are *never* powerless.

In my opinion, that's what being an investor is all about.

Bibliography

1990 NASDAQ Fact Book, National Association of Securities Dealers, Washington, D.C., 1990.

Addington, Larry H. *The Patterns of War Since the 18th Century,* Indiana University Press, Bloomington, IN, 1984.

Ahrari, Mohammed E. *OPEC: The Falling Giant,* University Press of Kentucky, Lexington, KY, 1986.

Alexander, Y. and Y. Nèeman. *Future Terrorism Trends*, Global Affairs, Washington, D.C., 1991.

al-Khalil, Samir. *Republic of Fear,* Pantheon Books, New York, NY, 1990.

Apodaca, "Japanese Investors Fuel Insurgence," *Investor's Daily*, December 4, 1987.

Arditti, F. D. and W. A. McCollough. "Can Analysts Distinguish Between Real and Randomly Generated Stock Prices," *Financial Analysts Journal*, November to December 1978.

Asia Week, May 11, 1994.

"Bad Blood in Germany—The Soviet Army Can't Leave Soon Enough," *Newsweek*, November 12, 1990.

Batra, R. *The Great Depression of 1990,* Simon & Schuster, New York, NY, 1987.

Beres, Louis R. *Terrorism and Global Security: the Nuclear Threat,* Westview Press, London, England, 1987.

Bone, J. "Experts Predicting Repeat of Tragedy," *South China Morning Post*, April 22, 1993.

Brodie, Bernard and M. Fawn. *From Crossbow to H-Bomb,* Indiana University Press, Bloomington, IN, 1973.

Bronfenbrenner, M. "Japan and Two World Economic Depressions," quoted in R. Dore and R. Sinha, *Japan and World Depression—Then and Now.*

Brown, Harold. *Thinking About National Security: Defense and Foreign Policy in a Dangerous World,* Westview Press, Boulder, CO, 1983.

Bulloch, J. and H. Morris. *Saddam's War,* Faber and Faber, London, England, 1991.

Busch, N. F. *Two Minutes to Noon,* Simon & Schuster, New York, NY, 1962.

Business Week, July 14, 1986.

Business Week, July 11, 1988.

Casey, Doug. *Crisis Investing for the Rest of the '90s*, Birch Lane Press, New York, NY, 1994.

"Cheap Oil Makes North Sea Waves," *International Herald Tribune*, April 13, 1994.

"Church of Doom Meets Bitter End," *South China Morning Post*, November 2, 1992.

Clark, R. C. *Technological Terrorism,* Devin-Adair Co., Old Greenwich, CT, 1980.

Cleary, M. N. and G. D. Hobbs. "The 50 Year Cycle: A Look at the Empirical Evidence," in *Long Waves in the World Economy* by C. Freeman.

Cooper, Chester L. *The Lion's Last Roar: Suez 1956,* Harper & Row, New York, NY, 1971.

Czeschin, Robert W. "Cashing In on the Coming Oil Shock: How to Profit From North Korea's Military Mischief," *Taipan*, Agora Inc., Baltimore, MD, July 1993.

Czeschin, Robert W. "Nuclear Weapons in North Korea," *Taipan*, Agora Inc., Baltimore, MD, April 1990.

Czeschin, Robert W. "Apocalypse Eclipsed," *Taipan*, Agora Inc., Baltimore, MD, May 1993.

Davidson, James D. and W. Rees-Mogg. *Blood in the Streets,* Summit Books, New York, NY, 1987.

Davies, Thomas (Rear Admiral). "Terrorism's Nuclear Potential: What Might the Means and Targets Be?", Conference on International Terrorism: The Nuclear Dimension, Nuclear Control Institute, Washington, D.C., June 1985.

"Decapitation 'Widespread,'" *Eastern Express*, May 20, 1994.

Deese, David A. "Oil, War, and Grand Strategy," *Orbis*, Vol. 25, Fall 1981, Foreign Policy Research Institute.

"The Devil's War Against Islamic Iran," published by the Revolutionary Guard Corps, Teheran, 1982.

Dore, R. and R. Sinha. *Japan and World Depression—Then and Now,* St. Martin's Press, New York, NY, 1987.

Dreman, D. A. "Psychology and Markets," in *Readings in Investment Management.*

Dunnigan, James F. *How to Make War: A Comprehensive Guide to Modern Warfare for the Post-Cold War Era*, 3rd Edition, William Morrow, New York, NY, 1993.

Dunnigan, James F. and Austin Bay. *A Quick & Dirty Guide to War: Briefings on Present and Potential Wars,* William Morrow, New York, NY, 1986.

Dupuy, Colonel Trevor N. *Future Wars: The World's Most Dangerous Flashpoints*, Warner Books, New York, NY, 1992.

Economic Stabilization Board, *Taiheiyo senso ni youru waga kuni no higai sogo hokokusho*, 1949.

Emerson, S. "The Postwar Scud Boom," *Wall Street Journal*, July 10, 1991.

Emerson, S. and B. Duffy. *The Fall of Pan Am 103,* Futura, London, England, 1990.

Fabozzi, F. A. *Readings in Investment Management,* Richard D. Irwin, Homewood, IL, 1963.

Festinger, L., H. W. Riechen, and S. Schachter. *When Prophecy Fails,* Harper & Row, New York, NY, 1956.

Fialka, J. J. "Airliners Can Exploit U.S. Guidance System, But So Can Enemies: GPS Could Be Used to Direct Cheap, Accurate Missiles," *Wall Street Journal*, August 26, 1993.

Freedman, Lawrence Z. and Alexander Yonah, eds. *Perspectives on Terrorism,* Scholarly Resources Inc., Wilmington, DE, 1983.

Friedman, Thomas L., *From Beirut to Jerusalem,* Farrar, Straus, and Giroux, New York, NY, 1989.

Fullick, Roy and Geoffrey Powell. *Suez: The Double War,* Hamish Hamilton, London, England, 1979.

Georges-Abeyie, D. E. "Women As Terrorists," in L. Z. Freedman and Y. Alexander, *Perspectives on Terrorism.*

Gersh, Seymour M. *The Samson Option,* Faber & Faber, London, England, 1991.

Girardet, Edward R. *Afghanistan: The Soviet War,* St. Martin's Press, New York, NY, 1985.

"Gold 1994," Gold Fields Mineral Services, Ltd., London, 1994.

Goralski, R. and R. Freeburg. *Oil and War,* William Morrow and Co., New York, NY, 1987.

"Grey Clouds on the Horizon," *Asia Magazine*, October 1, 1993, U.S. Bureau of the Census, International Data Base.

Guderian, Heinz, translated by C. Fitzgibbon. *Panzer Leader,* E.P. Dutton, New York, NY, 1952.

Gumbel, Peter. "Anthrax: The Survivors Speak," *Asian Wall Street Journal*, October 24, 1991.

Hadfield, Peter. *Sixty Seconds That Will Change the World*, Sidgwick & Jackson, London, England, 1991.

Herz, Martin F., ed. *Diplomats and Terrorists: What Works, What Doesn't —A Symposium,* Institute for the Study of Diplomacy, Edmund A. Walsh School of Foreign Service, Georgetown University, Washington, DC, 1982.

Herzog, Chaim. *Arab-Israeli Wars: War and Peace in the Middle East From the War of Independence Through Lebanon,* Random House, New York, NY, 1982.

"How to Survive As a Hostage," *Diplomats and Terrorists: What Works, What Doesn't—A Symposium*, Institute for the Study of Diplomacy, Georgetown University, 1982.

Ibbotson, R. G. and G. P. Brinson. *Global Investing*, McGraw-Hill, 1993.

Ibbotson, R. G. and R. A. Singuefield. "Index of Year-End Cumulative Wealth 1925-1986," *Dow Jones-Irwin Business and Investment Almanac 1987.*

Inoguchi, Rikihei, Tadashi Nakajima, and Roger Pineau. *The Divine Wind: Japan's Kamikaze Force in World War II*, Greenwood Press, Westport, CT, 1978.

International Energy Agency. *World Energy Outlook*, OECD, Paris, 1993.

Kaufman, Henry. *Interest Rates, the Markets, and the New Financial World,* Times Books, New York, NY, 1986.

Kennedy, Paul. *The Rise and Fall of the Great Powers: Economic Change and Military Conflict From 1500 to 2000,* Random House, New York, NY, 1987.

Kindel, Stephen. "Catching Terrorists," *Science Digest,* September 1986.

Kondratieff, Nickolai. *The Long Wave Cycle,* translated by Guy Daniels, Richardson & Snyder, New York, NY, 1984.

"Korean Missile Near Completion," *South China Morning Post*, November 13, 1993.

Laffin, J. *War Annual I,* Brassey's Defense Publishers, London, England, 1988.

Lewis, B. *The Assassins: A Radical Sect in Islam,* Weidenfeld and Nicolson, London, England, 1967.

Lewis, Bernard, ed. Islam: *From the Prophet to the Capture of Constantinople, Vol. 1: Politics and War*, Harper & Row, New York, NY, 1974.

Livingston, Neil C. *The War Against Terrorism,* Lexington Books, Lexington, MA, 1982.

Los Angeles Times, February 1, 1987.

MacDonald, E. *Shoot the Women First: Inside the Secret World of Female Terrorists*, Random House, New York, NY, 1992.

Macksey, Kenneth. *Technology and War: the Impact of Science on Weapon Development and Modern Battle,* Prentice Hall, New York, NY, 1986.

Macksey, Kenneth and John H. Batchelor. *Tank: A History of the Armored Fighting Vehicle*, Ballantine Books, a division of Random House, New York, NY, 1970.

Malkiel, B. G. *A Random Walk Down Wall Street.*

Martin, David C. and John Walcott. *Best Laid Plans: The Inside Story of America's War Against Terrorism,* Harper & Row, New York, NY, 1988.

Mason, P. R. and R. W. Tryon. "Macroeconomic Effects of Projected Population Aging in Industrial Countries," *International Monetary Fund Staff Papers*, Vol. 37, No. 3, September 1990.

Maurice, C. and C. W. Smithson. *The Doomsday Myth: 10,000 Years of Economic Crisis,* Hoover Institution Press, Stanford University, Stanford, CA, 1984.

McConatha-Douglas. "Japan's Coming Crisis: Problems for the Honorable Elders," *Journal of Applied Gerontology*, Vol. 10, No. 2, June 1991.

McIntosh, M. *Japan Rearmed,* St. Martin's Press, New York, NY, 1986.

Miller, Judith and L. Mylroie. *Saddam Hussein and the Crisis in the Gulf,* Times Books, New York, NY, 1990.

Miller, Marshall Lee. "How the Soviets Invaded Iran," *Armed Forces Journal International*, February 1987.

Miller, Marshall Lee. "Soviet Military Developments—The Soviet General Staff's Secret Plans for Invading Iran," *Armed Forces Journal International,* January 1987.

"Missiles in North aimed at Beijing, report claims," *South China Morning Post*, April 8, 1993.

Modderno, Francine. *Traveler's Health & Safety Handbook,* Agora Inc., Baltimore, MD, 1986.

Mohr, Anton. *The Oil War*, Harcourt Brace, New York, NY, 1926.

Murray, A. and U. C. Lehner. "U.S. Japan Struggle to Redefine Relations As Resentment Grows," *Wall Street Journal*, June 13, 1990.

Nelon, B. W. "Fighting Off Doomsday," *Time*, June 28, 1993.

Niebuhr, G. "On the Horizon, Apocalypse Dates Still Being Set by Prophets of Doom," *Washington Post*, March 4, 1993.

Nixon, Richard M. *Beyond Peace*, Random House, 1994

"North Korea Alarms U.S. Over Mideast Missile Sales," *Asian Wall Street Journal*, July 19, 1993.

"Nuclear Weapons on Sale for Hard Currency in Eastern Europe," *Taipan*, Agora Inc., Baltimore, MD, August 1990.

O'Ballance, Edgar. *Language of Violence: The Blood Politics of Terrorism,* Presidio Press, San Rafael, CA, 1979.

O'Connor, Harvey. *World Crisis in Oil,* Monthly Review Press, New York, NY, 1962.

Odell, Peter R. *Oil and World Power,* 7th Edition, Richard Clay (The Chaucer Press) Ltd., Bungay, Suffolk, U.K., 1983.

"Oil Output Fell to 35-Year Low in U.S. in First Half," *Wall Street Journal,* July 15, 1993.

O'Sullivan, Noel, ed. *Terrorism, Ideology, and Revolution,* Westview Press, Boulder, CO, 1986.

Overholt, William H. *China: The Next Economic Superpower,* Weidenfeld & Nicolson, London, 1993.

Palance, D. *Mutual Funds... Legal Pickpockets?,* Vantage Press, New York, NY, 1963.

Pipes, D. *In the Path of God,* Basic Books, New York, NY, 1983.

Princeton Alumni Weekly, October 25, 1976.

"Pyongyang Food Crisis Fears Grow," *South China Morning Post,* September 24, 1993.

"Pyongyang says Tokyo is prime nuclear target," *Eastern Express,* March 10, 1994.

Reading, Brian. *Japan: The Coming Collapse,* Orion, London, 1992.

"The Reconstruction of Tokyo," Tokyo Municipal Office.

Rubinfien, E. "Reverse Land Rush: Americans Pitch Property to Japanese," *Wall Street Journal,* June 15, 1988.

Rustow, Dankwart A. *Oil and Turmoil: America Faces OPEC and the Middle East,* W. W. Norton & Co., New York, NY, 1982.

Savage, Peter. *The Safe Travel Book—A Guide for the International Traveler,* Lexington Books, Lexington, MA, 1993.

Schemmer, Benjamin F. "Was the U.S. Ready to Resort to Nukes for the Persian Gulf in 1980?", *Armed Forces Journal International,* September 1986.

Segal, Gerald. *World Affairs Companion,* Simon & Schuster, London, 1993.

Seib, Gerald F. "Soviets' Big Stick Gets Better Results Than That of U.S. Gulf Actions Show," *Wall Street Journal,* August 10, 1987.

Shansab, Nasir. *Soviet Expansion in the Third World: Afghanistan: a Case Study,* Bartleby Press, Silver Spring, MD, 1986.

Shultz, George P. *Turmoil and Triumph: My Years as Secretary of State,* Charles Scribner's Sons, New York, NY, 1993

Sifrag, M. L. and C. Cerf, eds. *The Gulf War Reader,* Times Books, New York, NY.

Singer, Max and Aaron Wildavsky. *The Real World Order: Zones of Peace/Zones of Turmoil,* Chatham House Publishers, Inc., Chatham, NJ, 1993.

Special National Intelligence Estimate, prepared by CIA analyst J. Azrael, 1981.

Spector, L. "Treaties Target China's Arms Trade," *Asian Wall Street Journal,* September 9, 1991.

Springer, J. L. *The Mutual Fund Trap,* Henry Regnery Co., Chicago, IL, 1973.

Sterling, Claire. *The Terror Network: The Secret War of International Terrorism,* Holt, Rinehart and Winston, New York, NY, 1981.

Stockholm International Peace Research Institute. *Weapons of Mass Destruction.*

Stoff, Michael B. *Oil, War, and American Security: The Search for a National Policy on Foreign Oil, 1941-1947,* Yale University Press, New Haven, CT, 1980.

Talbot, Strobe, ed., trans. *Khrushchev Remembers,* Little, Brown & Co., Boston, MA, 1970.

"Task Force's Brady Says Japanese Sales of U.S. Bonds Touched Off October 19 Crash," *Wall Street Journal,* April 22, 1988.

Taubman, P. *New York Times Magazine,* April 14, 1985.

This is Korea, Vol. 5, No. 6, December 25, 1991, Intraco, Seoul, South Korea.

Thomas, Gordon and Max Morgan-Witts. *Pontiff,* Doubleday & Co., New York, NY, 1983.

Timmerman, K. R. "China's Comrades in Arms," *Asian Wall Street Journal,* April 3-4, 1992.

Timmerman, K. R. "Time to Stop Russia's Nuclear Gangsters," *Wall Street Journal,* December 1, 1992.

"Tomorrow's Pensions," *The Economist,* June 20, 1992.

Tuchman, Barbara. *The Guns of August,* Bantam, New York, NY, 1976.

Tulfah, Khairallah. "Three Whom God Should Not Have Created: Persians, Jews, and Flies," Dar al-Hurriyya, 1981.

Uchino, Tatsuro. *Japan's Postwar Economy: An Insider's View of Its History and Future,* Kodansha International Ltd., Tokyo, Japan, 1978.

Venn, Fiona. *Oil Diplomacy in the 20th Century,* St. Martin's Press, New York, NY, 1986.

Viner, Aron. *The Emerging Power of Japanese Money,* Dow Jones-Irwin, Homewood, IL, 1988.

"Waiting for the Big One," *The Economist,* December 7, 1991.

Washington Post, September 23, 1981.

"Weapons Rise Raises Concern," *South China Morning Post,* September 23, 1993.

Webster, W. Speech before American Bar Association meeting, Toronto, August 9, 1988.

White, David. "Uphill Battle to Tighten Biological Weapons," *Financial Times,* September 6, 1991.

Wigmore, B.A. *The Crash and Its Aftermath—A History of Securities Markets in the United States 1929-1933,* Greenwood Press, Westport, CT.

Wright, Peter and Paul Greengrass. *Spycatcher,* Dell, New York, NY, 1987.

Wright, Robin. *Sacred Rage: The Wrath of Militant Islam,* Simon & Schuster, New York, NY, 1986.

Yamaguchi, M. "Dateline Tokyo: Fears Grow Over 'Messiah,'" *South China Morning Post,* October 18, 1992.

Yergin, D. *The Prize,* Simon & Schuster, New York, NY, 1991.

Acknowledgments

Like most writers, I owe countless debts that I can never repay. Books are never a one-man show, and this one rests upon the labors of many. Many of my sources of inspiration appear in the bibliography and in dozens of footnotes throughout.

I am especially grateful to Bill Bonner, president of the Agora, Inc./Newstar Orient Ltd. Group of Companies, who has been the guiding light of this project since the beginning, and who paid my salary during the many prior editions of this work. I am also indebted to dozens of thoughtful readers both inside and outside the United States for insightful comments and suggestions.

Others to whom I own special debts include Loray Greiner, Rachel Wong, Bernard Chu, Adrienne Locke, Christoph Amberger, and James Dale Davidson. I am also grateful to Judith Strauss for careful proofreading, Kimberlee Lansdale for typesetting and production, and Katie Yeakle of Shot Tower Books for shepherding this entire enterprise on to its logical conclusion.

To all these people, I owe credit for what is worthy of merit in this slim volume. That which is not, I cheerfully acknowledge as mine alone.

About the Author

Robert W. Czeschin is the editor of the WORLD MONEY ANALYST, Hong Kong's leading investment advisory service with readers in 114 countries. For nearly five years, he has been Director of Research for *Taipan*, the futurist journal of business and investment opportunity. In 1994, he became editor of the recently launched *Czeschin's World Investor*.

Mr. Czeschin is the former editor of the prestigious *World Financial Review*.

In addition to six previous editions of *The Last Wave*, he is the author of a second book, the *Complete Report of Banking Safety and Privacy*. A recognized expert in the field of investments, Mr. Czeschin has addressed dozens of financial conferences in Canada, China, Hong Kong, Jamaica, Malaysia, Singapore, Switzerland, Thailand, the United States, and Vietnam.

Interviews with him have appeared regularly on American radio and television. He presently appears as a guest investment expert on WGN-AM, Chicago's 50,000 watt, clear-channel superstation.

Mr. Czeschin was educated in the United States. He earned a Bachelor of Arts degree from the University of Chicago in 1974. Ten years later, he was awarded a Master of Business Administration degree from the University of Illinois at Chicago.

A registered investment advisor, he also manages money for a select group of private clients. He is investment advisor to the Luxembourg-listed fund, SAX-Asia, and director of Jaguar Investment Services, Limited, an investment management and consultancy company with a worldwide clientele.

Jaguar Investment Services, Limited
GPO Box 10943
Hong Kong

A note from the publisher:

If this kind of analysis appeals to you — and you don't want to wait until Czeschin's next book — perhaps you'd like to join the readers of Czeschin's *World Investor*. This monthly newsletter brings you Czeschin's easy, low-risk methods for making major profits in global markets. In each issue you will:

- Discover the easiest ways to get double-digit yields for high income

- Find out about stocks that regularly double and triple in price

- Learn how to protect your money from a dollar decline and bear market on Wall Street

- Read about the fastest-growing companies in Thailand, Malaysia, Vietnam, New Zealand, Australia, South Africa, Latin America, and much, much more.

Just as important as what you will get, what you won't get is second-hand information from brokers, fund managers or advisors new to global investing. Instead you'll cash in on proven strategies of global investing success, explained in easy-to-follow action plans — so simple anyone can follow them!

Over, please ...

As a reader of *The Last Wave*, you are entitled to a special low introductory rate of only $59 for 12 issues. Fill in the coupon and **mail it today**. You never know where the market will be by this time tomorrow.

Special Introductory Offer

____ Yes! Please begin my subscription to *Czeschin's World Investor* immediately for the low introductory price of only $59 for 12 issues.

____ Enclosed is my check for $59

____ Please charge my

___AMEX   ___MasterCard   ___VISA

Signature _____Exp. Date_____

NAME _____

ADDRESS _____

CITY/STATE/ZIP_____

Mail to:
   Robert Czeschin's World Investor
   U.S. Subscription Services
   824 East Baltimore Street
   Baltimore, MD 21202 USA

Or fax your order to 410-539-7348   LW794